100 GREATS

KENT
COUNTY CRICKET CLUB

DAVID ROBERTSON, HOWARD MILTON
& DEREK CARLAW

TEMPUS

Frontispiece: Kent's trio of Batsmen to score one hundred first-class hundreds – Coiln Cowdrey, Frank Wolley and Leslie Ames.

Front cover: Colin Blythe bowling, a detail from Kent v. Lancashire at Canterbury in 1906, by Albert Chevallier Tayler.
Back cover: From the top: Lord Harris; Frank Woolley; Colin Cowdrey.

First published 2005

Tempus Publishing Ltd
The Mill, Brimscombe Port
Stroud, Gloucestershire GL5 2QG
www.tempus-publishing.com

© David Robertson, Howard Milton, Derek Carlaw, 2005

The right of David Robertson, Howard Milton, Derek Carlaw,
to be identified as the Authors of this work has been asserted in
accordance with the Copyrights, Designs and Patents Act 1988.

British Library Cataloguing in Publication Data.
A catalogue record for this book is available from the British Library.

ISBN 0 7524 3454 3

Typesetting and origination by Tempus Publishing
Printed and bound in Great Britain

100 GREATS

KENT
COUNTY CRICKET CLUB

To Mark

David Robertson

PREFACE

Few words in the English language are more misused than 'great' but working to the dictionary definition 'considerably above the normal or average', Kent has had more than its share of great cricketers. In its long history the County has also had an abundance of players who from time to time have crossed the shadowy line between great and very good and from this company of greats, near-greats and very goods we have been granted the privilege of choosing our top 100.

Some explanation of our selection criteria might help disarm some of the inevitable criticism. Although performances in Test cricket and contributions to the game in a wider sense have not been ignored, our main concern has been achievements for Kent. It is on this basis that Percy Chapman, for example, is included in our 100 but does not make our top twenty. One Test captain and thirteen other Test cricketers are excluded wholly or partly on this basis. Overseas players were considered only if they played for two or more seasons. Perhaps more controversially, we have not picked any player who appeared for the County in 2004. We agonised long and hard over this decision but concluded that, what with peaks and troughs in form, injuries etc, it would be wrong to assess a player until his career with the County was over. Several of those selected might not have made it if judgement had been made at some intermediate low point in their careers. Conversely, following a purple patch, some of those excluded might have merited selection.

When statistics for players from earlier eras are considered, it must be remembered that the majority of our selections played entirely on uncovered wickets. Wickets were less batsmen-friendly pre-1914 and even though during the 1920s and 1930s wickets at the main centres were for the most part prepared to suit the bat, far more use was made of out-grounds where 'natural' pitches predominated. As for batting on the rough wickets of the Mynn/Pilch/Wenman era, to arrive at a twenty-first century comparison it is probably advisable to multiply the figures by two.

Finally, although we have consulted widely before making our final selections, the choices are ours and ours alone.

ACKNOWLEDGEMENTS

Our grateful thanks are due to the many people who have helped us in the research and preparation of this book. For kindly agreeing to write the foreword, especial thanks were due to one of Kent's true greats, Brian Luckhurst, who died, deeply mourned, shortly before this book went to print. We are similarly grateful to Rob Sharman, James Howarth and Holly Bennion of Tempus Publishing for their guidance through the several pitfalls awaiting the unwary in the world of publishing. We are deeply indebted to Kent County Cricket Club in general for the use of photographs from the Club's library and providing access to the committee minutes and to Jon Fordham, Jean Owens and Jean Cryer of Kent CCC in particular for their help in numerous ways, not least with the collation and scanning of photographs. Among many others who have helped we would like to single out Shaun Caveney for reading through and commenting on sections of the text. The numerous authors whose books were consulted are acknowledged in the bibliography. Photographs are an important feature of this book and we thank and acknowledge Tom Morris and Anthony Roberts for permission to use some of their excellent work. If we have inadvertently used any copyright material we apologise unreservedly.

STATISTICAL NOTES

All career statistics and best performances relate only to matches played for Kent by the individuals concerned. Best performances may have been bettered in matches elsewhere. Performances in limited-overs matches are noted in italics. Bowling performances are only included if three or more wickets are taken; career best performances of ten wickets in a match are also included.

The status of matches for all statistics and performances are as defined by the Association of Cricket Statisticians and Historians for first-class and important matches and for List A limited-overs games.

Because of the varying numbers of balls per over covered, bowling records list balls rather than overs and maidens. The alternative, to reconstruct overs on a six-ball premise, would give a false impression. In the early nineteenth century, full bowling analyses as of now were not kept or have not survived, balls are then ignored and 'other wickets' when even runs conceded are not known are noted.

KEY:

RHB – right-handed batsman
LHB – left-handed batsman
RF/LF – right/left-arm fast bowler
RFM/LFM – right/left-arm fast medium bowler
RMF/LMF – right/left-arm medium fast bowler
RM/LM – right/left-arm medium pace bowler
RSM/LSM – right/left-arm slow medium bowler
SRA/SLA – slow right/left-arm bowler
OB – off break bowler
LB(G) – leg break (and googly) bowler
WK – wicketkeeper

GC – Gillette Cup
NWT – NatWest Trophy
C & G – Cheltenham & Gloucester Trophy
SL – Sunday League
NL – National League
B & H – Benson & Hedges Cup

FOREWORD
BY BRIAN LUCKHURST

In the early to mid-1950s Kent were going through difficult times on the field. Retiring from the game were Leslie Ames, Bryan Valentine, Leslie Todd (who incidentally was an international table tennis player), Ray Dovey, Doug Wright and Arthur Fagg. Kent found it very difficult fielding a side capable of success in the County Championship. However, new faces were emerging such as Colin Cowdrey, Fred Ridgway, Bob Wilson, Arthur Phebey, Alan Dixon, Stuart Leary and Dave Halfyard.

I mention that particular era as it was then that I was given the opportunity to become a very young professional, being offered a playing contract at the age of fifteen years and two months. The then-secretary, Nevill Christopherson, was asked to write to all state schools enquiring if they had any possible future Kent cricketers. My form master at Westlands Secondary School, Sittingbourne, Denis Jarrett, replied straightaway suggesting I was worth looking at. That was the winter of 1953/54. The County Coach, Claude Lewis, picked me up outside the school gates at 2 p.m. every Thursday afternoon and took me to the only indoor cricket school in the County at that time, Eltham Baths. In April 1954 I was offered a trial and the rest, as they say, is history.

The Kent successes were in the distant past, having won the County Championship on four occasions: 1906, 1909, 1910 and 1913. The outstanding players of that era were Frank Woolley, 'Wally' Hardinge, James Seymour, Jack Mason, C.H.B. Marsham, Colin Blythe, Bill Fairservice (who when eighty years old was Second XI scorer when I started!), Arthur Fielder, Jack Hubble and Fred Huish.

With the wonderful combination of the talents of Les Ames, Colin Cowdrey and Colin Page running Kent Cricket, on the field an incredible period of success started in 1967 with the winning of the Gillette Cup at Lord's when playing in the final against Somerset. The following twelve years saw Kent winning eleven trophies; this period was to become known as 'The Glory Years'. It was a great thrill to be part of that success, playing with three of the Kent greats, Colin Cowdrey, Derek Underwood and Alan Knott. That was something very special. Add to that the names of players like Mike Denness, Asif Iqbal, Bob Woolmer, Graham Johnson, Stuart Leary, Alan Ealham, Bob Wilson, John Shepherd, Alan Brown and Norman Graham. You can see why we won trophies!

Between the periods of the early 1900s and the more recent successes of the 1970s there have been many wonderful Kent cricketers, players who didn't have the thrill or experience of playing in a Championship-winning team. It doesn't seem possible, for example, that 'Tich' Freeman, who played between 1914 and 1936, taking 3,340 wickets, was one such player.

The putting together of this book has taken a great deal of time and effort by Derek Carlaw, Howard Milton and David Robertson. It has been done very, very professionally. You will, I am sure, very much enjoy going through their thoughts and views.

Brian Luckhurst

Kent and England
President of the Kent County Cricket Club 2004-2005
Died 1 March 2005

100 KENT GREATS

Tom Adams	Ray Dovey
Terry Alderman	Alan Ealham
Les Ames	Mark Ealham
Bill Ashdown	Richard Ellison
Asif Iqbal	*Godfrey Evans*
'Farmer' Bennett	*Arthur Fagg*
Mark Benson	Bill Fairservice
Colin Blythe	Nicholas Felix
'Bill' Bradley	Arthur Fielder
Alan Brown	Matthew Fleming
Jack Bryan	*'Tich' Freeman*
'Pinky' Burnup	Norman Graham
Douglas Carr	Dave Halfyard
Gerry Chalk	*'Wally' Hardinge*
Percy Chapman	*Lord Harris*
George Collins	Dean Headley
Chris Cowdrey	Alec Hearne
Colin Cowdrey	George Hearne
Graham Cowdrey	William Hillyer
Arthur Day	Simon Hinks
Sammy Day	*Carl Hooper*
Mike Denness	Jack Hubble
Graham Dilley	Fred Huish
Ted Dillon	'Punter' Humphreys
Alan Dixon	Kenneth Hutchings

Alan Igglesden

Kevin Jarvis

Graham Johnson

Manley Kemp

Alan Knott

Stuart Leary

'Hopper' Levett

Claude Lewis

Brian Luckhurst

Martin McCague

William McCanlis

Frank Marchant

'Father' Marriott

Steve Marsh

Cloudesley Marsham

'Nutty' Martin

Jack Mason

Alfred Mynn

Colin Page

Harry Patterson

Tony Pawson

Frank Penn

Arthur Phebey

Roy Pienaar

Fuller Pilch

William Rashleigh

Peter Richardson

Fred Ridgway

David Sayer

James Seymour

John Shepherd

Chris Tavaré

Neil Taylor

Les Todd

Edward Tylecote

Derek Ufton

Derek Underwood

Bryan Valentine

Trevor Ward

Alan Watt

Ned Wenman

Ned Willsher

Bob Wilson

Frank Woolley

Bob Woolmer

Jimmy Wootton

Charlie Wright

Doug Wright

Walter Wright

Bill Yardley

The top twenty, who appear here in italics, have longer entries.

Thomas Miles (Tom) Adams

RHB & RM (round-arm) 1836-58

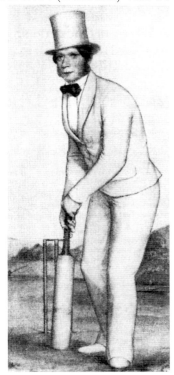

Born: Gravesend, 2 May 1808
Died: Milton, Gravesend, 20 January 1894

Batting

M	I	NO	Runs	Av	100	50
99	187	5	2,291	12.58	–	7

Bowling

Runs	Wkts	Av	Other Wkts
418	31	13.48	59

5wI	10wM	ct/st
2	–	78

Best Performances
78 v. Sussex (Hove) 1849
6-39 v. Sussex (Gravesend) 1854

Although not eulogised as some of his more famous Kent contemporaries, Tom Adams was a vital element in the Grand Old Kent XIs that dominated English cricket in the late 1830s and 1840s. He played more games for the County than anyone else in that period, as well as making many appearances in the various England XIs of the time and playing five times for the Players against the Gentlemen at Lord's.

Adams was born and died a Gravesend man. In appearance, he was just under six foot (about 180cm) tall, with a distinctive gypsy or kiss–curl. Today, Adams would be regarded something of a 'bits and pieces' player. *Cricket Scores and Biographies* noted, 'As a batsman he proved himself to be a fine and punishing hitter... His round–arm bowling was plain but straight, always delivering over the wicket and holding the ball extending nearly at arm's length in front of him in a line with his face. His fielding was also very good indeed, either at point, long-stop or middle wicket.'

By the standards of the time Adams' batting record was above average , making scores of 20 or more in one in five innings, good for the time and comparing favourably with Alfred Mynn at least. His hard hitting was well known, in one instance at Lord's sending the ball to the top of the tennis court (where the Mound Stand now is) with a leg hit, leaving a mark that remained there for some time. Many of his bowling performances are lost in the restricted bowling analyses that survive but he did bowl unchanged throughout a match with Hillyer, taking Kent to a big victory over Nottinghamshire at Canterbury in 1845. He was also one of the most accomplished long fielders of his generation with a tremendous throw.

Adams' legacy is the Bat and Ball Ground in his hometown. He is purported to have spent three years after 1845 in its careful levelling and preparation. Thereafter he remained closely associated with the management of the ground and the various fairs and sports meetings that appeared there. Even beyond the Bat and Ball, Adams was renowned for his concern over the pitches on which he played, carefully supervising rolling of the turf. The cynical view was that this dictated his preference for opening the innings, which he generally did to good effect, for then the pitch was at its smoothest and the bowling most wayward. Given this, it is perhaps no coincidence that his best overall record on any ground was on his own pitch. For five seasons in the 1850s, he was a practice bowler for the MCC, and he was also employed for a short time at Southampton. Adams was also a first-rate shot and a keen follower of the Sport of Kings, walking every year from Gravesend to the Epsom Derby.

Tom Adams lies buried in Gravesend Cemetery, his final resting place marked by a tombstone with a still clearly visible distinctive cricket motif. His portrait is to be found in the pavilion at Canterbury.

Terence Michael (Terry) Alderman
RHB & RFM 1984-86

Terry Alderman was Kent's leading wicket taker during his two seasons as their overseas player. His tally of wickets was far ahead of Derek Underwood, the next most successful bowler in those two years. In fact, there is a widely held view that, possibly with the exception of Arthur Fielder, he was probably the best seam bowler to play for the County. With Kent, he enjoyed two outstanding seasons in a notably successful domestic and international career during which he played in 41 Test matches for Australia. The feature of his right-arm fast medium bowling was how close he got to the stumps and the resulting high proportion of lbw decisions he achieved. In his two seasons, close on forty per cent of his dismissals were adjudged lbw.

In the second of his two seasons he finished seventh in the national bowling averages with 98 wickets at an average of 19.20. Without doubt he would have passed the 100 wickets mark had it not been for an arm injury which kept him out of the last two matches. He topped the Kent bowling averages in both seasons with Kent. Only Derek Underwood bowled more overs. He achieved his career-best figures in the match at Derby in 1986 when he returned 8-46 in Derbyshire's first innings. Four weeks later he again took eight wickets in the first innings of the opening match of Canterbury Week against Leicestershire, finishing with an analysis of 14-144 in a match that Kent won by just five runs.

He was a reliable close-to-the-wicket fielder, frequently in the slips, and averaged almost a catch a match during his time with Kent. Although very much a tail end batsman, of his forty-eight innings he was not out on twenty-one occasions and recorded a highest score of 52 not out.

Born: Subiaco, Perth, Western Australia, Australia, 12 June 1956
County Cap: 1984

Batting

M	I	NO	Runs	Av	100	50
40	48	21	322	11.92	–	1
23	7	5	25	12.50	–	–

Bowling

Balls	Runs	Wkts	Av
7,018	3,607	174	20.72
1,212	812	38	21.36

5wI	10wM	ct/st
15	3	38
1	–	12

Best Performances
52* v. Sussex (Hastings) 1984
11 v. Lancashire (Maidstone) 1984 (SL)
8-46 v. Derbyshire (Derby) 1986
14-144 v. Leicestershire (Canterbury) 1986
5-36 v. Leicestershire (Maidstone) 1984 (SL)
Tests: 41 for Australia
Limited-Overs Internationals: 65 for Australia
Wisden Cricketer of the Year: 1982 (for Australia)

His early career success was down to his out-swinger, but he improved his skills with an in-swinger and leg cutter and moved the ball in off the seam as his career progressed. He was just a few months past his eighteenth birthday when he made his debut for Western Australia. Despite outstanding performances for his State side, it was seven years before he won national recognition due to the presence in Australian teams of Dennis Lillee and Jeff Thomson and perhaps Max Walker, who was a fairly similar type of bowler. By all accounts, one of the turning points in his career resulted from a season playing league cricket as a professional in Scotland in 1980. He returned a different bowler, tougher in mental outlook, eager for work, and with a variety of additional deliveries that he had worked hard to perfect.

Terry Alderman played for Western Australia for almost twenty years from 1974/75 to 1992/93. Two of his mentors were John Inverarity and Daryl Foster, both of whom have had close ties with Kent cricket. He made his international debut on the 1981 tour of England when he took 42 wickets in the six-Test series – a record for an Australian bowler in England. Somewhat injury prone, his career looked to be in serious jeopardy when he was badly hurt after a pitch invasion during the Perth Test against England in 1982.

The decision not to invite him back for a third season with Kent was questioned by many. The concerns voiced at the time seemed fully justified when in 1988 with Gloucestershire, he took 75 wickets at 22.81.

Leslie Ethelbert George (Les) Ames CBE

RHB, LB & WK 1926-51

Born: Elham, 3 December 1905
Died: Canterbury, 27 February 1990
County Cap: 1927

Batting

M	I	NO	Runs	Av	100	50
430	717	64	28,951	44.33	78	139

Bowling

Balls	Runs	Wkts	Av
1,190	697	22	31.68

5wI	10wM	ct/st
–	–	512/330

Best Performances
295 *v.* Gloucestershire (Folkestone) 1933
3-23 *v.* Surrey (Oval) 1946
6 dismissals (ct 4 st 2) in an innings *v.* Sussex (Maidstone) 1929 and *v.* Sussex (Folkestone) 1930
9 dismissals (ct 8 st 1) in a match *v.* Oxford University (Oxford) 1928
9 dismissals (ct 5 st 4) in a match *v.* Sussex (Maidstone) 1929
Tests: 47 for England
Wisden **Cricketer of the Year:** 1929

As the leading wicketkeeper–batsman of his day and as an administrator, few have contributed as much to cricket as Leslie Ames. When he was first picked for England there were some who, deceived by his unobtrusive technique, believed he owed his selection to his batting, but by the mid-1930s it was generally agreed that wicketkeeping ability alone justified his selection. Apart from a selectors' aberration in 1935, he was England's first choice from 1931 until the end of the 1938/39 South African tour when, due to persistent back trouble, he gave up behind the stumps. In Test matches he hit 2,434 runs at 40.56 with eight centuries, taking 74 catches and completing 23 stumpings. He toured Australia three times, South Africa once and West Indies twice. After giving up wicketkeeping he continued to play for Kent as a batsman until a final back spasm on a cold, dank day at Gillingham forced him to retire.

As a 'keeper he saw the ball early, taking it without histrionics or acrobatics. Between the wars wicketkeepers generally stood up to everything except genuine pace and, although Kent's emphasis on leg spin undoubtedly boosted his number of dismissals, fifteen of his stumpings were from the lively fast-medium of Watt and Ashdown. Even so, he was equally accomplished standing back, notably to England's

Tonbridge 1938: Les Ames whips off the bails to run out Worcestershire's South African all-rounder Sid Martin (61)

pace-orientated attack on his last two tours of Australia. On the 1932/33 bodyline tour he was said to have missed only one chance in the entire series and at Melbourne in 1937 he allowed only one bye in a total of 604. As a batsman he was quick on his feet, excelling in the drive and never afraid to lift the ball over the in-field. During his epic hundredth hundred against Middlesex at Canterbury in 1950 he repeatedly went down the wicket and drove the pace bowling of John Warr back over his head. The game was notable for another reason. Ames took over behind the stumps when Godfrey Evans was injured. He excelled on turning wickets, playing spinners as well as anyone of his generation. He twice won the Lawrence Trophy for the fastest hundred of the season. The highest of his nine double-hundreds, 295 against Gloucestershire at Folkestone in 1933, was scored in just over 240 minutes. Between the wickets he was one of the quickest of his era.

Encouraged by his father, himself no mean left-arm spinner with the Elham club, and the old Kent and England cricketer Francis Mackinnon, who lived locally, Ames hit his first century at the age of fourteen for Harvey Grammar School, Folkestone. On the strength of an innings of 46 for Ashford against Kent Club and Ground, the Kent coach, the famously eccentric Gerry Weigall, invited him to play for the Club and Ground against Hythe in 1924. One of a swarm of bees in Weigall's bonnet – or in his case straw boater – was that a professional needed two strings to his bow and, with limited experience, Ames found himself a reluctant wicketkeeper. Three catches, one stumping, no missed chances and a useful, if modest, contribution with the bat got him started. By the end of the season he had made his Second XI debut and by 1926 was regular reserve to Jack Hubble.

Progress was rapid. In 1926 he played two first-class matches as a batsman and next year made his debut as first-team wicketkeeper in the opening game of the season against Worcestershire at Folkestone. He hit 90, shared a sixth-wicket partnership of 155 in 65 minutes with Percy Chapman, caught one and stumped two, both off Freeman. This launched a partnership destined to account for 343 wickets, 82 caught, 261 stumped. In June he registered his first century, by August he had reached 1,000 runs and within two years had gained his first England cap – *v.* South Africa at The Oval. Apart from recurrent back trouble, his subsequent career was almost unbroken success. He scored a thousand runs in every season from 1927 to 1950 except 1936 when he missed a lot of cricket due to a displaced vertebra. He exceeded 2,000 runs six times – twice post-war when he was over forty – with a highest of 3,048 in 1933 when he hit nine hundreds. Behind the stumps he three times achieved the wicketkeeper's 'double': 1928 – 1,919 runs, 122 dismissals; 1929 – 1,795 runs, 128 dismissals; 1932 – 2,482 runs, 104 dismissals.

Offered the Kent captaincy when Bryan Valentine retired, he declined when, belatedly, he discovered it would entail relinquishing his professional status. He led a Commonwealth team to India and Ceylon (as it then was) in 1950/51 when, despite his back, he hit his final two hundreds. During the Second World War Ames served with the RAF, reaching the rank of Squadron Leader. In a wartime club match he performed the hat-trick with rarely used leg spinners. When Jack Hubble, Ames's predecessor as Kent 'keeper retired, he offered his successor a partnership in a sports business in Gillingham. The enterprise prospered, providing valuable experience of the wider world and, when his playing days ended, Ames turned to administration. With minimal back-up staff he was manager of Kent CCC between 1957 and 1959, Secretary Manager between 1960 and 1972 and had a major share in the Club's successes during the 1970s, not just on the field but off it in the setting up of a sound administrative structure. Not the least of his virtues was his *rapport* with players half his age. His even-handed approach during the Packer imbroglio did much to avert the schisms suffered by less fortunate counties. He was President in 1975. He managed three MCC touring teams and was the first professional (and second Kent cricketer) to be appointed a Test selector. He was also one of the first professionals to be elected an Honorary Life Member of MCC. He was made CBE in 1973 for his services to cricket and in 1988 was awarded an Honorary MA by the University of Kent and Canterbury. Until 1932 Les Ames played professional football for Folkestone, Clapton (subsequently Leyton) Orient and Gillingham. In later years he was hard to beat on the golf course.

William Henry (Bill) Ashdown
RHB & RMF 1920-37

Bill Ashdown is unique in having played first-class cricket before the First World War and after the Second. In 1914, at the age of fifteen, playing for Gerry Weigall's XI *v.* Oxford University he showed, in the words of *Wisden*, 'considerable promise. In 1947, ten years in retirement, he scored 42 and 40 and took 5-73 for Morris Leyland's XI against a strong 'the Rest' team in the short-lived Harrogate Festival.

An unselfish player, between 1925 and his retirement in 1937 he hit a thousand runs in a season eleven times, his most prolific year being 1928, when he totalled 2,247 runs at 43.21. He is not merely the only player to score 300 for Kent. He did

Born: Bromley, 27 December 1898
Died: Rugby, Warwickshire,
   15 September 1979
County Cap: 1922

Batting

M	I	NO	Runs	Av	100	50
482	804	76	22,309	30.64	38	105

Bowling

Balls	Runs	Wkts	Av
43,030	19,290	595	32.42

5wI	10wM	ct/st
12	–	398/1

Best Performances
332 v. Essex (Brentwood) 1934
6-23 v. Gloucestershire (Maidstone) 1924

W. ASHDOWN (KENT.)

so twice. His highest score of 332 was in the 1934 Brentwood run feast when Kent totalled 803-4 in seven hours at 5.5 an over. He added 352 with Woolley (172) and 243 with Ames (202★). Essex bowled only six maidens. This was the first county match played at the constricted Brentwood ground – according to the Essex skipper Tom Pearce, at one end it was only possible to score a single or four. In the previous week Jim Swanton had played there in a club match and reputedly declared it unfit for cricket! In the second match of the Brentwood Week, Surrey were skittled for 115! At Dover in 1935 he carried his bat for 305★ (47 fours) out of 560 scored at 4.1 an over, outpacing renowned stroke players such as Bryan Valentine and Percy Chapman against a Derbyshire attack that within a year would give them the Championship. He hit a century in each innings against Middlesex at Lord's in 1931.

Ashdown took part in forty-eight century opening partnerships, twenty-six of them with Wally Hardinge and lacked only consistency to lift him to a higher class. The off side was his favourite area but, although never dismissed for 'a pair', he had a tendency towards rash ventures outside off stump on first going in. Cover and square drives were among his most profitable strokes while his devastating square cut brought on palpitations in gully fielders all round the county circuit. He was an enthusiastic hooker. Good enough to be considered a genuine all-rounder, he bowled on the brisk side of medium, swinging the new ball both ways and often opening the bowling. Twice he exceeded 60 wickets in a season. In his young days he was a good all-round fielder but later settled in as a reliable slip.

The nearest Ashdown came to honours was selection for the Players v. the Gentlemen in the 1933 Folkestone Festival when he hit 117 and added 204 in 195 minutes with Les Ames (201). On retirement he was an exceptionally fine coach/groundsman at Rugby, served three years on the umpires list then moved to Leicester where he was coach between 1951 and 1961, chief scout in 1965 and scorer between 1966 and 1969. His services for the Midland's county were rewarded by honorary life membership.

Asif Iqbal (Jimmy) Razvi

RHB & RM 1968-82

Born: Hyderabad, Andhra Pradesh, India, 6 June 1943
County Cap: 1968
County Captain: 1977 & 1981-82

Batting

M	I	NO	Runs	Av	100	50
243	399	42	13,231	37.06	26	69
241	229	28	5,544	27.58	3	27

Bowling

Balls	Runs	Wkts	Av
4,083	2,096	73	28.71
4,199	2,728	106	25.73

5wI	10wM	ct/st
–	–	168
1	–	91

Best Performances
171 *v. Gloucestershire (Folkestone)* 1978
106 *v. Gloucestershire (Maidstone)* 1976 (SL)
4-11 *v. Lancashire (Canterbury)* 1968
5-42 *v. Middlesex (Lord's)* 1980 (B & H)
Tests: 58 for Pakistan (6 as captain)
Limited-Overs Internationals: 10 for Pakistan (6 as captain)
***Wisden* Cricketer of the Year:** 1968 (for Pakistan)

Many have been the exciting and talented cricketers who have graced Kent grounds and enthralled its supporters over the years. High on the list of those is Asif Iqbal, a batsman who entertained, was brilliant and fleet of foot in the field, and a right-arm swing bowler with a slinging action who could surprise the best of batsmen. When the sun shone everything was done with a smile, but on cold days he wore so many sweaters his upper body looked too big for the lower and one felt he was not wholly enjoying life. Equally at home in both first-class and limited-overs cricket, he was a vital member of Kent's 'Glory Years' teams, captaining the side in 1977 when the Championship was shared with Middlesex, and again in the 1981 and 1982 seasons.

It was during the Pakistan tour of England in 1967 that Asif was approached by Leslie Ames and Colin Cowdrey to join Kent, thus beginning a fifteen-year career in English domestic cricket. In six of those seasons he exceeded 1,000 runs and scored twenty-six hundreds. His best with the bat, when he scored 1,379 runs, coincided with Kent's first Championship for fifty-seven years. He won the Walter Lawrence Trophy in 1973 for the fastest hundred of the season, scored in 72 minutes against a strong MCC side at Canterbury.

Asif's exciting brand of cricket coincided with the early years of the limited-overs game and the County's success in those years owes much to him. By the standards of limited-overs cricket his performances were significant, not the least in the almost match-winning innings in the 1971 Gillette Cup final. He bowled his overs at an economical 3.89 runs and scored his runs at a fast rate. He was superb between the wickets particularly with other good runners such as Knott, Alan Ealham and Tavaré, although one wondered how he achieved such a turn of speed given his loosely tied pads that were surely an encumbrance and made him look bow legged! Despite that, ones frequently became twos, twos were turned into threes, and all-run fours were not unusual. But when there was obviously just a single he often strolled it.

After spending his early playing days in India, Asif emigrated to Pakistan. Selected for the tour of Australia in 1964/65, he is probably best remembered for an outstanding innings in the final Test of the three-match series on his first tour to England in 1967. Batting at number eight with Pakistan's second innings score standing at 53-7 and a further 167 runs being required to make England bat again, Asif scored a magnificent 146. He put on 190 with Intikhab Alam, thus creating a new record ninth-wicket partnership in Test cricket that stood for thirty years. Kent supporters will remember him for his many enthralling and entertaining performances. Two particular incidents in the victorious 1970 season epitomise Asif's approach: at Cheltenham in mid August, Kent required 340 to win on what was described as a 'broken' wicket. Victory was achieved by just one wicket with Asif scoring a brilliant 109. A week after the victory at Cheltenham, Kent met Surrey at Blackheath. In a typically tight local derby encounter, Surrey needed twelve runs to win in the penultimate over with one wicket standing. In attempting a six off the fifth ball of that over, Pocock was the victim of a brilliant running catch with outstretched hands after a sprint round the boundary: a catch described as unforgettable by those privileged to witness it.

George (Farmer) Bennett

RHB & SRA (round-arm) 1853-73

Born: Shorne Ridgeway, 12 February 1829
Died: Shorne Ridgeway, 16 August 1886

Batting

M	I	NO	Runs	Av	100	50
126	234	22	3,143	14.82	–	10

Bowling

Runs	Wkts	Av	Other Wkts
7,784	456	17.07	5

5wI	10wM	ct/st	
30	8	88	

Best Performances
82 *v.* MCC (Maidstone) 1859
9-113 *v.* Sussex (Hove) 1871
14-82 *v.* Sussex (Hove) 1858

George Bennett, nicknamed 'Farmer' because friends thought his appearance suitably rustic, has several claims to fame. He conceded the first run in Anglo–Australian cricket when, playing for the first English touring team *v.* Eighteen of Victoria at Melbourne on 1 January 1862, the home captain George Marshall drove his second ball (the sixth of the match) for a single. Shortly afterwards he took the first wicket, Jerry Bryant lbw. When England batted he faced the first delivery and next day he became the first Englishman to lose his wicket, c Butterworth b Conway 11. As David Frith points out in his book *The Trailblazers,* Bennett might easily have found himself in Australia before the English team arrived. In his youth he had spent time in prison for burglary, which often meant transportation. It should be said that by 1862 George was perfectly respectable. When not playing cricket, he earned a living as a brick-maker and later as a gardener on Lord Darnley's estate at Cobham.

'Farmer' made his debut for Kent *v.* England at Canterbury in 1853 alongside Kentish legends such as Mynn, Pilch etc, but his greatest contribution came later when Kent cricket was in near-terminal decline. With the more famous Ned Willsher, he virtually carried the county's attack in the difficult years between the break up of the 'Grand Old Kent XI' and the establishment of the present club in 1870.

He bowled slow round-arm at a time when almost all round-arm bowlers bowled fast or tried to. His bowling looked easy, Lord Harris termed it 'ground bait', but between 1860 and 1871 with a limited county programme he captured more than thirty wickets in a season eight times. Statistically his best performances were all at Hove against Sussex, 7-37 and 7-45 in 1858, 5-9 in 1857 and 9-113 in 1871. At The

Oval in 1863 he bowled one (four-ball) over that accounted for the cream of Surrey's batting, Stephenson (stumped), Caffyn (run out), Dowson (bowled) and Griffith (caught). He finished with 7–39. Quick-footed batsmen often punished him. In 1864 for Eighteen of Hastings *v.* the United All England XI the same 'Ben' Griffith hit all four balls of a Bennett over out of the ground. As a defensive batsman he was 'stiff as a block of wood' according to Lord Harris but useful, generally in the middle order. His highest score was 100 for South *v.* North at Lord's 1865. In 1861 for Players of Kent *v.* Gentlemen of Kent at Maidstone (non-first class) he pushed and prodded his way to 160. Stiffness notwithstanding, he was fast between the wickets and lively in the field with a long throw. He was picked four times for Players *v.* Gentlemen, twice at Lord's, twice at The Oval and played for the two major wandering sides, the All England and United All England XIs. In 1873 the county granted him a benefit, Kent *v.* W.G. Grace's XI at Gravesend.

100 GREATS

Mark Richard Benson

LHB & OB 1980-95

Born: Shoreham-by-Sea, Sussex, 6 July 1958
County Cap: 1981
County Captain: 1991-96

Batting

M	I	NO	Runs	Av	100	50
290	488	34	18,284	40.27	48	98
265	254	10	7,810	32.00	5	53

Bowling

Balls	Runs	Wkts	Av
479	493	5	98.60
–	–	–	–

5wI	10wM	ct/st
–	–	140
–	–	68

Best Performances
257 *v.* Hampshire (Southampton) 1991
119 v. Sussex (Hove) 1995 (B&H)
Test: 1 for England
Limited-Overs International: 1 for England

One of the unluckiest of cricketers, Mark Benson suffered a series of injuries which seriously affected his career. During his captaincy four runners-up positions were achieved and one title – the Sunday League in 1995. He is one of a number of Kent players who appeared for England in a single Test match. Despite his misfortunes, his record places him in the top flight of Kent batsmen. He made his debut in 1980 and was capped the following season. Only ten players have scored more runs for the County while his average is the fourth highest for those who have scored more than 10,000 runs. He was the model of consistency, passing 1,000 runs in eleven of his fifteen seasons. In 1987 he exceeded 1,700 runs with five hundreds while two years later in twenty-nine innings he averaged 54.12 with another five centuries. His highest score coincidentally equalled that of another Kent opener, Arthur Fagg, also against Hampshire on the same ground in 1936.

As a boy, he was an outstanding all-round sportsman, excelling at rugby, hockey and tennis, but it was not until his early teens that his ability as a cricketer came to the fore. Encouraged by his father, he attended Alf Gover's indoor school and at the age of fourteen he secured a place in his school First XI. He joined the Kent staff in 1978. A left-handed batsman, he could aptly be described as cautious and watchful with the ability to know which balls outside his off stump he could safely leave. He is still cited as a master of the technique. It was difficult even for the most experienced of spectators to fathom which were deliberate 'leaves' and which he played at and missed! Never flustered, he could spend long periods at the crease content to let his partner keep the scoreboard moving, but able to push the game along when necessary. If he played a bad shot or got a good ball, it did not bother him, and he was never inconvenienced by fast bowling. He shares with Neil Taylor the record first-wicket partnership for the County of 300, achieved against Derbyshire at Canterbury in 1991. Belying his cautious and watchful approach, he was a highly successful exponent of the limited-overs game in which he hit five hundreds and averaged 32. In 1995 he dominated the early stages of the Benson & Hedges Cup competition, sharing five successive opening stands of 100 with Trevor Ward. The injury jinx hit him again in the run up to the final when a finger fracture prevented his appearance at Lord's to the immense disappointment not only of him, but Kent's supporters.

At a time when the Kent side suffered from limited bowling and batsmen did not play to their full potential, Mark Benson's record as captain stands favourable comparison with his predecessors. During his five seasons in charge (injury prevented him appearing at all in 1996) he led the team to victory in thirty-two Championship matches and seventy-three in the limited-overs competitions. He is now proving himself as an outstanding umpire having already achieved international recognition.

Colin (Charlie) Blythe

RHB & SLA 1899-1914

Contemporaries such as Ranjitsinhji and Jessop rated 'Charlie' Blythe above any other left-arm spinner. Pelham Warner wrote 'Peel, Briggs, Peate, Rhodes and Ferris were in their day great bowlers but he would be a rash man who would aver that even Peel was a greater bowler than Blythe'. Writing in 1909 Philip Trevor considered him 'better than any other bowler on a good wicket and much better than any other bowler on a bad wicket'. Yet in 2000 when *Wisden* published its 'Five

Born: Deptford 30 May 1879
Died: Forest Hall to Pimmern military railway
line near Passchendaele, Belgium,
8 November 1917
County Cap: 1900

Batting

M	I	NO	Runs	Av	100	50
381	506	11	3,964	10.03	–	5

Bowling

Balls	Runs	Wkts	Av
90,274	36,859	2,210	16.67
5wI	10wM	ct/st	
195	64	183	

Best Performances
82* v. Nottinghamshire (Nottingham) 1904
10-30 (17-48) v. Northamptonshire
(Northampton) 1907
Tests: 19 for England
Wisden **Cricketer of the Year:** 1904

Cricketers of the Century' Blythe did not receive a single vote. In 19 Test Matches he took exactly 100 wickets at 18.63 and of the twenty-eight bowlers nominated, only Sydney Barnes has a better Test career average and strike rate! Devastating when the ball turned, Blythe differed in his ability to trouble good batsmen on, in modern jargon, flat wickets. His action was near perfect, running in from behind the umpire and bringing his arm over from behind his back in a long arc. Blessed with a good cricketing brain and long fingers, strengthened he claimed by playing the violin, he could turn the ball on most wickets but his cardinal virtues were flight, change of pace and accuracy. Against Sussex at Tunbridge Wells in 1904 his first 12 overs cost 1 run.

Many wickets came through catches at cover or mid off from batsmen driving at balls pitching a foot or so shorter than expected. Never allowing the batsmen to settle, he sometimes delivered from a yard or more behind the crease. As well as the stock delivery spinning away from the bat and the ball going on with his arm, he bowled a medium-pace in-swinger, often a yorker. He bowled faster to quick-footed batsmen and faced with one reluctant to play strokes, used an occasional in-swinging full toss targeted on the off-bail. When two batsmen were set he sometimes switched to over the wicket leg-theory.

Playing on Blackheath, Blythe started bowling seriously around the age of eleven. On leaving school he played club cricket at modest level while apprenticed as a fitter

Arguably the greatest of all left-arm spinners, 'Charlie' Blythe joined the Kent Fortress Engineers immediately on the outbreak of war in 1914. As a sergeant attached to the King's Own Yorkshire Light Infantry he was one of thousands killed near Passchendaele in 1917.

and turner at Woolwich Arsenal where his father worked. His opportunity came in 1897 when William McCanlis saw him bowling to Walter Wright before Kent's game with Somerset at Rectory Field, Blackheath. The upshot was a trial at the Tonbridge Nursery and an invitation to sign for the following season. He bowled Yorkshire's Frank Mitchell with his first ball in first-class cricket and in 1900 captured a hundred wickets as he did in all but one subsequent season. In 1909 he took 215 wickets at 14.54. Statistically his most remarkable bowling was 17-48 from 31.1 overs in a single day at Northampton in 1907 but, considering the strength of the opposition and the flat wicket, equally good was 7-138 from 52.1 overs when Lancashire totalled 475 at Old Trafford in 1914. Fifteen times he took 13 or more wickets in a match, nine in an innings five times, eight in an innings nine times. Five times he bowled unchanged through a match. His two hat-tricks were both in 1910.

His introduction to Test cricket with MacLaren's 1901/02 team in Australia brought him eighteen wickets at a respectable 26.11 but on his second visit in 1907/08 he played only one Test. Rhodes was preferred but overall did little better. In all matches Blythe took 41 wickets at 21.28 against 31 at 34.48. Matting wickets in South Africa were more to his liking. On two tours, 1905/06 and 1909/10 he took 33 Test wickets at 21.69 with a best performance of 11-118 at Cape Town in

1906. At home, Blythe's 15-99 against South Africa at Leeds in 1907 virtually decided the three-match series in which he took 26 wickets at 10.38. Against Australia at Edgbaston in 1909, bowling in tandem with George Hirst, his 6-44 and 5-58 were crucial in England's only victory. Afterwards he was taken ill, probably with some form of fit and on medical advice missed the next two Tests while continuing playing for his county. In the fifty-eight days between his illness and his return for the Fourth Test at Old Trafford, he took 99 wickets for Kent at 15.39 plus 12-103 for Players *v.* Gentlemen at The Oval. In his final Test appearance in England, another seven wickets gave him 18 at 13.44 for the series.

A competent batsman, Blythe shared several notable late-order partnerships including 106 for the ninth wicket with Bill Fairservice at Trent Bridge in 1904 when he hit his top score of 82★. Against Sussex at Canterbury in 1906, again for the ninth wicket, he added 111 in 35 minutes with his captain 'Slug' Marsham.

Blythe apparently suffered from epilepsy. According to his specialist, Test matches were liable to trigger an attack but county cricket seldom affected him. This might explain why he was only once selected for Players *v.* Gentlemen. It all seems odd but until quite recently a certain stigma was attached to epilepsy. Diagnosis and treatment were in their infancy and such matters tended to be hushed up. Blythe is sometimes portrayed as highly strung. One writer even labelled him 'the shrinking Blythe'. Shrinking violets seldom flourish in Deptford and his fellow cricketers regarded him highly. Contemporary evidence shows a clever, self-reliant Cockney with a love of prizefights and a devotion to music. He owned an expensive Italian violin, practised two hours daily in winter and took lessons from a noted local teacher. Although happy to play the popular songs of the period, he was first violin in the Tonbridge Orchestra and won praise when performing Brahms and Mozart.

Epilepsy and experience at Woolwich Arsenal could have kept him safe at home but in September 1914 Blythe missed the last game to join the Kent Fortress Engineers and quickly rose to Sergeant. In August 1917 he played at Lord's, and took his final wicket, Charles Macartney. Shortly afterwards he embarked for France and three months later was killed by shellfire. His splinter-riddled wallet with a hole through the middle of his wife's picture adds a poignant note to the display cabinets in the Canterbury pavilion and every Cricket Week his memorial on the ground is the scene of a simple wreath-laying ceremony.

William Morris (Bill) Bradley

RHB & RF 1895-1903

| Born: Lower Sydenham, 2 January 1875 |
| Died: Wandsworth Common, 19 June 1944 |
| County Cap: 1895 |

Batting

M	I	NO	Runs	Av	100	50
123	185	50	795	9.80	–	50

Bowling

Balls	Runs	Wkts	Av
23,351	11,886	536	22.17
5wI	10wM	ct/st	
39	10	71	

Best Performances

67* v. Yorkshire (Canterbury) 1897
9-87 v. Hampshire (Tonbridge) 1901
14-134 v. Lancashire (Manchester) 1901
Tests: 2 for England

A product of South London club cricket with Lloyds Register and Forest Hill, 'Bill' Bradley was for a few seasons one of the most destructive fast bowlers in the country. Son of a grocer and wine merchant, he was not quite the archetypal public school/Oxbridge amateur. He worked in a City office, lived all his life in South London, spoke with a South London accent and had an encyclopaedic knowledge of pubs and beer. At his school, Alleyn's, he bowled medium pace but he taught himself to bowl fast and in June 1895 for Lloyds v. Mitcham Second XI took six wickets in six balls. Shortly afterwards he made his debut for Kent, against Somerset at Blackheath. Despite only one wicket and 'a pair' he stayed in the side for Canterbury Week where he impressed with 4-35 and 5-51 against Warwickshire and 5-92 against Yorkshire. Thriving on hard work, at The Oval he bowled 80 overs for 8-228. Batting was not his forte: his first eight innings for Kent were 0,0,0*, 0,1,0,1,1.

Work restricted his county cricket for the next three seasons but Lord Harris took him under his wing and thanks to an arrangement whereby he was employed by Consolidated Goldfields (chairman: Lord Harris!) and Kent paid part of his salary, he played full time from 1899 to 1902. Among his notable performances were 9-87 in Hampshire's first innings at Tonbridge in 1901, 12-83 v. Nottinghamshire at Trent Bridge in 1899 and 14-134 v. Lancashire at Old Trafford in 1901. He twice took a hundred wickets in a season and did the hat-trick three times including one at Tonbridge in 1899 when his victims were Yorkshire legends Hirst, Rhodes and Lord

Hawke. When fielding point at Cheltenham in 1896, a square cut hit him on the forehead en route to the boundary, despite which he finished with 6-31.

In his first Test at Old Trafford in 1899, Bradley dismissed Frank Laver with his first ball and ended with 5-67 from 33 overs. When Australia followed-on his captain MacLaren bowled him into the ground – 46 overs for just one wicket. Picked again for The Oval, his figures were 0-86. He made six appearances in Gentlemen v. Players. Taking a long run with arms pumping and finishing with a grunt, Bradley relied almost entirely on pace and lift although towards the end of his career he began, probably unwittingly, to move the ball in. Many of his wickets came from catches high on the bat – 'perchers' in Bill's own private vocabulary. Bradley considered himself the worst batsman in the game but against Yorkshire at Canterbury in 1897 he hit 67*, putting on 95 in 45 minutes for the last wicket with Walter Wright. He toured the USA with Kent in 1903 where his 28 wickets cost 8.28. On returning, he gave up his job with Consolidated Goldfields when something better turned up, thereby ending his county career. Troubled by his heart in later life, he was an inveterate cricket watcher and the centre of a group of friends whose freely expressed views on cricket and life were a feature of the Lord's Long Room between the wars.

Alan Brown

RHB & RF 1957-70

Alan Brown's career with Kent included two quite memorable performances, both against Midlands counties. In his third season, in the final championship match of 1958 against Nottinghamshire at Folkestone he took nine wickets, five in the first innings, which included four in five balls. Five years later, this time at Nuneaton against Warwickshire, he recorded his best return in an innings, with 8-48, which included the first five batsmen all dismissed with only 14 runs on the board.

Coming from a mining background, as once was the tradition with fast bowlers, Brown was a thoroughly enthusiastic cricketer, an exceptionally cheery and outgoing character, popular with spectators and opponents, always ready for a chat. He came to Kent through serving in the Army at Gravesend Barracks where he met and married a local girl. He bowled fast-medium, with a pronounced drag of his right foot. With Norman Graham, John Dye and David Sayer he was part of a formidable quartet of seam bowlers. His 707 wickets place him firmly in the top ten of post-war players. His most successful season was 1965 when he took 114 wickets at 19.07. Only Alan Dixon took more, but at greater cost. Surprisingly, this was the only season in which he achieved the 100 landmark. The five occasions on which he took ten in a match included 12-112 against Lancashire at Maidstone in 1962, 12-68 against Derbyshire at Derby in 1965 followed by 11-112 against Essex at Maidstone including seven in the first innings. In the memorable match against Worcestershire at Tunbridge Wells in 1960, which was completed in a single day, he shared with David Halfyard 38 of the 43 overs bowled and took 9-34. He played in the early days of limited-overs cricket and his best performances were in the Gillette Cup, with 3-17 against Sussex at

Born: Rainworth, Nottinghamshire, 17 October 1935

County Cap: 1961

Batting

M	I	NO	Runs	Av	100	50
237	301	81	2120	9.63	–	3
31	24	4	194	9.70	–	–

Bowling

Balls	Runs	Wkts	Av
38,723	17,534	707	24.80
1,516	945	37	25.54

5wI	10wM	ct/st
25	4	97
–	–	40

Best Performances

81 *v. Glamorgan (Folkestone)* 1968

37 *v. Northamptonshire (Northampton) 1969 (SL)*

8-46 *v. Warwickshire (Nuneaton)* 1963

12-68 *v. Derbyshire (Derby)* 1965

4-17 *v. Warwickshire (Maidstone) 1969 (SL)*

Tests: 2 for England

Canterbury in the 1967 semi-final (the season in which Kent won the Trophy) while it was in the John Player League that he recorded his best limited-overs bowling performance of 4–17.

He normally batted at ten or eleven and just failed to reach a double-figure average in his 301 innings. Nevertheless, he entertained with lusty blows and had an average of 18.54 in 1967, his best season with the bat. In the match against Yorkshire at Canterbury that year he hit Fred Trueman for 4,6,4,4, off successive balls in an innings of 33. His career-best score of 81 against Glamorgan at Folkestone in 1968 was a remarkable innings. Joining Alan Ealham at 170-8 on a pitch affected by rain, they put on 158 runs in double-quick time to demoralise Glamorgan and lay the foundation of an innings victory. He missed the whole of the 1964 season through a cartilage injury and appearances in his final seasons were restricted due to the emergence of a group of promising young players and to a broken leg while playing football. However, he played in 13 matches during the 1970 Championship winning season, taking 35 wickets.

Alan Brown toured with the MCC to India, Pakistan and Ceylon in 1961/62, playing in two Test matches and taking three wickets. An accomplished association footballer, his winters were spent playing as a centre forward for Kent non-League sides, notably for Gravesend and Northfleet, for whom he scored 26 goals in 43 matches. Following retirement he worked in the cement industry and the Post Office.

John Lindsay (Jack) Bryan MC

LHB & OB 1919-32

Born: Beckenham, 26 May 1896
Died: Eastbourne, Sussex, 23 April 1985
County Cap: 1920

Batting

M	I	NO	Runs	Av	100	50
119	187	17	6,174	36.31	12	30

Bowling

Balls	Runs	Wkts	Av
330	239	5	47.80

5wl	10wM	ct/st
–	–	67

Best Performances
236 *v.* Hampshire (Canterbury) 1923
Wisden **Cricketer of the Year:** 1922

Jack Bryan was the eldest of three brothers, all left-handed, all of whom played for Kent. A fourth brother appeared for Kent Seconds. Sound rather than brilliant, he had a strong defence, drove hard and was severe on anything loose on middle and leg. He seldom cut but had a powerful square drive which brought him a lot of runs in the arc from square to fine third man. An excellent player of fast bowling, he averaged 45.36, including three hundreds against Nottinghamshire in the days when they had Larwood, Voce, Barratt etc, to call on. Bryan was outstanding in the outfield or covers and occasionally bowled rather erratic leg breaks.

Bryan captained Rugby to victory over Marlborough at Lord's in 1914, his final year, and in the holidays appeared for Kent Second XI. In 1914 he was commissioned into the Manchester Regiment and was sent to the Western Front in October where he survived the murderous First Battle of Ypres, thus becoming an 'Old Contemptible' at eighteen-and-a-half. He subsequently served in Gallipoli and Egypt, then returned to France. He was awarded the MC while commanding a battalion of the Machine Gun Corps.

Before going up to Cambridge in 1919, he played three times for Kent without doing anything remarkable. In 1920 he missed his Blue but hit his first hundred for the County, 125 *v.* Worcestershire. In 1921 he not only got his Blue, he finished fifth in the national averages with 935 runs for Cambridge including a double-hundred against Surrey and another 923 for Kent. From 1921 onwards his cricket was for the most part confined to the holidays but he was three times selected for Gentlemen *v.* Players at Lord's. In 1923 he hit over 900 runs in all matches including his career best 236 *v.* Hampshire in Canterbury Week with 2 sixes, 1 five and 38 fours. One six went through an open pavilion window, narrowly missed a waiter and ricocheted into the picture of the 1877 Week. It still carries the mark.

In 1924 Bryan was chosen to tour Australia with MCC under Arthur Gilligan but, although playing well, with a batting line up of Hobbs, Sutcliffe, Hendren, Woolley, Hearne, Chapman, Sandham and Whysall, he did not manage to break into the Test team. Nevertheless, the class was there and had St Andrew's School, Eastbourne, where he taught for sixty years, not had priority, he might well have played regularly at top level. He rejoined the Army in 1939, served in France in 1940 and ended his career with the rank of Lieutenant Colonel. After giving up county cricket he played for Eastbourne as late as 1950.

Cuthbert James (Pinky) Burnup

RHB & RM 1896-1907

Cuthbert 'Pinky' Burnup is one of a select few 'best batsman never to play for England'. He had strong claims, not least on grounds of consistency, averaging over 30 in every one of his nine full seasons between 1896 and 1907 and only once failing to reach a thousand runs. He hit 1,505 runs at 40.12 in 1899, 1,780 at 35.60 in 1901 and 2,048 at 39.38 with six centuries in 1903. In his last year, 1906, he headed the national averages with 1,207 runs at 67.05

Three years in the XI at Malvern, Burnup failed to get his Blue at Cambridge in 1895 but was selected for the Gentlemen *v.* I Zingari at Lord's. Batting number nine, he hit 66★ and, opening the bowling, picked up three wickets. Next year he became a Double Blue, for cricket (1896-98) and for Association Football (1895-98). Opening against the MCC in 1896 he hit 95 and 93. On his debut for Kent, *v.* Gloucestershire at Gravesend in the opening game of the 1896 season, he was top scorer with 54 and an innings of 101 out of a total of 196 against the Australians in Canterbury Week added to his reputation. Possibly his finest performance was 171 and 65★ at Tonbridge in 1899 when Yorkshire, previously on course for the Championship, lost by eight wickets. Against Surrey at The Oval that year he carried his bat for 103★ out of 209. In 1900 he hit Kent's first double-hundred, 200 in 320 minutes (28 fours) at Old Trafford which included a partnership of 211 for the fifth wicket in 110 minutes with T.N. Perkins. His six-hour 179 at Bournemouth in late August 1906 clinched Kent's Championship.

Shortish and lightly built, Burnup kept the score moving without taking risks, providing solidity to a team of brilliant strokemakers. Against Nottinghamshire at Gravesend in 1897 he hit a hundred before lunch almost without anyone noticing. Unlike most public school amateurs of the period, he played back and across, holding the bat low down. Strong on the on side, he played the ball very late and was particularly good at scoring from good-length balls pitching middle and leg. He cut well and drove hard through extra cover. His medium-pace out-swingers could

Born: Blackheath, 21 November 1875
Died: North End, Golders Green, London,
5 April 1960
County Cap: 1896
County Captain: 1903

Batting

M	I	NO	Runs	Av	100	50
157	271	17	9,668	38.06	20	57

Bowling

Balls	Runs	Wkts	Av
3,189	1,795	41	43.78
5wI	10wM	ct/st	
1	–	74	

Best Performances
200 *v.* Lancashire (Manchester) 1900
5-44 *v.* Australia (Canterbury) 1899
***Wisden* Cricketer of the Year:** 1903

be useful. When Kent beat the Australians at Canterbury in 1899, used as fifth change, he took 3-7 in four overs and 5-44 when the visitors folded in the second innings. He was an outstanding fielder with safe hands and rated by many the best deep third man of his day. He captained Kent in 1903 and on their (unbeaten) ground-breaking tour of the USA that autumn. He was picked for Gentlemen *v.* Players at Lord's only once but played four times at The Oval, hitting 123 in 1900. He also hit a hundred for the Gentlemen at Scarborough in 1902. As a footballer, he played outside left for the Corinthians in their great days and gained one full England cap against Scotland. He was red-headed but why he was called 'Pinky' remains unclear.

———————————————— **Douglas Ward Carr**

RHB & LBG 1909-14

Kent's first leg-break and googly bowler, Douglas Carr was a late developer. Originally a useful all-rounder bowling mainly medium pace, he was in the XI at Sutton Valence and played in the Freshman's match at Oxford in 1891 but progressed no further beyond some success for the Mote, Band of Brothers, Free Foresters etc. For Blue Mantles in 1896 he finished off Newbury's first innings with a hat-trick and took wickets with his first two balls in the second innings to make it five in five. He was a good enough batsman to hit 165 for Free Foresters *v.* Royal

D.W.CARR (KENT)

Born: Cranbrook, 17 March 1872
Died: Salcombe Hill, Sidmouth, Devon,
   23 March 1950
County Cap: 1909

Batting

M	I	NO	Runs	Av	100	50
49	54	13	398	9.70	–	–

Bowling

Balls	Runs	Wkts	Av
8,948	4,529	290	15.61
5wI	10wM	ct/st	
27	8	18	

Best Performances
48 v. Somerset (Taunton) 1911
8-36 v. Somerset (Taunton) 1909
13-74 v. Gloucestershire (Dover) 1912
Test: 1 for England
Wisden **Cricketer of the Year:** 1910

Engineers in 1897 and in that year appeared for Kent Second XI. After playing against the father of the googly, Bernard Bosanquet, Carr, a teacher by profession, began experimenting, initially 'just for a rag'. Hard work throughout the 1905/06 winter paid off and by 1908 he had gained sufficient control of his new toy to baffle club batsmen. Invited by Kent to play against Oxford University in May 1909, match figures of 7-95 resulted in selection for the Gentlemen v. Players matches. Faced with the cream of England's professional batting he took 8-138 at The Oval and 7-128 at Lord's. Still without experience of county cricket, he was in the party for the Fourth Test match at Manchester but left out of the final eleven. A highly successful Canterbury Week (8-106 v. Middlesex, 6-99 v. Hampshire), was followed by selection for the Fifth Test at The Oval. Opening the bowling, he dismissed Gregory, Armstrong and Noble for 18 runs but his captain Archie MacLaren kept him on for an hour and a half and his final figures were 34-2-145-5 and 35-1-136-2.

Carr was in his thirty-eighth year and no lightweight but he troubled the Australians again with 4-27 and 4-78 when Lord Londesborough's XI beat them at Scarborough and he finished second in the Kent averages with 61 wickets at 16.21, including 8-36 v. Somerset at Taunton. Never available for more than half a season, he claimed 50 or more wickets at under 20 runs each year from 1910 to 1913. 1912 was his best with 7-46 v. the Australians and 8-36 v. Gloucestershire at Dover. He ended top of the Kent averages with fifty-six wickets at 9.21. The end came suddenly. Against Surrey at Blackheath in 1914, his only appearance, his analysis was

28-1-134-0. Although in club cricket he could still bowl a leg break, the googly hurt his shoulder.

More accurate than his contemporaries, Carr's googly seems to have been tossed up more than his leg break, coming out of the back of the hand in the usual way but, according to Carr himself 'more an action break' with spin 'put on by cutting under the ball with the third finger'. It does not seem to have turned much and he estimated that some seventy-five per cent of his wickets came from the leg break. Presumably, with the googly still a novelty, the mere threat was enough.

100 GREATS — Frederick Gerald Hudson (Gerry) Chalk DFC

RHB 1933-39

Born: Sydenham, 7 September 1910
Died: Louches near Calais, France,
   17 February 1943
County Cap: 1933
County Captain: 1938-39

Batting

M	I	NO	Runs	Av	100	50
101	169	12	4,436	28.25	5	24

Bowling

Balls	Runs	Wkts	Av
165	137	2	68.50

5wl	10wM	ct/st
–	–	40

Best Performances:
198 v. Sussex (Tonbridge) 1939

Cricket probably never saw the best of Gerry Chalk. The son of a master butcher with a chain of shops in South-East London, he captained Uppingham and gained a Blue in each of his four years at Oxford. Captain in 1934, he played a brilliant innings of 108 in the University match, adding 230 in 170 minutes with D.C.H. Townsend. Chalk made his debut for Kent v. Surrey at Blackheath in 1933 and proved a useful member of the side, not least for his fielding. After University, three years teaching at Malvern restricted his county cricket and it was not until 1937 that he hit his first hundred for Kent, 107 v. Middlesex at Lord's. Appointed captain in 1938, he scored a thousand runs in his first full season, hit 167 v. Worcestershire at Dudley and saw his team rise from twelfth to ninth in the table. 1939 was even better. Chalk hit 1,288 runs at 30.66, set a fine example in the field and Kent finished fifth. Against Sussex he hit 198 in four hours with 23 fours at Tonbridge and 104 in the return at Hastings, adding 215 for the third wicket with Bryan Valentine. He reached his peak in the final games at Dover in that strange, unreal August of 1939. Having put Yorkshire in, Chalk saw his side following-on 229 behind on the second day. Facing Hedley Verity on a turning wicket, he carried his bat for 115★ out of a total of 215 with only Doug Wright (34) passing 20. In the second match, set 382 by Lancashire, Kent won by five wickets from 520 balls with an hour to spare. Opening with Arthur Fagg, Chalk was first out with 94 (13 fours) in a partnership of 181. In 1939 he was picked for Gentlemen v. Players at Lord's and for the Gentlemen v. the Australians.

Chalk had a wide range of strokes, particularly on the off side, and in the field excelled in the covers and at mid off. As a captain he had a gift for getting the best out of everybody and was particularly good with nervous newcomers. With a flair for field placing and changing bowlers at exactly the right time, he always endeavoured to keep at least one bowler fresh.

In 1939 he joined the Army, subsequently transferring to the RAF. In July 1941, as a commissioned air gunner, he was awarded the DFC when, as the rear gunner in a Wellington returning from a raid on Hanover, he fought off and probably destroyed a German night fighter. Retrained as a fighter pilot, Flight Lieutenant Chalk was reported missing after an encounter with German fighters in 1943. At the time he was thought to have crashed in the Channel but in 1989 his remains were found, still in his Spitfire, deep in a French field. His funeral in France was attended by Leslie Ames, 'Hopper' Levett, Godfrey Evans and his brother-in-law Peter Foster, who played for Kent in 1939 and 1946.

Arthur Percy Frank Chapman ——————————— 100
LHB & LM/SLA 1924-38

Briefly the Golden Boy of English cricket, Percy Chapman arrived at Cambridge from Uppingham in 1920 with a considerable reputation. Awarded his Blue as a Freshman, he hit a hundred on first-class debut and was selected for Gentlemen v. Players. Next season brought another Blue and a place in MacLaren's all-amateur team that triumphed over the previously all-conquering Australians at Eastbourne. In 1922 he led Cambridge to an innings victory over Oxford to which he contributed a brilliant 102★. He was still playing for Berkshire when he made his Kent debut against Oxford in 1924. When he qualified for Kent in 1926 he had already toured Australia and had six Test caps. Selected for four Tests in 1926, in the last at The Oval he displaced Arthur Carr as captain amid much controversy but silenced criticism by winning the Ashes.

Six feet two (188cm) with powerful wrists and forearms, his batting depended more on physical strength than technique. Whatever happened, he kept playing strokes and, although lacking Woolley's classicism, he shared the latter's ability to drive the good-length ball over mid off, mid on, straight or square on the off side. When he flashed, as he did frequently, the result was likely to be six over point or third man. On the leg side he favoured the pull and short-arm hook. Outstanding at slip, gully

Born: Reading, Berkshire, 3 September 1900
Died: Alton, Hampshire, 16 September 1961
County Cap: 1925
County Captain: 1931-36

Batting

M	I	NO	Runs	Av	100	50
194	269	21	6,681	26.93	8	29

Bowling

Balls	Runs	Wkts	Av
207	151	3	50.33

5wl	10wM	ct/st
—	—	173

Career-Best Performances
260 *v.* Lancashire (Maidstone) 1927
Tests: 26 for England (17 as captain)
***Wisden* Cricketer of the Year:** 1919 (for Public Schools)

or cover, he had a flair for improbable catches. Even when, all too soon, his batting became a pale shadow of what had been, he remained inspirational near the wicket.

His great days lasted only a few seasons. In 1926 he averaged 49.50 for Kent and in 1927 hit 985 runs at 70.35 with three hundreds including one of the truly great innings. Coming in at 70-5 against eventual champions Lancashire at Maidstone, he hit 260 (5 sixes, 32 fours) in just over three hours. With Geoffrey Legge (101) he added 284 in 150 minutes. Ted McDonald, the world's best fast bowler, was treated like a Saturday afternoon trundler. In 1928 he averaged 38 but decline was setting in. From 1930 he never again averaged over 30 for Kent, three times below 20. Business and a crowded social life often intervened, but from 1931 to 1936 he was a popular Kent captain. While no great tactician, he had a gift for leadership, willing to listen to senior players while remaining his own man. He led a happy side, bringing, in the words of Robertson-Glasgow 'breadth and humour to what was in danger of becoming narrow and parochial'. Leslie Ames wrote, 'you just had to enjoy yourself'. As England captain he retained the Ashes in Australia, winning the 1928/29 series 4-1. Against the Australians in 1930, after winning one, losing one and drawing two, he lost the captaincy. At Lord's he hit a spectacular 121, becoming the only man to hit hundreds in the University match, Gentlemen *v.* Players and for England.

The rest was tragedy. His business life was mainly linked to brewing or distilling and that he drank too much was no secret. The break-up of his marriage in 1942 plus that scourge of sportsmen late in life, arthritis, accelerated the slide. By the end he was an embarrassment to his friends and probably himself. He died following a fall.

George Christopher Collins

LHB & RFM 1911-28

Born: Gravesend, 21 September 1889
Died: Rochester, 23 January 1949
County Cap: 1920

Batting

M	I	NO	Runs	Av	100	50
212	316	37	6,237	22.35	4	33

Bowling

Balls	Runs	Wkts	Av
17,473	8,964	178	23.71

5wI	10wM	ct/st
24	3	79/1

Best Performances

110 v. Leicestershire (Leicester) 1926
10-65 (16-83) v. Nottinghamshire (Dover) 1922

George Collins had cricket in the blood. Three generations played for the county, a unique record for Kent. Father Christopher was a promising fast bowler and played eight times between 1881 and 1885 before doubts about his action ended his career. He was subsequently groundsman at Gravesend. Uncle George, a fastish round-arm bowler and useful batsman, appeared intermittently between 1874 and 1882. Grandfather Ben played one match in 1856.

The younger George was essentially a journeyman cricketer, his value to the side not always reflected in figures. Tall, heavily built and looking rather clumsy, he was immensely strong. Although presumably not often having cause to do so, he was said to be able to lift a pavilion chair with his teeth. As a left-handed batsman he was no stylist but adaptable. He could take the shine off as an opener or bat lower down when the full quota of amateurs was available later in the season. Here he was equally happy to stick or go for quick runs. As a bowler he took a long run, worked hard and on his best days his out-swinger often brought him early wickets but his pace was never more than fast medium. In the field he never gave anything less than his best but his build was against him. He could also keep wicket.

Collins joined the Tonbridge Nursery in 1908 and played one match in 1911, opening the batting against Gloucestershire on his home ground, Gravesend. He made seven appearances in 1912 with a top score of 80 at Northampton where he added 122 for the eighth wicket with Bill Fairservice. According to *Wisden,* the two batted in 'masterly style'. Nobody else achieved double figures. Despite this, and a steady 59 against Essex at Leyton, he only played once in 1913 and left the staff at the end of the season. In 1919 he rejoined and became a first-team regular from 1920 to 1926. Opening the batting at Old Trafford in 1922 he hit 108, his last 50 coming in 55 minutes, as well as taking six wickets. Two months later at Dover with the wind aiding his out-swinger, he claimed 6-58 and followed up with 10-66 against a Nottinghamshire batting order beginning with five Test cricketers. When he had taken nine he missed a sitter off Freeman and was almost in tears in case people thought it deliberate. The fact that Freeman took the catch for his tenth cannot have helped. In his next match, *v.* Middlesex at Lord's, he began with five wides.

Although never doing anything comparable, he was always useful. In 1923 he came near to a double with 1,036 runs and 90 wickets. Against Worcestershire at Gravesend that year he hit 101★ and took 5-55. His last game was in 1928 *v.* Nottinghamshire, yet again at Gravesend. Due to injury he was unable to bat in either innings. Subsequently he was groundsman at the Officer's Club, Aldershot.

100 GREATS — Christopher Stuart (Chris) Cowdrey

RHB & RM 1976-91

Christopher Cowdrey came close to playing in the same Kent XI as his distinguished father. The title of his autobiography, *Good Enough?* posed what for him was an important question which in some respects dominated his career. After fourteen years with the County, six of which he served as Captain, there could be few Kent followers who would not respond to that question in the affirmative.

Like so many Kent players, Chris Cowdrey was educated at Tonbridge, where his cricketing talent was encouraged and developed. At his preparatory school, Wellesley House, he was selected for the first XI when just nine; at Tonbridge, he was playing in the first XI at fourteen. He writes in his autobiography of the pressures and expectations at an early age, becoming aware of being under the spotlight. This is not surprising, being the son of Colin, baptised by former England captain and Bishop of Liverpool David Sheppard, and having as Godparents another England captain, Peter May, and the one-time Kent and England opener Peter Richardson!

With those expectations he joined Kent, playing his first Second XI match in 1973 when just fifteen years old. Three years later he made his first-team debut in a Sunday League match against Yorkshire at Scarborough, and his first-class debut against the Australians in a rain-affected match at Canterbury in 1977. Few have played with more enthusiasm. His approach was especially suited to the limited-overs game where his versatility as a forcing batsman, right-arm medium pace bowler and brilliant fielder (few were so good in so many different positions) was used to good effect. His 309 matches in this form gives him an all-round record which compares with the best for the County. In the first-class game he scored 1,000 runs in a season four times, the best in 1983 with 1,364 at an average of 56.83. His aggregate of 11,869 first-class runs places him in the top thirty of the County's outstanding batsmen. He was appointed vice-captain of the side in 1984 and served as captain from 1985 to 1990. In 1988 he led the side to within two points of winning the

| Born: Farnborough, Kent, 20 October 1957 |
| County Cap: 1979 |
| County Captain: 1985-90 |

Batting

M	I	NO	Runs	Av	100	50
280	430	64	11,869	32.42	21	5
309	279	45	6,518	27.85	2	41

Bowling

Balls	Runs	Wkts	Av
13,259	7,216	181	39.86
7,152	5,472	186	29.41

5wl	10wM	ct/st
2	–	274
1	–	100

Best Performances

159 v. Surrey (Canterbury) 1985
122* v. Essex (Chelmsford) 1983 (NWT)
5-46 v. Hampshire (Canterbury) 1988
5-28 v. Leicestershire (Canterbury) 1984 (SL)
Tests: 6 for England (1 as captain)
Limited-Overs Internationals: 3 for England

County Championship. Between 1984 and 1988 he played in six Test matches, five of which were against India on the 1984/85 tour. He was unexpectedly appointed England captain for the final two Tests in the disastrous series against the West Indies in 1988. In the event, injury prevented him from playing in the second. In 1991 he appeared in only three first-class and 13 limited-overs matches and when fit was unable to gain a regular place in the side. He was not re-engaged at the end of that season and subsequently signed a one year contract with Glamorgan.

He became a member of Kent's General Committee in 2001, thus maintaining a family link with the County that, with a very short break, goes back to 1950.

Graham Robert Cowdrey

RHB & RM 1984-98

When Graham Cowdrey left the field at the end of a limited-overs match against Sri Lanka in August 1998, Kent supporters said farewell to a family dynasty that spanned almost fifty years of the Club's history. Between them, the Cowdrey family, Colin, Christopher and Graham, had made 861 first-class and 651 limited-overs

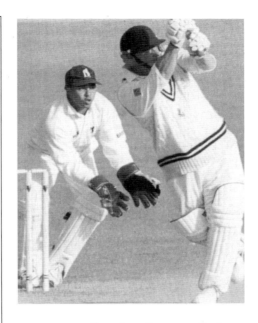

Born: Farnborough, Kent, 27 June 1964
County Cap: 1988

Batting

M	I	NO	Runs	Av	100	50
179	284	29	8,858	34.73	17	46
261	230	33	5,144	26.11	3	24

Bowling

Balls	Runs	Wkts	Av
1,206	872	12	72.66
1,279	920	35	26.28

5wI	10wM	ct/st
–	–	97
–	–	80

Best Performances

147 *v. Gloucestershire (Bristol)* 1992
105* *v. Hampshire (Southampton)* 1995 (SL)
4-15 *v. Essex (Ilford)* 1987 (SL)

appearances for the County. Graham retired at the relatively early age of thirty-four and it was perhaps appropriate that his final appearance should be against the side captained by Kent's popular overseas player of 1995, Aravinda de Silva, for it was in him that Graham found his kindred spirit. They became great friends, and shared one of the County's outstanding batting performances, certainly of the post-war period, with a record partnership at The Mote of 368 against Derbyshire for the fourth wicket; the highest ever stand by a Kent pair for any wicket.

Maybe no-one in Kent's history can have enjoyed his cricket more. He gave much pleasure to supporters especially in the limited-overs game, in which his natural talent came to the fore. His record, for the most part, justified the confidence placed in him, although one is left with the feeling that his was a talent not wholly fulfilled, especially in first-class matches. While his average with the bat was marginally better than that of his elder brother, he was no first-class bowler! But he had some unexpected successes when he bowled in limited-overs matches. In the three seasons between 1990 and 1992 he exceeded 1,000 first-class runs, his best being in 1990 with an aggregate of 1,576 at 47.76. Despite those three good years, he was unable to maintain any degree of consistency and could not hold down a regular first-team place in the four-day game. But it will be as a successful one-day batsman that he will be best remembered by Kent supporters. His 5,144 runs were scored in style and many were the occasions when he was able to turn a match by his aggressive batting, or a piece of spectacular fielding, be it a catch or a run out. In the final Refuge Assurance League match against Leicestershire at Folkestone in 1989 he single-handedly rescued Kent with an innings of 102 off 76 balls that included six sixes and eight fours, with his second 50 coming off just 17 balls. Only two players have hit more sixes for the County in limited-overs matches. He shares with Christopher the record fifth-wicket partnership in the Benson & Hedges competition and for a number of years uniquely shared with him record wicket partnerships in all three limited-overs competitions.

Since his retirement he has developed a strong association with the horse racing industry, in which his wife Maxine was one of the first female National Hunt jockeys.

100 ——— Michael Colin Cowdrey CBE (Baron Cowdrey of Tonbridge)
GREATS
RHB & LBs 1950-76

In the pantheon of Kent's heroes Colin Cowdrey's place is assured. He played for twenty-seven successive seasons, captaining the County from 1957 to 1971, a period equalled only by Lord Harris. Only the latter can match Cowdrey's service to Kent and country as a player and cricket administrator. Cowdrey stands sixth in the all-time list of Kent run-scorers, his career average beaten only by Les Ames of those who scored over 10,000 runs. He is fourth in the list of Kent century-makers. This despite the fact that for the best part of half of his career Cowdrey played in a Kent side that was at best indifferent, at worst weak. It was largely a period of uncovered wickets and at a time when there was a succession of very wet summers. There were also Test calls and, too often, injury and illnesses that interrupted his Kent career.

While there were often questions over his captaincy of England, such doubts were never so pre-eminent in Kent. For this the shrewd appointment of Les Ames as the Kent manager has much to answer. Ames provided the perfect match to the often diffident Cowdrey, not the least in the firm control of discipline off the field, never Cowdrey's greatest strength. Together they raised Kent from the depths of 1957 to the remarkable summer of 1970, when, having been bottom of the table mid-season, they brought the County Championship back to the hop county for the first time since 1913.

The legend is that his cricket-fanatic father gave his only child his very distinctive initials quite deliberately. Certainly the elements of the game were instilled from an early age on the tea plantation in India where he was born. That is until aged five, when his parents transported him back to England for school, only to be parted by war for the next seven years. The cricket potential was apparent the moment he went to Tonbridge School, although at this stage his leg break and googly bowling was attracting as much attention as his batting. While at Tonbridge, he became almost certainly the youngest player ever to appear in a competitive match at Lord's, scoring 75 and 44 and taking 3-58 and 5-59. For the next four seasons he rewrote the Tonbridge record books, making almost 3,000 runs. It was Tonbridge that cemented his attachment to Kent.

A man of great sensitivity and modesty, Cowdrey probably never realised how good a cricketer he was. This uncertainty often brought caution and introspection

Born: Ootacamund, India, 24 December 1932

Died: Angmering Park, Littlehampton, Sussex, 4 December 2000

County Cap: 1951

County Captain: 1957-71

Batting

M	I	NO	Runs	Av	100	50
402	651	85	23,779	42.01	58	128
81	72	11	1,921	31.49	3	12

Bowling

Balls	Runs	Wkts	Av
1,905	1,285	27	47.59
59	43	3	14.33

5wI	10wM	ct/st
–	–	406
–	–	37

Career-Best Performances

250 v. Essex (Blackheath) 1959

116 v. Suffolk (Ipswich) 1966 (GC)

4-22 v. Surrey (Blackheath) 1951

Tests: 114 for England (27 as captain)

Limited-Overs International: 1 for England

Wisden Cricketer of the Year: 1956

that could bedevil his performances. But at his best he was one of the outstanding English batsmen of the twentieth century. To a generation of cricket followers, notably in Kent, Cowdrey was the master. Most will recall to their dying day at least one Cowdrey innings played at his superb best. A hundred in eighty minutes in the gloom of a Gravesend evening with Kent facing an innings defeat, or, in his last full season, a magnificent 151 not out to give Kent their first victory over the Australians in seventy-six years. No-one played the cover drive more elegantly. No one could handle short-pitched bowling with such breathtaking hooks. No one caressed the ball with more perfect timing to the boundary. Cowdrey was the supreme master of orthodox strokeplay, allowing only a dalliance with the irregular, his distinctive 'paddle'. Despite being plump and unathletic on first sight, he was an excellent judge of a quick single and in the slips his lightning reactions brought him many catches, the ball often characteristically sliding into his pocket before any realisation of its fate. The early promise of a high-class bowler never bore fruit.

Cowdrey played Test cricket for England over a period of twenty years. When he retired he had scored more runs and more hundreds than any other Englishman, and played in more Tests and taken more catches than anyone anywhere. He was the first player to play in a hundred Tests, a distinction he celebrated with a hundred. But it was an England career of serious highs and lows, of a potential that was perhaps never

*Lord's, 1960.
Colin Cowdrey
cuts Middlesex
left-arm spinner
Bob Hurst for
four. The
wicketkeeper is
John Murray.*

fully fulfilled, of issues such as the captaincy and his role as an opener that too often seriously distracted. For a man of his sensitivity to be for ever at the whim of selectorial indecision did not help his confidence. Cowdrey had no fewer than five stints as England captain. He permanently had trouble convincing the England selectors that he had the necessary determination for the post. Most disappointingly for him was that despite a record–equalling six tours of Australia, he never achieved his ultimate ambition of leading a side there. Perhaps he lacked the guidance of an Ames as a foil – he was noticeably most successful on the 1967/68 West Indies tour when Ames was the manager. Time and time again gross ill-fortune intervened, not the least a succession of injuries and illnesses.

In his latter years, Cowdrey's enthusiasm and commitment to the game was given rein in cricket administration. As President of the MCC in 1987, the Club's bicentenary, he oversaw a year of discontent between the MCC and the Test and County Cricket Board. As President of the International Cricket Council (twice) he travelled the world using cricketing high diplomacy to resolve seemingly intractable issues such as the return of South Africa to the world arena, the introduction of an international code of conduct, and the appointment of match referees to oversee international games. Cowdrey was awarded a CBE in 1972, a knighthood in 1992 and then in 1997 he was raised to the peerage taking, in deference to his old school, the title of Baron Cowdrey of Tonbridge.

In 2000 Cowdrey became President of the Kent County Cricket Club. During Canterbury Festival Week he suffered a severe stroke from which he seemed to be making an encouraging recovery when he died quite suddenly in his sleep four months later.

Arthur Percival (Happy) Day

RHB & LB/RF 1905-25

Born: Blackheath, 10 April 1885
Died: Budleigh Salterton, Devon.
  22 January 1969
County Cap: 1905

Batting

M	I	NO	Runs	Av	100	50
143	217	22	6,532	33.49	13	33

Bowling

Balls	Runs	Wkts	Av
6,847	3,236	129	25.08

5wI	10wM	ct/st
4	–	85

Best Performances
184* v. Sussex (Tonbridge) 1921
8-46 v. Middlesex (Lord's) 1911
Wisden Cricketer of the Year: 1910

A. P. DAY. (KENT)

When Frank Woolley was asked to name the best Kent bowler of his time he replied, 'For a month, Mr Day.' Up to 1910 Arthur Day was considered a batsman who bowled a bit. After six seasons he had just ten expensive wickets to his credit. The change came in 1911 at Lord's in Kent's first county fixture of the season. Day was not given the ball until the second innings when Middlesex, chasing 452, were 122-0. Bowling 'fastish' with a high action and swinging the ball away, he immediately had Tarrant (72) lbw, bowled Hendren (4) and finished with 8-49. Little used in his next two outings, he repeated the performance at Sheffield, ripping out Yorkshire's middle order and tail with figures of 7-66. Playing only ten matches, he ended the season with 33 wickets at 16.38. For the rest of his career he was useful – he claimed 30 wickets at 19.33 in 1914 – but never again approached this form.

Like elder brother Sam, Day gained a considerable reputation as a batsman at Malvern where he was in the XI from 1901 to 1904, the last two years as captain. He made his debut for Kent in 1905 and ended the season with 1,149 runs at 32.82 including two centuries, both against Gloucestershire. Next year saw a decline. He was dropped towards the end of the season and played only a few games in 1907. Returning to form in 1908, he hit 118 in a partnership of 246 for the seventh wicket with 'Punter' Humphreys v. Somerset at Taunton and in 1909 passed a thousand runs averaging 41 and hitting three hundreds. When scoring 177 v. Essex at Leyton he put on 107 for the fifth wicket with Humphreys and 189 for the sixth with brother Sam (79).

In 1910 he shared another long partnership with Humphreys, 254 *v.* Lancashire at Tunbridge Wells and in the following year he reached 100★ in 55 minutes *v.* Hampshire at Southampton. He was selected six times for Gentlemen *v.* Players and hit 52 for the Rest of England in one of the Test Trial matches staged in 1912. He played occasionally after the First World War. In just four matches in 1921 his scores were: 48 and 184★ *v.* Sussex at Tonbridge; 31 and 44 *v.* Nottinghamshire at Catford; 101 and 3★ *v.* Surrey at The Oval; 67 and 77★ *v.* Surrey at Blackheath.

Like most Malvern-trained batsmen Arthur Day was strong on the off side and a good fast-wicket player. Much taller than Sam, he used his height to drive the short ball in the best Malvern tradition. Like his brother but unlike many of his public school contemporaries he was also good when the ball was turning. On a wet wicket at Hull in his debut season he scored 54 and 58★ against Rhodes, Haigh, Hirst, Jackson and co. Only one other Kent batsman passed 30. Although never officially captain, he led Kent on six occasions, six times to victory.

Samuel Hulme (Sam/Sammy) Day

RHB & RFM 1897-1919

| Born: Peckham Rye, 29 December 1878 |
| Died: Chobham, Surrey, 21 February 1950 |
| County Cap: 1899 |

Batting

M	I	NO	Runs	Av	100	50
128	206	18	5,893	31.34	5	38

Bowling

Balls	Runs	Wkts	Av
252	201	7	28.71

5wI	10wM	ct/st	
—	—	35	

Best Performances
152* *v.* Gloucestershire (Bristol) 1904
3-46 *v.* Hampshire (Bournemouth) 1914

Son of a successful wine merchant and elder brother of Arthur and Sydney, who also played for the county, Sam Day was still at Malvern when he hit 101★ in the second innings *v.* Gloucestershire at Cheltenham on his debut for Kent in 1897. Captain of Malvern in 1897/98, he was awarded his Blue as a Freshman at Cambridge in 1899, played against Oxford four times, as captain in 1901. He contributed 117★ to the Cambridge victory in 1902. Although Cambridge and subsequently teaching ruled out a full season, he was always a valuable addition to the side, not least for his fielding at which, unlike brother Arthur, he was outstanding, especially in the outfield. In 1901 he hit 118 against Hampshire at Tonbridge, sharing a second-wicket partnership of 210 in 135 minutes with C.J. Burnup (144). 1904 was his best season when he headed the Kent averages with 735 runs at 45.93 in only 11 matches. Although normally a strokeplayer, he could get his head down when necessary. In the second innings at Bristol in 1904 with the odds on a Gloucestershire victory, he batted five hours for 152*.

Day was abroad on a football tour for most of 1906 but between 1907 and 1909 and in 1914 he averaged over 30 despite restricted appearances. Against Sussex in Canterbury Week 1908 he scored a chanceless 114 in 150 minutes, adding 118 in fifty minutes with Jack Mason. His last hundred for Kent was against Worcestershire at Canterbury sixteen days after the outbreak of war. In a fourth-wicket partnership with Frank Woolley, 200 runs came in 100 minutes. – Day 109, Woolley 160*. His final innings for Kent was 68 against Hampshire at Bournemouth in 1919. Surprisingly, he was never selected for any of the major Gentlemen *v*. Players matches.

Very quick on his feet, some considered him even better when the wicket was helping the spinners than on hard pitches. He shared with 'Punter' Humphreys, a positive relish for genuine sticky wickets. Among a wide array of off-side strokes were the square drive and the more unusual cut off the front foot. So well did he play the cut in all its forms, it was said that, when he settled in, to post a third man was wasting a fielder. Like Bill Ashdown of a later generation, his greatest strength was also his main weakness. He often got out early on caught at slip or behind the wicket through playing ambitious off-side shots before he had settled.

He won four and lost none of his seven games as Kent captain. At Association Football he was considered one of the best of his time at what used to be called inside forward. He won a Football Blue at Cambridge in 1901 and played three times for England in 1906. In 1903 he was in the Corinthians side that beat the FA Cup holders Bury 10-3 to win the Sheriff of London Charity Shield.

Michael Henry (Mike) Denness

100 GREATS

RHB & OB/RM 1962-76

As a nineteen-year-old, Mike Denness had his first experience of international cricket in 1959, albeit for Scotland. *Wisden* records that he was the first schoolboy to be capped by Scotland. He came to Kent for a month's trial in 1961, making his Second XI debut in the first match of the season against Essex, scoring 48 in Kent's second innings. The following year he joined Kent on a special registration and for his debut match Essex were again the opponents. In his first appearance he did not distinguish himself, largely because he encountered a rampant Jim Laker, and managed just three runs in two innings. But one week later he top-scored with 51 in a first-innings total of 198 against Surrey. This was the start of a fifteen-year career with Kent during which he developed an opening partnership

Born: Bellshill, Lanarkshire, Scotland,
  1 December 1940
County Cap: 1964
County Captain: 1972-76

Batting

M	I	NO	Runs	Av	50	100
333	562	44	17,047	32.90	21	103
158	150	17	4,001	30.08	5	22

Bowling

Balls	Runs	Wkts	Av
72	55	2	27.50
–	–	–	–

5wI	10wM	ct/st
–	–	308
–	–	74

Best Performances
178 v. Somerset (Maidstone) 1973
118* v. Yorkshire (Scarborough) 1976 (SL)
Tests: 28 for England (19 as captain)
Limited-Overs Internationals: 12 for England
(all as captain)
Wisden **Cricketer of the Year:** 1975

with Brian Luckhurst that lasted from the final matches of the 1964 season up to mid-1971 when he took over the captaincy and dropped down the batting order. They opened together in 147 first-class matches and shared century partnerships on twenty-three occasions. This opening partnership also served the County well in the two limited-overs competitions of that period, often with stands which laid the foundation for match-winning scores in the early years of Kent's dominance in this form of the game. They still hold the record for an opening partnership of 182 created in the then-John Player League against Somerset in 1970.

Regarded as one of the most graceful batsmen of his day, Denness scored 1,000 runs in a season on twelve out of fifteen occasions, his best being in 1965 with just over 1,500. His aggregate of 17,047 runs puts him thirteenth among the County's batsmen. In all, he scored thirty-three first-class hundreds. He was technically very orthodox and it has been said he played like one of the best pre-war amateurs. He played in 28 Tests, was vice-captain of the MCC tour of India, Pakistan and Sri Lanka in 1972/73 and went on to captain England on 19 occasions including the tours of 1973/74 to the West Indies and 1974/75 to Australia and New Zealand. On that tour he topped the batting averages with a total of 1,136 runs despite loss of form and criticism of his captaincy, much of it ill-informed and technically ignorant. Given the quality of the opposition, it is doubtful if anyone else would have done significantly better. Because of his loss of form he dropped himself for the Fourth

Test, returning for the final two matches when he scored a first-innings 50 in the Fifth Test followed by a first-innings 188 in the final match. He followed this with an innings of 181 in the First Test in New Zealand. Although, as with virtually every other England batsman, he had so much trouble with Lillee and Thomson, an outstanding feature of his batting was his footwork which served him particularly well against the spinners. This was much in evidence during the three-match Test series against India in 1974, when he averaged 96.33.

Mike Denness was captain of Kent from 1972 to 1976 during which the County won the Championship once, the Gillette Cup once and the Sunday League and Benson & Hedges Cup twice. In his first full season as captain he led the side to the Sunday League title for the first time. During his period of captaincy the team won 29 out of 100 Championship matches and 83 out of 116 (71.5%) in the three limited-overs competitions. But he gained considerable experience of captaining the side before his formal appointment. In 1969 he took over the captaincy early in the season following a serious injury to Colin Cowdrey which kept him out of the side until the final match of that year. He also deputised as captain on seven occasions in the 1970 Championship winning side when Colin Cowdrey was on Test match duty, and when the team was additionally weakened with Knott, Luckhurst and Underwood also appearing for England. Three of those matches, played in the second half of the season when the side was progressing from bottom place in the Championship, were won. In that 1970 Championship winning season, he scored 1,445 runs at an average of 41.28. In the match against Essex he played a not out

Middlesex 'keeper John Murray sees Mike Denness cut to the boundary during his innings of 26 against Middlesex at Lord's in 1966.

innings of 167 in an emphatic innings victory and in the mid–August match against Gloucestershire at Cheltenham he scored a masterly 97 on a difficult wicket to help win a match that made Kent favourites for the title. Those were two occasions when he captained the side.

His outstanding performances were not confined to the first-class game. He was a vital part of the Club's successes in the limited-overs triumphs of the late 1960s and the 1970s. His record in the three competitions was outstanding, including century partnerships on fourteen occasions. He was a brilliant fielder, taking over 400 first-class catches and seventy-four in limited-overs matches. When Kent defeated Somerset to win the Gillette Cup – their first title in more than fifty years – Mike Denness was judged Man of the Match for his innings of 50 in an opening partnership of 78 with Brian Luckhurst.

He left the County at the end of the 1976 season in controversial circumstances, going on to play for Essex for four years, during which he recorded his highest first-class score of 195 against Leicestershire in his first season with them. In 1988 he was elected to the Kent Committee and served as chairman of the Cricket Committee in recent years.

Graham Roy Dilley

LHB & RF 1977-86

In recent years Kent has not been generally regarded as a nursery for England fast bowlers, but in Graham Dilley the County produced an outstanding player who appeared in forty-one Tests. Such was the immediate promise of his fast bowling that he was selected for England before being awarded his County Cap. But given his international recognition at such an early stage, that he played in so few matches must be attributed to a succession of injuries, a bout of glandular fever, losing the whole of the 1984 season with a serious neck injury and a loss of confidence at crucial times in his career.

He made his first-team debut for Kent at the age of eighteen against Cambridge University at Canterbury in 1977. The following season he played in four Championship matches, taking seven of his eight first-class wickets that season in his first Championship match at Lord's. His one Sunday League appearance that season, against Surrey at The Oval, yielded him three wickets in six overs at a cost of just 13 runs. In 1982 he took 57 wickets for the County with a haul of five in an innings on three occasions. His best return was in 1986, his final season with Kent, when at Canterbury in Lancashire's first innings he took 6-57, following it with a further four in the second innings. He took two hat-tricks, against Surrey at The Oval in 1985 and Essex at Chelmsford the following year. His career-best performance was in South Africa playing for Natal against Transvaal in the 1985/86 season, when he took 7-63. He was no less effective in the limited-overs game, with a total of 131 wickets in 101 matches. His economy rate of 3.60 runs per over is in the top six of all Kent's specialist bowlers since the introduction of the shorter game. As a

Born: Dartford, 18 May 1959
County Cap: 1980

Batting

M	I	NO	Runs	Av	50	100
109	116	39	993	12.89	–	1
101	58	18	454	11.35	–	–

Bowling

Balls	Runs	Wkts	Av
14,179	7,145	257	27.80
4,799	2,886	131	22.03

5wI	10wM	ct/st
12	2	51
1	–	28

Best Performances
81 v. Northamptonshire (Northampton) 1979
37* v. Hampshire (Canterbury) 1983 (SL)
6-57 (10-110) v. Lancashire (Canterbury) 1986
5-29 v. Scotland (Edinburgh) 1986 (NWT)
Tests: 41 for England
Limited-Overs Internationals: 36 for England

lower-order left-hand batsman he played a number of significant innings for Kent as well as for England. His career-best score of 81 was achieved against Northamptonshire in 1979 when, with Derek Underwood, he added 129 for the ninth wicket. With his long stride, turn of speed and fast, accurate throw, he developed into a brilliant out fielder, particularly suited to the one-day game.

For those not necessarily associated with Kent cricket, he will be best remembered for his part in the Headingley Test of 1981. After following on 227 runs behind the Australian first-innings total of 401 and being 135-7, Graham Dilley joined Ian Botham in a stand of 117 in 80 minutes with a personal contribution of 56. It is a part of cricket history that this remarkable stand turned the series England's way. In the year prior to this he had earned recognition as Young Player of the Year. His first appearance in Test cricket was in Perth, when he became at 20 years and 210 days the youngest England debutant in thirty years. Had he enjoyed an injury-free career, he would undoubtedly have taken many more than 138 Test wickets.

After ten years with Kent he moved to Worcestershire, for whom he appeared in 52 matches and in recent years he has been one of the team of England bowling coaches.

Edward Wentworth (Ted) Dillon

LHB & LB 1900-23

Born: Penge, 15 February 1881
Died: Totteridge, London, 20 April 1941
County Cap: 1901
County Captain: 1909-13

Batting

M	I	NO	Runs	Av	100	50
223	348	22	9,415	28.88	12	46

Bowling

Balls	Runs	Wkts	Av
2,014	1,321	27	48.92

5wI	10wM	ct/st
–	–	195

Best Performances

141 *v.* Gloucestershire (Catford) 1905
3-20 *v.* Gloucestershire (Cheltenham) 1901

Edward Dillon was Kent's most successful skipper. His record reads: champions 1909, 1910 and 1913, second 1911, third 1912. In each of five seasons he missed a half-dozen or more matches due to the calls of business (insurance and ship-broking) but he won 64.4 per cent of the matches in which he led the side. Among other regular captains only Troughton (55.5 per cent), Marsham (51.7 per cent) and Cornwallis, (51.3 per cent) have a better than fifty per cent success rate. Despite the then obligatory public school/Oxbridge background, Dillon had a democratic approach and led a happy side, relaxed by mutual respect and confidence in each other's ability. Tactically astute apart from one or two misjudgements when inserting the opposition, he was always willing to take advice from experienced professionals such as Blythe and Huish.

Making full use of his height, Dillon excelled in the drive, straight and on both sides of the wicket, backed by the full range of left-hander's strokes between midwicket and fine leg. Restless at the crease, constantly adjusting his pads, fiddling with his gloves and patting the wicket, he was sound in defence and a regular opener until the Hardinge/Humphreys partnership settled in. Although he rarely bowled his leg spinners for Kent, he topped the Oxford University bowling averages in 1902.

Dillon learned his cricket at Abbey School, Beckenham, before going on to Rugby where he was in the XI from 1898 to 1900, captain in the last two years. In his final year at Rugby he hit a century on his first-class debut, 108 for W.G. Grace's London County *v.* Worcestershire at Crystal Palace. In the same week he played his first game for Kent, *v.* Somerset at Taunton and on his next appearance, against Hampshire at Tonbridge, he scored 90 and 59. He gained a Blue as a Freshman at Oxford in 1901 and hit 85 and 59 when his side lost to Cambridge in the following year. After Oxford he played for Kent as often as business permitted. In 1905 he headed the Kent averages with 1,310 runs at 48.51 including four centuries. Of his twelve hundreds for Kent none was more valuable than his 138 *v.* Yorkshire at Dewsbury in 1910 after the home side had been skittled for 81. Batting for four hours when no other batsman passed 35, he set up Kent's nine-wicket victory. He took part in three double-hundred partnerships, two for the first wicket with C.J. Burnup, 243 *v.* Hampshire at Tunbridge Wells in 1902 and 210 *v.* Worcestershire at Worcester in 1901 and 261 with James Seymour for the second wicket *v.* Somerset at Taunton in 1905. Less happy was his experience playing for Oxford University *v.* Kent in 1902 when he had his nose broken by Bill Bradley. He toured the West Indies with B.J.T. Bosanquet's team in 1902 and the USA with Kent in 1903. He played Rugby for Blackheath and was capped three times for England. During the First World War he served with the Royal West Kent Regiment.

100 GREATS — Alan Leonard Dixon

RHB & OB/RM 1950-70

At the age of 16 years and 248 days, Alan Dixon is the third youngest player to have made his first-class debut for Kent. His maiden appearance was against Essex at Clacton in early August 1950 just weeks after his first match with the Second XI at Canterbury. It was not exactly an auspicious start, with scores of 3 and 0, no wickets for 19 runs in two overs and defeat by ten wickets. That was his only first-class match in his debut season and between then and 1955 he played in just one more. He was awarded his Second XI Cap in 1951 but his career was on hold in the early 1950s due to national service.

A product of the Alf Gover/*Evening News* coaching scheme, he was a very dedicated cricketer who worked hard at his game. By 1955 there were signs that he would develop into a genuine all-rounder although his early promise was as a batsman. Even then, five years after his debut appearance, he still struggled to achieve a regular first-team berth although he had a promising season in 1956 with almost 900 runs and 32 wickets. But two poor seasons followed. Then in 1959 he established himself, playing in 27 matches and scoring more than 1,000 runs. This was the first of three successive seasons when he achieved 1,000 runs with a maiden hundred in 1960. Although he played a number of important and crucial innings he was becoming a more important member of the side as a bowler. Initially, he bowled off-breaks but also developed into an extremely useful medium-pace seamer. As his bowling developed so his batting fell away and his three most successful seasons with the bat were followed by three equally successful with the ball. He delivered more overs than any other Kent bowler in 1964 and finished the season with 122 wickets, followed by 117 in 1965 and 115 in 1966. With his record of runs and wickets he is

Born: Dartford, 27 November 1933
County Cap: 1960

Batting

M	I	NO	Runs	Av	100	50
378	576	71	9,561	18.93	3	37
22	18	7	122	11.09	–	–

Bowling

Balls	Runs	Wkts	Av
54,605	23,869	929	25.69
1,070	640	34	18.82

5wI	10wM	ct/st
46	10	155
2	–	5

Best Performances
125* v. Worcestershire (Worcester) 1960
23* v. Surrey (Canterbury) 1967 (GC)
8-61 v. Northamptonshire (Dover) 1964
12-49 v. Essex (Blackheath) 1964
7-15 v. Surrey (Oval) 1967 (GC)

in the top ten of Kent's all-rounders. His all-round ability also extended to his fielding, where he excelled in the covers. In 1967 he was appointed vice-captain to Colin Cowdrey, a position he held until his retirement at the end of the 1970 season. Although he played in only nine matches in the 1970 Championship winning season, his contribution to that success especially in encouraging the younger players, was of immense value.

Limited-overs cricket was just getting into its stride at his retirement. The Sunday League was only two years old, but he made his mark in the first one-day competition, the Gillette Cup, with a sensational bowling performance. His 7-15 against Surrey at The Oval in the third-round match of 1967 stood as a record until beaten by Derek Underwood who took 8-31 against Scotland in 1987.

Following his retirement from the first-class game he built up a very successful career in the financial services industry. He was elected to Kent's General Committee in 1979 on which he served for some fifteen years.

Raymond Randall (Ray) Dovey

LHB & OB/RM 1938-54 s

Born: Chislehurst, 18 July 1920
Died: Tunbridge Wells, 27 December 1974
County Cap: 1946

Batting

M	I	NO	Runs	Av	100	50
249	391	72	3,768	11.81	–	5

Bowling

Balls	Runs	Wkts	Av
53,483	20,489	751	27.28

5wI	10wM	ct/st
25	2	76

Best Performances

65* v. Northamptonshire (Dover) 1951
8-23 (13-75) v. Surrey (Blackheath) 1950

Tall, bespectacled and with a scholarly air, Ray Dovey was one of those cricketers whose career was just developing at the outbreak of the Second World War. He joined the Kent Nursery in 1936 and first played for the County in 1938, but had only five matches before hostilities intervened. A player who gave an impression of lacking in confidence, he was reluctant to sign for the County after the war, doubting as to whether he was good enough. He only became convinced after another trial. He was an invaluable right-arm stock bowler at a time when Kent's attack was weak, used mainly as an off spinner, but occasionally bowling medium pace. Only on drying wickets did he markedly turn the ball although when bowling seam he tended to move the ball into the batsman off the pitch and with some in-swing, but at a fairly gentle pace. From 1946 until he was released to take up an appointment as coach at Sherborne School, he was an ever-present in the side. His height, military bearing, spectacles, and sleeves rolled high up his arms, made him easily distinguishable in the field. Like most of his generation he showed no emotion on taking a wicket.

His 751 wickets put him in fifteenth place among Kent's all-time bowlers, and seventh in the list of those who played post-war. He was a lower-order left-handed batsman whose average in all but two of his post-war seasons was in double figures. In three seasons he exceeded 500 runs and in two others came close to that figure. He took 100 wickets only once, in 1950, but was within two of achieving it in 1951 and just one away the following season. In his first post-war season he achieved his best bowling average with 89 wickets at 19.04, taking five in an innings five times. His best bowling performance was 8-23 against

Surrey at Blackheath in 1950, the best by a Kent player on that ground. He followed it with a further 5-52 in the second innings, thus providing Kent with its first victory at Blackheath in sixteen years. This was against a side with five Test players destined to share the Championship that season and to dominate it throughout the 1950s. It was the second of two occasions when he took ten wickets in a match, the first being in the immediate post-war season with 10-113 against Somerset at Bath. He had a further eight-wicket haul the following season in the Glamorgan second innings at Swansea. On that occasion he conceded just 38 runs in 14.4 overs.

Following his retirement from the first-class game, he took up coaching and played Minor Counties cricket with Dorset. At the time of his sudden death at the early age of fifty-four he was a coach at Tonbridge School and a popular figure running the school shop.

Alan George Ernest Ealham

RHB & OB 1966-82

| Born: Willesborough, 30 August 1944 |
| County Cap: 1970 |
| County Captain: 1978-80 |

Batting

M	I	NO	Runs	Av	100	50
305	466	68	10,996	27.62	7	59
237	231	38	4,070	21.08	–	14

Bowling

Balls	Runs	Wkts	Av
229	189	3	63.00
12	9	1	9.00

5wl	10wM	ct/st
–	–	175
–	–	102

Best Performances

153 *v.* Worcestershire (Canterbury) 1979
94* *v.* Sussex (Canterbury) 1977 (B & H)

A loyal servant of Kent cricket for many years, Alan Ealham played his first match for the Second XI in 1962, but did not perform consistently until two years later. Some fine performances at that level in 1964 and 1965 earned him a first-team place the following year when he played in 23 Championship matches. Although not making many big scores he showed considerable promise as an aggressive middle-order batsman. He was an outstanding fielder in the deep, a talent with which he was to thrill his many admirers in the following fifteen years.

Alan Ealham's father recognised his potential and was instrumental in him being accepted as an Ashford player at the age of thirteen. This placed him in the Association of Kent Cricket Clubs' coaching scheme and drew him to the attention of Leslie Ames. Although offered terms by Kent, his father insisted that he should complete his apprenticeship as a welder and panel beater before committing himself to cricket. A popular player, he captained Kent from 1978 to 1980. In the first of those years he had a magnificent season, achieving the 'double' of County Championship and the Benson & Hedges Cup. A specialist outfielder, he was consistently an inspiration in the field and on many occasions turned a match with a brilliant catch, often running long distances to pull off the seemingly impossible. There was an occasion against Yorkshire at Canterbury with Fred Trueman in aggressive mood with the bat and Ealham fielding under the Woolley Stand at third man. A shot from Trueman was hit square on the off-side, travelling like a bullet at waist height. Ealham ran some thirty yards with right arm fully stretched, arriving at the same second as the ball to achieve a spectacular catch. Trueman left the field, head shaking in disbelief. It was not just his deep-field catching that inspired his teammates. It is claimed that he had one of the best throws in cricket history, strong and accurate and achieving many run outs. His prowess as a fielder was recognised by the England selectors inviting him to act as twelfth man in a number of Test matches. In all, he took 175 catches for Kent, a remarkable figure for an outfielder, and at Folkestone in 1966 he took five, all in the deep, off the bowling of Derek Underwood.

Although not scoring as heavily or as consistently as his ability seemed to warrant, he exceeded 1,000 runs in three seasons, the best being in 1971 with 1,363. In hitting his 153 against Worcestershire at Canterbury in 1979 he put on 251 for the fourth wicket with Chris Tavaré. His whole approach made him particularly suited to the limited-overs game. He won the Benson & Hedges Gold Award on four occasions and was Gillette Cup Man of the Match once. His 102 catches set him apart from all his contemporaries, except for wicketkeepers, and he shares with Graham Johnson a record 68 catches in the Sunday League. In that competition he also created record fourth and fifth-wicket partnerships of 146 with Chris Tavaré and 163 with Bernard Julien.

Following his retirement from the first-class game in 1982 he took on the responsibility for the Second XI and throughout the nineties was the Director of Youth Coaching.

Mark Alan Ealham

RHB & RMF 1989-2003

Born: Willesborough, 27 August 1969
County Cap: 1992

Batting

M	I	NO	Runs	Av	100	50
173	274	40	7,459	31.87	7	48
259	223	54	4,529	26.79	1	23

Bowling

Balls	Runs	Wkts	Av
23,617	11,227	396	28.35
11,397	7,766	291	26.68
5wI	10wM	ct/st	
19	1	88	
2	–	74	

Best Performances

153* v. Northamptonshire (Canterbury) 2001

112 v. Derbyshire (Maidstone) 1995 (SL)

8-36 (10-74) v. Warwickshire (Birmingham) 1996

6-53 v. Hampshire (Basingstoke) 1993 (SL)

Tests: 8 for England
Limited-Overs Internationals: 64 for England

Not for the first time, an outstanding Kent player produced a son who has made a name for himself in first-class cricket. Mark Ealham joined the Kent staff in 1989 having made his Second XI debut three years earlier. He quickly developed into a true all-rounder with the ability to score runs quickly and to bowl accurately with great economy. These talents were employed to good effect in both first-class and limited-overs cricket. As a batsman he was more technically correct than his father, and played straighter. As a bowler he moved the ball away from the batsman.

His first-class debut match was at Old Trafford when he was second highest scorer with 45, and shared with Steve Marsh a seventh-wicket partnership of 74, the best of the innings. For fifteen seasons he performed consistently in both forms of the game. While not achieving 1,000 runs or 100 wickets in a season, his first-class record puts him high among Kent's all-rounders. In 1993 his average was 51.23 from twelve matches while four years later in thirteen matches he scored 924 runs at an average of 57.75. His highest score, 153★ against Northants at Canterbury in 2001, came in a remarkable match. He joined David Fulton at 202-5 with Kent needing a further 47 to avoid an innings defeat. By the time he was out they had put on 219 runs towards a Kent total of 576-8. A lunch-time declaration on the final day almost gave Kent a sensational victory with Northants hanging on, having lost nine wickets.

His right-arm medium-pace seam bowling was often the key to Kent victories in Championship matches. On 19 occasions he took five in an innings with an outstanding performance against Warwickshire at Edgbaston in 1996 when he took 8-36 in 20 overs, demolishing their first innings. He excelled in the one-day game, both for his County and his country. Like his father he was a big hitter; his 119 sixes in limited-overs matches gives him the County record for the number of sixes in that form of the game. In Kent's Sunday League Championship-winning season of 1995, Ealham broke the record for the fastest hundred. Against Derbyshire at Maidstone, he went in to bat with the score on 105 for 5 and only 14 overs remaining. His innings of 112, scored off 44 balls, included nine sixes and nine fours. In the Benson & Hedges Cup he won the Gold Award on six occasions and was named Man of the Match twice in the National Westminster Bank Cup.

He proved a valuable all-rounder in the England one day team, his 64 appearances including the 1999 World Cup in which he played in all five of England's matches, taking a total of 10 wickets, equal second to Darren Gough's 11. He created a new one-day international bowling record for England on the 2000 tour of Zimbabwe, with a return of 5-15, all five being lbw. At the end of the 2003 season he left Kent to join Nottinghamshire, following a disagreement over terms.

100 GREATS — Richard Mark Ellison

LHB & RFM 1981-93

A series of back injuries severely restricted, and eventually curtailed, the career of Richard Ellison, who showed great promise as a forcing middle-order left-hand batsman and right-arm fast-medium swing bowler. He had the ability to swing the ball both ways and on his day could produce a particularly good well-controlled out-swinger. After a sensational season in 1985 when he topped the national bowling averages, he was selected for the final two Test matches. He struggled for form and against injury the following year then missed the whole of the 1987 season when he should have been at the peak of his career.

In his debut championship match for the County, against Hampshire in Canterbury Week, he scored an undefeated first-innings 55 and helped Derek Underwood put on 108 for the ninth wicket. In that first season he played eleven innings and was not out on six occasions. With a top score of 61 not out he was second in the batting averages with 247 runs at 47.40. In 238 innings for Kent he was not out on 65 occasions, a high percentage for a middle-order batsman. Three times he took 7 wickets in an innings: 7-87 against Northants at Maidstone in 1985, 7-75 against Nottinghamshire at Dartford in 1988 and a remarkable 7-33 in just 14 overs against Warwickshire at Tunbridge Wells in 1991. In the limited-overs game he maintained his remarkable record of being undefeated, with forty-eight not out innings. His 174 wickets were at the highly economical rate of just 3.94 runs per over. He won five Benson & Hedges Gold Awards and was named Man of the Match

Born: Willesborough, 21 September 1959
County Cap: 1983

Batting

M	I	NO	Runs	Av	100	50
176	238	65	4,274	24.70	1	19
154	120	48	1,851	25.70	—	4

Bowling

Balls	Runs	Wkts	Av
24,729	11,412	393	29.03
6,918	4,552	174	26.16

5wI	10wM	ct/st
14	1	76
—	—	24

Best Performances
108 v. Oxford University (Oxford) 1984
84 v. Gloucestershire (Canterbury) 1984 (SL)
7-33 v. Warwickshire (Tunbridge Wells) 1991
11-164 v. Northamptonshire (Maidstone) 1985
4-19 v. Cheshire (Canterbury) 1983 (NWT)
Tests: 11 for England
Limited-Overs Internationals: 14 for England
Wisden Cricketer of the Year: 1986

in the National Westminster Bank Trophy match against Essex in 1985.

Richard Ellison played in 11 Tests and will be especially remembered for his Ashes-winning performance in the final two matches of the 1985 series when he topped the England bowling averages with seventeen wickets at 10.88. In the Fifth Test at Edgbaston, under heavy cloud cover and ideal conditions for him, he took 10 for 104 with six in the first innings, which included a devastating spell of 4 for 15. He followed this in the second innings with four wickets for 1 run in half an hour, reducing Australia to 36 for 5. In the last match at The Oval he took a further seven wickets. But despite all the promise, he never quite lived up to expectations as an all-rounder. His height and solid build provided the potential for lots of runs as a powerful middle-order batsman. They never came in abundance. He hit only one century and never approached 1,000 runs in a season, his best being 546 in 1984. His bowling was similar. Largely due to the back injuries he sustained his success was not consistent. He exceeded 50 wickets in only three seasons, his best being in 1988 when he took 71 wickets at 21.90. But when fully fit and when conditions suited, he could be devastating.

In spite of his many setbacks, he remained a cheerful and popular character both on and off the field. He joined the teaching profession in 1985, becoming master-in-charge of cricket at Millfield School.

Thomas Godfrey Evans

RHB, LB & WK 1939-67

Born: Finchley, Middlesex, 18 August 1920
Died: Northampton, 3 May 1999
County Cap: 1946

Batting

M	I	NO	Runs	Av	100	50
258	451	15	9325	21.38	4	43

Bowling

Balls	Runs	Wkts	Av
241	215	2	107.50

5wI	10wM	ct/st
–	–	451/103

Best Performances
144 v. Somerset (Taunton) 1952
5 dismissals in an innings five times
9 dismissals (ct 8 st 1) in a match v. New
Zealand (Canterbury) 1949
Tests: 91 for England
Wisden **Cricketer of the Year:** 1951

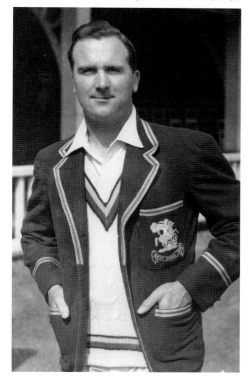

Every Kent schoolboy's hero: that was Godfrey Evans. If anyone epitomised the spirit and optimism of those early post-war years, it was Godfrey. His popularity with the youngsters had much to do with his willingness to spend post-play time behind the Canterbury Pavilion cheerfully signing autographs for as long as the demand was there. Of course, there were other reasons for his popularity: his effervescent personality, his fun-loving nature, his approach to both wicketkeeping and batting and his obvious enjoyment of the game.

It was at Kent College, Canterbury, where he was educated and became captain of cricket, football and hockey, that his love of cricket was encouraged. At school, he shone as a batsman and had little opportunity to keep wicket. In a schools match he played an innings of 132 for which he won a Jack Hobbs bat, which was offered by a London newspaper to promising schoolboys. In his early days he had to make up his mind between cricket and boxing. For a short period he performed as a professional boxer, having three fights, all of which he won, and during the last of which he broke his nose. At that point, when just seventeen years old, he was required by the Kent Committee to make the choice: boxing or cricket.

His first-class career lasted for just five matches before it was interrupted for six years by the Second World War. But it was not as wicketkeeper that he made his debut. Nevertheless, in the final pre-war match it was noted that 'Evans showed promising form behind the wickets'. He also received favourable notices in *Wisden* for performances at Lord's in wartime representative matches, in which he appeared while serving as a Sergeant in the Royal Army Service Corps, so that by the end of the war he was regarded as England's wicketkeeper-in-waiting.

So effectively the distinguished career of Godfrey Evans began in 1946. Having been awarded his County Cap, and after just three months of first-class experience, he was selected for the third and final Test match against India. At the end of that first season he was chosen for the tour of Australia. He went as understudy to the then-Yorkshire wicketkeeper Paul Gibb, but after the First Test he became an automatic choice, winning 91 Test caps and claiming 219 victims, 173 caught and 46 stumped. This stood as a world record until exceeded by his Kent successor, Alan Knott. After the 1946/47 tour of Australia, he became England's first-choice wicketkeeper for the next fourteen years, although he was replaced for the final two Tests on the 1948/49 tour of South Africa by S.C. (Billy) Griffith. This ended a record sequence of 22 consecutive appearances for a wicketkeeper.

His Test batting average of over 20 included two hundreds, the first of which was in 1950 against the West Indies. On a very difficult Old Trafford pitch, and coming in when England were 88-5, he made 104 in a stand of 161 with Trevor Bailey. The second of his hundreds came at Lord's against India two years later, when he scored a remarkable 98 runs before lunch and equalled his previous best score in a stand of 159 with Tom Graveney. But possibly his most famous batting achievement was in the Adelaide Test on his first tour of Australia when, with Denis Compton as his partner, he remained for 95 minutes before scoring his first run. In a stand realising 85 runs, his contribution was just 10, scored off seven of the 98 balls he received. This, however, was a performance not really in character but of immense value in that it made safe a game that would otherwise have been lost. He toured Australia

Godfrey Evans stumped the great Frank Worrell in both innings of the First Test match at Old Trafford in 1950. Bill Edrich is at slip.

and New Zealand on three further occasions, the West Indies in 1947/48 and 1953/54, South Africa in 1948/49 and in 1956/57.

Godfrey Evans maintained a long line of Kent wicketkeepers of outstanding ability for both county and country. But he was really a 'big time' performer. Winding him up to perform for his County could be difficult and he was not always at his best if the crowd was small. Although he completed in excess of 1,000 runs on four occasions, he only did this once for Kent, probably because of the extra incentive of a bet, with 1,241 at 28.86 in 1952. His Adelaide performance notwithstanding, he was generally an entertaining batsman, who scored his runs at a more than respectable rate, while his running between the wickets was always exciting. His career's highest score of 144 was against Somerset at Taunton in 1952, while in the match against the New Zealand tourists at Canterbury in 1949 he claimed nine dismissals, 8 caught and 1 stumped. In his early years he regularly exceeded 50 dismissals for the county in a season, and had a remarkable understanding with Doug Wright, not the easiest of bowlers to keep to. Indeed, his keeping to Wright was always an entertaining highlight of any match. Some of his dismissals, particularly down the leg side, bordered on the sensational and many of his stumpings were certainly in that category. His agility and speed behind the stumps probably compare with any past or present. He had a superb pair of hands and was always full of energy. He was a born entertainer, had a flair for the spectacular and was a favourite wherever he played in the world. He would have been a great success in limited-overs cricket. His appeal was so great that some years after his retirement in 1959 he was still being selected for privately sponsored tours of South Africa and the West Indies. He was recalled to the Kent side for the match against Yorkshire during the 1967 Canterbury Week when Alan Knott was on Test duty. His presence attracted a large crowd, who were rewarded with two fine catches in Yorkshire's first innings.

Following his retirement he maintained his links with the game advising on the odds for Ladbrokes, the bookmakers, at Test matches. He was always recognisable on grounds with his long, thick whiskers down the sides of his face. He was appointed CBE in 1960 for services to cricket.

100 ——————————————————————— **Arthur Edward Fagg**
GREATS

RHB, RM & occasional WK 1932-57

Only one batsman throughout the world of first-class cricket has the distinction of scoring two double-hundreds in the same match. Arthur Fagg is that batsman. It is a record which has stood since 1938 when against Essex at Colchester he scored 244 and 202 not out. His first innings 244 was out of a total of 429 while his second innings score was out of 313-1 declared. His 446 runs represented over sixty per cent of Kent's total in the match.

As a youngster, Fagg's early days with the County were not plain sailing. After a trial he was initially turned down but during the 1931 season when the Club & Ground team were a player short he was called into the side and scored a half-

Born: Chartham, 18 June 1915
Died: Tunbridge Wells, 13 September 1977
County Cap: 1934

Batting

M	I	NO	Runs	Av	100	50
414	767	44	26,072	36.06	55	123

Bowling

Balls	Runs	Wkts	Av
72	47	0	–

5wI	10wM	ct/st
–	–	411/7

Best Performances
269* v. Nottinghamshire (Nottingham) 1953
Tests: 5 for England

century. In his third match, when still not sixteen years old, he went in to bat with the score 16-4 and hit 131 runs. This was soon after he had been seen by the then-Kent groundsman batting in the nets for the Beverley Club. On enquiring as to whether he scored many runs for them the reply was they did not think him good enough! He joined the Kent staff as a wicketkeeper-batsman, played as such in some of his early matches, and once for MCC on the tour of Australia in 1936/37. He made his first-class debut in 1932 and was a regular in the side until his retirement in 1957. A right-hand opening batsman, he has a record of consistency as impressive as any in Kent's long history. He and Leslie Todd made an outstanding opening partnership particularly in the four years between 1947 and 1950 when they shared fourteen three-figure stands including one of 230 against Northamptonshire in 1948, exceeded the following season by 251 against Leicestershire at Maidstone. That year they recorded ten partnerships in excess of 100. In all but one of the seasons when he appeared in twenty or more matches, he comfortably exceeded 1,000 runs. Included in his fifty-five three-figure innings were six double-hundreds, including two of more than 250. His personal best of 269 not out in 1953 on a Trent Bridge featherbed was in a Kent total of 507-6 declared. At the time it was the fifth-highest individual score by a Kent player and was his second double-hundred on that ground. It beat his previous best of 257 against Hampshire at Southampton some seventeen years earlier. Derbyshire is the only county against whom he did not score a century.

He was declared unfit for military service during the Second World War and spent the duration doing agricultural war work and coaching at Cheltenham College. He did not return to regular first-class cricket until 1947. But despite the eight-year break from 1939 to 1947 he continued his consistent performances right up to 1955. Only in 1954 and 1956 did he fail to score more than 1,000 runs while in four seasons he broke the 2,000-run barrier. His 26,072 runs place him in fifth place among Kent's highest-scoring batsmen.

In the mid–1930s, when England were seeking a new opening partnership, Fagg was favourite to succeed Herbert Sutcliffe. At that time he was considered a better prospect than Hutton and played twice against India in 1936. He was selected for the 1936/37 tour of Australia and played in the first two Tests of that series with moderate success. Unfortunately, he contracted rheumatic fever following the second match and was sent home. He missed the whole of the following domestic season, returning in 1938 when in addition to his two double-hundreds he scored seven hundreds and topped the batting averages with 2,322 runs at 52.77. He was selected as a member of the squad for the final Test against Australia but was not picked for the team. Following the 1938 season he turned down the chance to tour South Africa on the 1938/39 MCC tour. With Hutton and Washbrook firmly established in the immediate post-war period, and with lots of competition from others, Fagg was unable to win the approval of the selectors. His final international appearance was in 1939 against the West Indies when in a low-scoring match he scored 7 and 32. His short Test career was not distinguished and his Test record of just 150 runs from eight innings hardly does justice to his undoubted ability. But his record for the County certainly made him one of the outstanding batsmen on the circuit; hard hitting, very strong on the leg side and dismissive of anything short. He was particularly good against the new ball. As a specialist slip fielder and occasional wicketkeeper, he had

Arthur Fagg uses his feet to drive Walter Robins against Middlesex at Lord's in 1936. He was lbw to Robins for 40. The wicketkeeper is Fred Price.

quick reflexes. His 411 catches puts him in third place among Kent's fielders. Against Hampshire at Southampton in 1952 he took seven in the match.

In 1959 he was appointed a first-class umpire who was highly respected and at his peak regarded as one of the world's best. Serving until his death in 1977, he created a sensation during the Edgbaston Test against the West Indies in 1973. He protested at the attitude of the West Indies team when he gave Boycott not out and refused to stand at the start of play the following morning. However, having made his point he resumed after one over. There was also a famous incident involving Australian opener Bill Lawry who enquired as to how he was out. Having been told 'lbw' he claimed to have hit the ball, to which Fagg apparently responded, 'I know you damn well did, you're out caught'.

Arthur Fagg did not quite receive the reward his ability deserved and was a finer player than many people realised. He was one of the quiet men of Kent and will be remembered as a loyal and very valuable member of the Kent team for many years.

William John (Bill) Fairservice

RHB & OB 1902-21

Born: Nunhead, 16 May 1881
Died: Canterbury, 26 June 1971
County Cap: 1903

Batting

M	I	NO	Runs	Av	100	50
301	417	96	4,922	15.33	–	9

Bowling

Balls	Runs	Wkts	Av
44,718	19,272	853	22.59

5wI	10wM	ct/st
38	7	164

Best Performances
61* v. Essex (Leyton) 1906
7-44 v. Leicestershire (Leicester) 1920
13-125 v. Gloucestershire (Bristol) 1908

Turning the ball from the off at something approaching medium-pace, Bill Fairservice had a distinguished career with Kent but might have achieved wider fame with a county less well-endowed with bowlers. Uncovered pitches meant that wickets often favoured spin but left-arm spinners Blythe and Woolley generally had first use of a turning wicket and for Fairservice the chance often came late or not at all. And when the full quota of amateurs was available poor Bill was often the first to be left out; in Kent's great year of 1906 he was not picked at all in August.

Fairservice had his first trial at the Tonbridge Nursery in 1899 and was eventually engaged in 1901. His debut in 1902 was promising with 3-32 and 2-30 against MCC at Lord's but this proved to be his only game of the season. Next year he played against MCC again and distinguished himself further with figures of 4-40 and 3-56, including W.G. Grace (bowled) in both innings. In the next game at Leyton he took 5-64 and 2-32 and ended the season with 27 wickets at 23.78 in 14 matches. Whatever the conditions, Fairservice was seldom expensive and when given his chance on responsive wickets he could be destructive. At Leicester in 1906 with Blythe injured and Woolley not yet established, he had his best match return of 11-80. When Lancashire were overwhelmed by ten wickets at Old Trafford in 1913 he took 5-58 and 5-44 even though he only came on as second change. At Bristol in 1908, as well as 7-59 and 6-66, he was Kent's top scorer with 55, leading an ultimately decisive late-order rally. Although not perhaps on figures a genuine all-rounder, he was a competent batsman and shared in three century ninth-wicket partnerships.

During the First World War he, like Blythe, joined the Kent Fortress Engineers, subsequently transferring to the Military Police. Post-war, with no Blythe, Fielder or Mason, he found himself one of the mainstays of the attack and in 1920 took 113 wickets at 17.46. In that season when Surrey were beaten in two days at Blackheath he dismissed Jack Hobbs for 11 and 0 and, bowling unchanged with Woolley (all but one over), took 10-58.

He retired at the end of 1921. After two seasons with Northumberland, he established a reputation as a coach at Tonbridge, Lancing and Malvern. From 1946 until he retired at the age of eighty-seven he served as Kent Second XI scorer. For a while he followed tradition by becoming licensee of the White Horse at Bridge, near Canterbury. One hundred and fifty years earlier the pub had been kept by another Kent cricketer, James Aylward. His son Colin made 59 appearances for Kent, hitting one century but never quite managing to establish himself. He subsequently played a few games for Middlesex. When, later in life, Colin became sports master at King's School, Canterbury, his father assisted him by bowling in the nets until well into his eighties.

100 GREATS —————— Nicholas Felix (Nicholas Wanostrocht)

LHB & SLA (under-arm) 1834-52

Among cricketers not even the multi-talented Charles Fry could match Nicholas Wanostrocht (aka Felix) for sheer versatility. The best left-handed batsman of his day, he was also a painter good enough to turn professional in later life, author, linguist, teacher and musician. According to his friend and teammate Fuller Pilch he could 'make music on anything from a church organ to a pair of tongs.' In Canterbury Week he conducted the orchestra, acted, sang and danced (not necessarily all at once). He was even a ventriloquist. He invented the Catapulta

Born: Camberwell, 5 October 1804
Died: Wimborne Minster, Dorset,
   3 September 1876

Batting

M	I	NO	Runs	Av	100	50
52	94	3	1,528	16.79	1	6

Bowling

Other	Wkts	ct/st
2	–	48

Best Performances
113 v. Sussex (Brighton) 1847

bowling machine and designed some of the early pads and batting gloves. Above all, he was valued for his wit and sense of fun.

Felix was judged the most attractive batsman of his time, albeit not the most reliable. Five foot seven (170cm) and lightly built, he used his feet to the slow bowlers but to the predominantly fast round–arm bowling of the period his best stroke was the cut, square and late. He was good in the field, particularly at point, but was surprisingly sluggish between the wickets. His career figures are not impressive by today's standards but he was top scorer in approximately twenty-five per cent of innings in which he batted.

At the age of nineteen, following the death of both parents, Felix took over his father's Alfred House Academy in Camberwell, becoming responsible for six sisters, a brother and within a year a wife. Cricket came relatively late, possibly as an escape. His early cricket was in Camberwell and later, when he moved the school there, Blackheath. In 1830 he played his first 'important'/first–class match, MCC v. Suffolk at Lord's. Cricket was still looked upon by many as not quite respectable and to avoid offending the parents of pupils he began to play under the name 'Felix'. He quickly became prominent in the 'Grand Old Kent XI' despite being bowled for 0 in each innings by Frederick William Lillywhite in his first game for the County. 'Old Lilly' was England's greatest bowler but Felix was to play some of his best innings against him including his first major innings for Kent, 82* v. Sussex at Brighton in 1838 and 74 for Kent v. England in the first ever Canterbury Week in 1842. Lillywhite and Sussex had parted when Felix hit his only century for Kent, 113 at Brighton in 1847. Despite a somewhat dubious amateur status, he played twenty times for Gentlemen v. Players. Felix also played for Surrey and for William Clarke's itinerant All England XI but, probably due largely to his devotion to cricket, both his finances and private life suffered. By the late 1840s his connection with the school was ended and he became estranged from his wife and family. He wrote, 'Cricket was a mistress I loved not wisely but too well'. In 1857 he suffered a stroke and testimonials were launched in the sporting press. His final years were easier, at least financially. Following the death of his wife in 1863 he married the widow of a prosperous farmer.

Arthur (Pip) Fielder

RHB & RF 1900-14

Born: Plaxtol, 19 July 1877
Died: Lambeth, 30 August 1949
County Cap: 1903

Batting

M	I	NO	Runs	Av	100	50
253	329	154	2,000	11.42	1	1

Bowling

Balls	Runs	Wkts	Av
46,318	24,014	1,150	20.88

5wI	I0wM	ct/st
88	25	106

Best Performances
112* v. Worcestershire (Stourbridge) 1909
9-108 v. Lancashire (Canterbury) 1907
14-95 v. Derbyshire (Maidstone) 1907
Tests: 6 for England
Wisden **Cricketer of the Year:** 1907

Arguably Kent's most successful fast bowler, Arthur 'Pip' Fielder was one of the first batch of hopefuls tried at the newly opened Tonbridge Nursery in 1897. On the staff for the start of the 1899 season he made his debut the following year against Essex at Leyton. It was a tough baptism. Percy Perrin and Charlie McGahey put on 323 for the third wicket but Fielder emerged with credit bowling 20 overs for 40 runs, albeit without taking a wicket. This was his only first-team appearance in 1900 and it was not until Bradley dropped out in 1903 that Fielder's chance came. A wet season notwithstanding, he finished with 70 wickets at 18.41. His best efforts included 6-37 against Hampshire at Catford when, bowling unchanged with 'Charlie' Blythe, Hampshire were bowled out for 57, and 11-131 v. Worcestershire in Canterbury Week. He was a surprise choice for the MCC tour of Australia that winter but the trip was not a success. He played in only two Tests and took one wicket.

Another good season in 1904, 98 wickets at 22.56, was followed by only 55 expensive wickets in 1905 but 1906 brought a triumphant return to form. His 172 wickets for Kent at 20.55 were a major factor in their first ever Championship and for Players *v.* Gentlemen at Lord's he achieved the unique feat of taking 10-90 in the Gentlemen's first innings. 1907 was another good year with 159 wickets at 16.60 including 9-108 *v.* Lancashire at Canterbury. In the winter he toured Australia again, finishing second-highest wicket taker with 25 Test wickets at 25.08. Despite unhelpful wickets, local critics considered him the best English fast bowler they had seen.

Over the rest of his career he captured 100 wickets in 1911 and 1913 and only once claimed fewer than 70. 'Pip' Fielder was no batsman but he could do more than hold an end. Against Worcestershire at Stourbridge in 1909 he hit 112★ in a last-wicket partnership of 235 with Frank Woolley (185). He also shared two century tenth-wicket partnerships with James Seymour. In the Second Test at Melbourne in 1908, he contributed 18★ to a last-wicket partnership of 39 with Sydney Barnes to give England victory. Capable of bowling long spells and more than usually well served for catchers with Huish behind the stumps and Mason, Seymour, Hutchings and Woolley in the slips, Fielder was one of the first to use the out-swinger as his chief attacking weapon. He could also move the ball in off the seam, varied his pace and made good use of the new ball. He never played a Test Match in England but Pelham Warner considered him the most difficult of all fast bowlers.

Fielder was on the MCC staff from 1905 to 1921 and later coached at Rugby. During the First World War he served as a special constable. Latterly while living at Beckenham, he acted as Kent's scout in the Metropolitan area.

Matthew Valentine (Jazzer) Fleming ———————— 100
RHB & RM 1988-2002

Old Etonian Matthew Fleming played his cricket in the exciting tradition of the old-style amateur, with whom he shared many of their virtues – and some of their faults! As a competitive all-rounder he was highly entertaining and had the ability to turn the course of a match with inspired batting, a moment of brilliance in the field, or a sensational spell of bowling. His approach to the game, his enthusiasm and determination, made him an absolute natural for the limited-overs form of cricket. Whether batting, bowling or fielding something was always likely to happen. No-one who was at Kent's floodlit match against Surrey at Canterbury in their National League Championship winning season of 2001 will ever forget his astonishing feat of running out four batsmen with direct hits, three of them in four balls.

A great-grandson of C.F.H. Leslie (Middlesex and England) and great-nephew of Ian Fleming, creator of James Bond, Matthew Fleming joined Kent in 1989 after serving four years as a commissioned officer with the Royal Green Jackets, during which time he served in Northern Ireland, Germany and Hong Kong. His first-class debut was against Cambridge University and in his first season he played in eight matches, but without making his mark. However, the following year he scored 980 runs at an average of 37.68, which was to prove his best aggregate of first-class runs, and took

Born: Macclesfield, Cheshire, 12 December 1964
County Cap: 1990
County Captain: 1999-2002

Batting

M	I	NO	Runs	Av	50	100
219	348	43	9,206	30.18	11	42
301	270	30	5,993	24.97	4	28

Bowling

Balls	Runs	Wkts	Av
22,292	10,415	290	35.91
11,692	9,208	359	25.64

5wI	10wM	ct/st
2	–	83
3	–	79

Best Performances
138 v. Essex (Canterbury) 1997 and
v. Worcestershire (Worcester) 1999
125 v. Northamptonshire (Canterbury) 2001 (NL)
5-51 v. Nottinghamshire (Nottingham) 1997
5-27 v. Hampshire (Canterbury) 1997 (B & H)
Limited-Overs Internationals: 11 for England

22 somewhat expensive wickets. His value to the side was much more than a case of runs scored and wickets taken.

He was without doubt an inspirational figure, never more so than during his seasons of captaincy, a post he came to somewhat controversially in 1999. For three years he was designated as captain, then in 2002 he was appointed club captain and captain for the limited-overs matches. His leadership in those years was an important factor in maintaining Kent's first division status in both competitions: the last county to do so.

As a batsman he was always adventurous and had the reputation for scoring his runs quickly, be it in the first-class or limited-overs game, although when the situation demanded it, he could get his head down and play a defensive innings. But his natural tendency to play aggressively often got the better of him and there were occasions when a rash stroke brought about his downfall. He is one of six Kent players to win the coveted Walter Lawrence Trophy for the fastest hundred of the season, achieved in 2002 when, against Sri Lanka, he reached his century off 66 balls. For Kent, only Derek Underwood took more wickets in one-day cricket. He lies in sixth place for the number of runs scored – he was often used as a 'pinch hitter' to set the innings off on an aggressive note – and has hit more limited-overs sixes than all but one other Kent batsman.

He served as Chairman of the Professional Cricketers Association for a number of years and was known familiarly since schooldays as 'Jazzer'.

Alfred Percy (Tich) Freeman

RHB & LBG 1914-36

A. P. Freeman, Kent.   Flemons Tonbridge

Born: Ladywell, 17 May 1888
Died: Bearsted, 28 January 1965
County Cap: 1920

Batting

M	I	NO	Runs	Av	100	50
506	630	170	4257	9.25	–	2

Bowling

Balls	Runs	Wkts	Av
133,080	58,944	3,340	17.64

5wI	10wM	ct/st
348	128	202

Best Performances
66 v. Lancashire (Manchester) 1925
10-53 v. Essex (Southend) 1930
17-67 v. Sussex (Hove) 1922
Tests: 12 for England
Wisden Cricketer of the Year: 1923

Experts tend to disagree on 'Tich' Freeman's place in the hierarchy of English leg break and googly bowlers. What is beyond dispute is that he is second only to Wilfred Rhodes as the greatest wicket-taker of all time. No bowler has approached his 304 wickets in 1928. No one except Freeman himself. In 1933 he took 298. He dismissed 200 or more batsmen in every season between 1928 and 1935. In his least productive year, 1934, he claimed only (!) 205. In eight years his total bag was 2,124 wickets at 18.10, 2,111 of them when he was past forty. He captured 100 or more wickets every season from 1920 to 1936.

Freeman was originally on the Essex staff at Leyton where his uncle was groundsman but, unlike his brother John, he failed to get a contract due apparently to his height – only 62 inches (157cm). When he came to Tonbridge for a trial in 1911 he already had a reputation with the Upper Tooting club and, although he was older than most candidates, McCanlis considered him 'a promising googley (sic) bowler'. Twenty-one wickets at 8.00 for the Second XI in 1912 was a good start and in 1913 he topped the second-team averages with 44 at 13.72.

In 1914 he was picked for the First XI against Oxford. There have been happier debuts. His 18.2 overs cost 88 runs, the only reward number ten stumped. This was in a sense prophetic. By the end of his career 12.8 per cent of his wickets had fallen to stumpings. He continued to take wickets for the Second XI and when Douglas Carr dropped himself after his disastrous game against Surrey at Blackheath, Freeman was recalled for the return. The Oval having been commandeered on the outbreak of war, the match, Jack Hobbs' benefit, was moved to Lord's. Beaten by eight wickets, Kent had little to cheer about except Blythe's first innings 9-97 but Freeman had a distinguished first scalp in county cricket – Tom Hayward bowled. Going on to Birmingham he had his first five-wicket haul, 7-25. When the season ended he had 29 wickets to his credit at 27.55. In the immediate post-war years Fairservice, Woolley and Freeman were able to compensate in part for the loss of Blythe and the absence of a fast bowler but Fairservice retired at the end of 1921 and a knee injury restricted Woolley's bowling after 1924. As a result, until 'Father' Marriott joined the side in August, Freeman virtually carried the attack, supported mainly by a succession of not particularly penetrative seamers. Between 1925 and 1935 he delivered approximately thirty-five per cent of the overs bowled for the county and accounted for forty-four per cent of the wickets, including all ten three times, nine in an innings five times, 17 in a match twice, 16 twice. He took eight in an innings on 32 occasions and three hat-tricks. He appeared five times for Players v. Gentlemen at Lord's.

With a preliminary hitch of the trousers, 'Tich' took a five-pace run and bowled with a high arm and rotary action like, according to Ian Peebles, 'a spring snapping'. More accurate than most wrist spinners, his stock deliveries were the leg break, pitching middle and leg and the top-spinner, which tended to keep low. Seventeen per cent of his wickets were lbw. To left-handers he might bowl three or four googlies an over but otherwise it was reserved mainly for the inexperienced,

'Tich' Freeman bowling for Old England v. Surrey in the Centenary Match at The Oval in 1946. At the age of fifty-eight he bowled 15 overs for 58 runs and 1 wicket (England batsman Laurie Fishlock).

especially the 'fancy caps'. A well-disguised slower ball led to many of his stumpings. He was said to be intimidated by top quality batsmen. Certainly great players of spin such as Hammond, Hendren, Duleepsinhji and Jack O'Connor scored a lot of runs off him but equally he often took their wickets. He dismissed Hammond 19 times, more than any other bowler.

Freeman's success was not repeated at Test level. With MacLaren's side to Australia and New Zealand in 1922/23 he took 69 wickets (including a hat-trick *v.* South Australia) but the opposition varied in quality and there were no Test matches. With Arthur Gilligan in 1924/25 he took eight expensive wickets in two Tests. At Sydney he hit 50★ in a ninth-wicket partnership of 128 with Frank Woolley. In South Africa in 1927/28 his 14 wickets cost 28.50 and although he toured Australia again with Chapman in 1928/29 he did not make the Test side. He did however become the first Englishman to dismiss Bradman. At home he took 22 wickets at 13.72 against the West Indies in 1928 and 22 at 24.86 *v.* South Africa in 1929. The selectors probably erred by not choosing Freeman against Australia in this country. Bradman thought highly of him under English conditions and was troubled by him more than once, notably at Canterbury in 1930 when he was lbw for 18. On the other hand at Folkestone in 1934 Bradman hit him for thirty in an over.

Freeman was a useful late order batsman. When hitting 66★ against Lancashire at Old Trafford in 1925 he added 92 for the ninth wicket with George Collins. At Dover in 1933 he shared a ninth-wicket partnership of 105 with Leslie Ames. Although hardly athletic, he was a competent, occasionally brilliant cover point.

His career ended unhappily. After 1936 when his 110 wickets cost 25.41 the Committee suggested he continue on a match-to-match basis. The offer was not accepted and he was not re-engaged, although the county made a grant of £250 and paid his salary until the start of the 1937 season. He subsequently played in the Birmingham and District League. He was elected an honorary life member of the MCC in 1949. Discipline was strict for professionals in Freeman's day and in 'Tich's' case it extended to his domestic life. At home fixtures wife Ethel was invariably waiting to collect him, precluding any post-match socialising. At his funeral when the hearse was delayed, an irreverent former teammate suggested 'Perhaps Ethel wouldn't let him come.'

John Norman (Big Norm) Graham
RHB & RFM 1964-77

Known to all as 'Norm', this 6ft 8in (203cm) Northumbrian came to Kent as a right-arm fast-medium bowler whose height made him a difficult proposition on pitches which gave him lift. He had fourteen years with the County, although for six of those his number of first-class appearances was in single figures. Nevertheless, he played an important part in the successes of the late 1960s and the 1970s.

He made his Second XI debut in 1963 and had his introduction to the first-class game the following season, against Worcestershire at Dartford. That was one of only

Born: Hexham, Northumberland, 8 May 1943
County Cap: 1967

Batting

M	I	NO	Runs	Av	50	100
186	175	71	404	3.88	–	–
122	45	32	85	6.53	–	–

Bowling

Balls	Runs	Wkts	Av
35,756	13,462	600	22.43
6,182	3,183	169	18.83

5wI	10wM	ct/st
25	3	40
1	–	23

Best Performances

23 v. Cambridge University (Cambridge) 1968
13 v. Northamptonshire (Northampton) 1969 (SL)
8-20 v. Essex (Brentwood) 1969
12-77 v. Sussex (Tunbridge Wells) 1967
5-7 v. Northamptonshire (Tring) 1975 (SL)

two First XI matches he played in his debut season, but for the Second XI he took 54 wickets, well in excess of any other player. In his first three years he played in just fourteen Championship matches, while in his final three he played in only twenty. For a substantial part of his career he was dogged by injury and illness, but in 1967 and 1968 he was an ever-present. The first of these seasons proved to be his best with 104 wickets at 13.90; three times he took ten in a match. He did not again reach three figures but he passed 50 four times, 79 in 1969 and 78 in 1971. At Tunbridge Wells, where he was awarded his County Cap, he celebrated with 22 wickets in the Festival Week for a mere 141 runs, 12 in the match against Sussex, then a further ten against Worcestershire with 7-27 in their second innings. His third outstanding match performance in that prolific season was another 12 wickets against Essex at Dover in the final Championship match. Those 12 cost just 80 runs in 37.3 overs. His best innings performance was 8-20, achieved against Essex in their second innings at Brentwood in 1969 when they were dismissed for 34 on a wicket described as wet and drying under a hot sun. With 600 first-class wickets for the County he rates second to Derek Underwood for economy in the post–war period.

He was a key member of the one-day side, taking a total of 139 wickets in the three competitions. But his value was not just in the number of dismissals. For economy, he holds top spot among all Kent's bowlers in each of the three limited-overs competitions. Spectators got great enjoyment from his batting – he is one of a small number of cricketers who have scored fewer runs than wickets taken, while his regular sorties in the outfield enhanced his popularity as a cheery and amiable character, but sometimes evoked derision from spectators when his tall frame could not always get sufficiently low down to gather shots skimming along the surface.

He never lost his enthusiasm for his native North-East and on retirement returned there. He played for Northumberland in the Minor Counties Championship from 1981 to 1984.

David John (Dave) Halfyard
RHB & RFM 1956-64

Born: Winchmore Hill, London, 3 April 1931
Died: Westward Ho! Northam, Devon,
   23 August 1996
County Cap: 1957

Batting

M	I	NO	Runs	Av	100	50
185	274	31	2,538	10.44	–	2

Bowling

Balls	Runs	Wkts	Av
41,558	18,822	769	24.47

5wI	10wM	ct/st
49	13	88

Best Performances
79 v. Middlesex (Lord's) 1960
9-39 v. Glamorgan (Neath) 1957
15-117 v. Worcestershire (Maidstone) 1959

The appearance on any county ground of a Lambretta moped or a Messerschmitt bubble car heralded the arrival of David Halfyard. Despite what that must have done to his body, his fast-medium or medium-pace bowling in the late 1950s and early 1960s earned him the title of 'the human bowling machine'. His persistence and stamina became legendary and made him a captain's dream until it came to getting the ball away from him! He was able to operate for long periods, bowling with great accuracy and penetration. When performing at medium pace he bowled leg-cutters that turned a lot if the wicket helped him. In five of his seven full seasons he took well in excess of 100 wickets and in four of them he bowled more than 1,000 overs. He was just two short of a sixth successive season of reaching the 100 in 1962 when a serious road accident effectively ended his career with Kent.

In his first season, after joining Kent from the Surrey staff he took 58 wickets at an expensive 33.25, but from then on he became the mainstay of the attack. In his second season he took 117 wickets at 21.18. On nine occasions he took five or more in an innings and three times ten in a match. He demolished the Glamorgan first innings at Neath with 9-39 in early July and the following week against Worcestershire at Folkestone, he took 7-45 in their first innings including a hat-trick, and 6-49 in their second. The following season was his most successful with 135 wickets at an average of 19.91. Against Sussex he dismissed eight in their first innings, had a match haul of ten against Leicestershire in the following match including a hat-trick in the first innings. Later in the season there was another ten against Essex at Clacton immediately followed by a second innings 7-45 against Northamptonshire at Dover. He rounded off the season with 5-53 against the New Zealand tourists. Worcestershire were David Halfyard's 'rabbits'; 13 wickets in 1957, 15 in 1959, 9-27 in the celebrated match at Tunbridge Wells in 1960 which was completed in one day, a further 11 in the two matches of 1961 and ten in his final season. He dismissed 67 Worcestershire batsmen in just eleven matches.

Described as a 'rustic' tail-end batsman, he hit the ball hard and played some useful innings. His best season was 1958 when he scored 531 runs at 13.61 His top score of 79 was a remarkable innings. He came to the wicket at 88-7 and scored his runs out of 106 in 73 minutes, hitting three sixes and nine fours.

Following his car accident he missed the whole of the 1963 season and was unable to regain his form the following year. He was appointed a first-class umpire in 1967 but in 1968 returned to the first-class game with Nottinghamshire. He played Minor Counties cricket with Durham, Northumberland and finally Cornwall, for whom he had a remarkable match against Devon in 1974, taking 10-29 in the first innings and another six in the second. He returned to the umpires' list in 1977 on which he served until 1981. He remained active in club cricket, still bowling until a few weeks before his death.

100 GREATS ———————— Harold Thomas William (Wally) Hardinge

RHB & SLA 1902-33

'Wally' Hardinge was one of a now virtually extinct species, a double international. He played Association Football for England against Scotland in Glasgow in 1910 and cricket for England against Australia in 1921. He also became Kent's youngest debutant when he took the field against Lancashire at Tonbridge in 1902, 111 days past his sixteenth birthday. Starting as a left-arm spinner, he worked his way up the order to become one of the most reliable opening batsmen of his time. Blessed with an equable temperament, sound technique and good footwork, like Burnup, he added stiffening to a team of strokeplayers, some of whom could, on occasions, be carried away by their own brilliance. With a low grip, he was strong off his pads and, like most of his generation, off-drove and cut well. Although frequently acting as sheet anchor, he was adaptable and when runs were needed quickly his captains had no need to change the order. He twice hit hundreds before lunch. He participated in 149 three-figure partnerships, 54 for the first wicket, four over 200, 47 for the second

Born: Greenwich, 25 February 1886
Died: Cambridge, 8 May 1965
County Cap: 1907

Batting

M	I	NO	Runs	Av	50	100
606	990	98	32,549	36.48	75	153

Bowling

Balls	Runs	Wkts	Av
25,021	9,773	370	26.41

5wI	10wM	ct/st
8	1	286

Best Performances
263* *v.* Gloucestershire (Gloucester) 1928
7-64 (11-128) *v.* MCC (Lord's) 1932
Tests: 1 for England
Wisden **Cricketer of the Year:** 1915

wicket, one over 300 and nine over 200. In 1928 he put on a hundred for the first wicket twelve times with Bill Ashdown. He scored 1,000 runs in a season eighteen times and a century against every county except Glamorgan – eleven against Essex, ten against Hampshire. His total of 75 centuries includes four double-hundreds and two separate centuries in a match four times.

His bowling was little used pre-1914 but post-war he was a useful partnership breaker and twice took over 50 wickets in a season. Giving the ball a lot of air, he could achieve considerable turn in the right conditions. On a responsive wicket at Tunbridge Wells in 1929 he took 6-9 *v.* Warwickshire in 11.5 overs. As befits a man with a reputation for speed as a centre forward with Arsenal and Sheffield United, Hardinge was rated by *Wisden* as one of the best outfielders in the country, with safe hands and a fast return.

He had a long apprenticeship, playing only a handful of games each season from 1902 to 1906 but as early as 1903 he had shown his quality by hitting 69* batting number seven against Somerset at Gravesend when he added 159 for the sixth wicket with Burnup. Seconded from the Tonbridge Nursery that year, he also hit 202 for the Mote *v.* Stoics. In 1907 his career began to blossom. He was promoted to open with Frank Woolley at the start of the season and against Sussex at Hove the pair hit 214 in 130 minutes, 196 of them before lunch, Hardinge 129, his first century. Although later dropped down the order, he kept his place until the last month of the season when, as was customary, pros had to make room for Kent's array of talented amateurs. In 1908 he reached 1,000 runs for the first time, hit three hundreds including one in each innings *v.* Essex at Leyton and put on 219 for the first wicket with Cloudesley Marsham *v.* Derbyshire at Derby. Injury and loss of form restricted him in 1909 and 1910 but he made his place secure in 1911 again hitting two centuries in a match, 175 and 109 *v.* Hampshire at Southampton, and, when chosen for the Test Trial at Lord's, carrying his bat for 113★ for the Rest *v.* England. Pelham Warner wanted him in the MCC side to Australia that winter. He exceeded 2,000 runs in 1913, 1921, 1922, 1926 and 1928. Statistically his best year was 1928 when he amassed 2,446 runs at 59.65 and hit 263★ *v.* Gloucestershire at Gloucester and 205 *v.* Warwickshire at Tunbridge Wells. In 1921 his seven centuries included 207 and 102 against Surrey at Blackheath, his first double-hundred. He hit seven hundreds again in 1922, including 151 in a second-wicket partnership of 307 with Seymour (170) *v.* Worcestershire at Kidderminster. In 1926 he scored 160 in a fourth wicket partnership of 297 with Percy Chapman (159) and again passed three figures seven times.

In 1921 Hardinge was picked for England *v.* Australia at Headingley, one of sixteen batsmen called up during the series in an effort to deal with the fast bowling of Gregory and McDonald. His 25 and 5 was deemed insufficient and he was not asked again. It was said at the time and since that Hardinge had no relish for fast bowling. The evidence is at best inconclusive. He batted for two hours for 74 when facing the full Australian Test attack for Kent at Canterbury later that year but failed twice against them for South of England at Hastings. There were plenty of fast bowlers

Although only once finding favour with England's selectors, 'Wally' Hardinge was Kent's sheet anchor between the wars.

around in county cricket for most of his career and there are no indications of any particular problems. In 1926 at Dover Hardinge (132) and Woolley (137) caned the Lancashire attack including McDonald, then the best fast bowler in the world, for 253 in 170 minutes.

That Hardinge is a 'one-cap wonder' is all the harder to understand in that from 1921 until the Lindwall/Miller era the Australian attack was based almost entirely on spin. A possible explanation is the conviction embedded in the brains of generations of selectors that opening batsmen cannot bat down the order. Andy Sandham, Percy Holmes, John Langridge, Jack Robertson, Denis Brookes and Alan Jones are a random few of his fellow sufferers. Hardinge played six times for Players *v.* Gentlemen, three times at Lord's, three at The Oval. He hit 127 at The Oval in 1921.

After service in the First World War, when he reached the rank of Chief Petty Officer in the Royal Naval Air Service, Hardinge was for many years on the business staff of John Wisden & Co. On retirement he did some coaching and subsequently worked for the Cement Marketing Board.

George Robert Canning Harris GCSI GCIE CB ——— 100 GREATS
(Fourth Baron Harris)

RHB & RF (round & under-arm) 1870-1911

It is fashionable to belittle the achievements of Lord Harris. A man of his time and a complex character, he might not have found much common ground with the average modern *Guardian* reader, but, with hindsight, he was seldom wrong on major issues. A man of strong views, he was nevertheless willing to listen to others and if quick to anger he was equally quick to apologise. He espoused several 'liberal' causes both inside and outside cricket, notably in reforming Kent's benefit system to prevent a player being ruined by a couple of wet days. But for his persistence in guiding Seymour's case through to the House of Lords, cricketers' benefits would be taxable. Vilified for being over-zealous in matters relating to qualification, as far back as 1886 he tried to get the qualification period reduced to twelve months and he was in the forefront of the movement for modification of the lbw law. His lifelong stand against throwing has twenty-first-century echoes. Few did more to enhance the status of the professional cricketer, not least by ensuring that young players were not overworked and that injuries received the best medical attention. His contention that a professional was entitled to earn as much as he could without regard to county loyalty was heresy to many contemporaries. Captain 1875–89, President 1875, Chairman 1886–1931, secretary 1875-80, he dominated Kent cricket and was scarcely less influential at Lord's. He served on the committee of the MCC for twenty-four years, became a trustee in 1886, President in 1895 and Treasurer from 1896 until his death. Unlike most of cricket's grandees, he also made a considerable impact in the wider world.

The Harris family influence on Kent cricket dates from 1834 when the Second Lord Harris was one of the syndicate responsible for bringing Fuller Pilch to the

Born: St. Anne's, Trinidad, 3 February 1851
Died: Belmont, Faversham, 24 March 1932
County Cap: 1882
County Captain: 1875-89

Batting

M	I	NO	Runs	Av	100	50
157	278	17	7,842	30.04	10	45

Bowling

Balls	Runs	Wkts	Av
3,022	1,523	64	23.79

5wI	10wM	ct/st
1	–	155

Best Performances
176 *v.* Sussex (Gravesend) 1882
5-57 *v.* Lancashire (Rochdale) 1876
Tests: 4 for England (all as captain)

County. The Third Lord Harris was President when the present Club was formed in 1870. In 1870 Harris captained Eton and made his first appearance for Kent, *v.* Gentlemen of MCC. Next year he hit his first fifty for the County against Surrey at The Oval. At Oxford he gained Blues in 1871, 1872 and 1874 (he missed 1873 through injury). Inheriting the title in 1872, new responsibilities and marriage limited his county cricket until 1875 when he assumed the triple role of captain, President and Secretary. From 1875 he played regularly until 1885 when injury and politics intervened. Even so, up to 1889 he led the side whenever available. When Harris took over there were few professionals and many of the amateurs were reluctant to play outside Canterbury Week. Thanks almost entirely to Harris and a few devoted friends, a small professional nucleus emerged and the 'fancy caps' began to rally to the cause. The all-important Nursery, established in 1897, was largely Harris's brainchild.

An aggressive batsman excelling in the drive and cut, Harris was particularly good against fast bowling. Between 1875 and 1885 he headed the Kent averages seven times and in 1884 became the first Kent batsman to hit 1,000 runs in a season. At Derby in 1876 he hit 79 in a Kent total of 121 and against Middlesex in the 1882 Canterbury Week he scored 72 out of 114 and 101 out of 147. Next year *v.* Yorkshire at Gravesend he carried his bat for 80★ in a total of 148 and in the second innings hit 79 out of 105. His highest score, 176 *v.* Sussex at Gravesend in 1882, included an opening partnership of 208 with fellow aristocrat Lord Throwley. At The Oval in 1885, after breaking a bone in his right hand, he batted for 35 minutes using his left hand only.

Intimidating when in his prime but mellowing with age, Lord Harris remained, loathed by some but respected by all, the cornerstone of Kent cricket and an influential figure at Lord's until the end of his long life.

In 1878/79 he led a thoroughly unrepresentative side with only two professionals to Australia and lost the only Test Match. More significant was the pitch invasion at the New South Wales game in Sydney when, in trying to protect the umpire, Harris was hit with a stick. Such were the repercussions that when the Australians arrived in 1880 few counties wished to play them. The eventual reconciliation was due in part to Harris and at The Oval in September he led England to a five-wicket victory in the first ever home Test match with a personal contribution of 52. He captained England again in 1884 when they won at Lord's and drew at The Oval. He declined to play at Old Trafford because Lancashire's Jack Crosland of the dubious action had been selected.

He relinquished the Kent captaincy in 1889 on appointment as Governor of Bombay (now Mumbai) where, although subject to criticism – most of it non-contemporary – he did much to foster the game, particularly among the Parsi community and by encouraging Europeans to play against indigenous teams. Back in England he played three games for Kent in 1896, hitting 119 against Somerset at Taunton, adding 220 for the fourth wicket with his long-term ally 'Harry Pat' Patterson. He played against the West Indians in 1906 and made his last appearance for the County *v.* India at Catford in 1911, scoring 36 and sharing a partnership of 98 in an hour with Dillon. He continued playing for Band of Brothers, Old Etonians and his own Belmont side until he was seventy-nine.

On the progressive wing of the Tory party and a founder of the Primrose League, he was Under-Secretary of State for India in 1885 and Under-Secretary of State for War 1886–1889. On returning from India he became Chairman of Consolidated Goldfields, and a director of several other companies including the London,

Chatham and Dover Railway. He commanded the East Kent Yeomanry and served on the staff of the Imperial Yeomanry in South Africa during the Boer War. He was Lord-in-Waiting to Queen Victoria and ADC to Edward VII and George V.

In 1921 Harris wrote of cricket 'you will do well to love it, for it is more free from anything sordid, anything dishonourable, anything savouring of servitude than any game in the world. To play it keenly, honourably, generously, self-sacrificingly is a moral lesson in itself, and the classroom is God's air and sunshine.' Hardly the words of a hidebound reactionary and, even if the aims are a touch lofty for the modern world, few surely will disagree with the sentiments.

100 GREATS

Dean Warren (Deano) Headley
RHB & RFM 1993-99

Born: Norton, Stourbridge, Worcestershire, 27 January 1970
County Cap: 1993

Batting

M	I	NO	Runs	Av	100	50
83	118	32	1,550	18.02	–	4
111	44	24	207	10.35	–	–

Bowling

Balls	Runs	Wkts	Av
15,931	8,133	285	28.53
5,286	3,636	155	23.45

5wl	10wM	ct/st
14	1	41
2	–	19

Best Performances
81 *v. Hampshire (Canterbury)* 1998
29* *v. Gloucestershire (Moreton-in-Marsh)* 1996 *(SL)*
8-98 (11-165) *v. Derbyshire (Derby)* 1996
6-42 *v. Surrey (Canterbury)* 1995 *(SL)*
Tests: 15 for England
Limited-Overs Internationals: 13 for England

Uniquely, with a father and grandfather who became Test cricketers, Dean Headley had the genes to become an outstanding player. The fact that his career was cut short by a back injury, while on the England 1999/2000 tour of South Africa, deprived Kent and England of a potentially outstanding right-arm fast-medium, often fast, bowler who had not reached his peak.

Son of R.G.A. Headley (Worcestershire, Jamaica and West Indies 1958-74) and grandson of G.A. Headley, one of the West Indies all-time greats who was known as the Black Bradman, he came to Kent in the early 1990s after two seasons with Middlesex. He made his Kent First XI debut on the County's pre-season tour of Zimbabwe in 1993. Between 1996 and 1999 he played 15 Test matches and 13 limited-overs internationals. He toured with England A to Pakistan in 1995/96, Australia in 1996/97, and with the full England side in the West Indies 1997/98, Australia 1998/99 and South Africa 1999/2000. In the Ashes series of 1998/99 he took 19 wickets at 22.26 and topped the averages, as he did in all first-class matches on that tour with 29 at 22.93; no mean achievement in a series dominated by Australia. In the Melbourne Test his memorable spell of 5-9 in Australia's second innings sensationally turned round a match which until the final hour looked like a third successive Australian win. For his second innings 6-60 Headley won the Man of the Match Award. He went on to take a further eight wickets in the Fifth Test.

Dean Headley twice took 50 wickets in a season. The first occasion was in 1996, the highlight of which was a first-innings return of 8-98 (11-165 in the match) against Derbyshire at Derby. This included the first of three hat-tricks in the season, equalling a world record. The second was in the match immediately following, against Worcestershire at Worcester, then amazingly a few weeks later, both Headley and Martin McCague recorded hat-tricks against Hampshire at Canterbury, Headley in the first innings and McCague in the second. He developed into a more-than-useful lower-order batsman, sharing in a number of match-saving stands or scoring quick runs when the occasion demanded. He was an athletic outfielder able to gather the ball and throw with speed and accuracy. His most rewarding season overall was 1998 when he took 52 wickets at 21.26 and had a batting average of 18.71, including a personal-best score for Kent of 81. His overs in the one-day game were bowled at a highly respectable economy rate of 4.12. Twice in 1997 he won Gold Awards in the Benson & Hedges Cup. Remarkably for a hard-hitting batsman, in all his limited-overs innings he did not hit a single six.

Philosophical about his premature retirement, he has developed a number of business interests, mainly in the field of design and printing.

Alec Hearne ——————————————————————————— 100

RHB & OB/LB 1884-1906

GREATS

Unlike brothers George and Frank, Alec Hearne learned his cricket in Kent, on the ground of the Private Banks Club at Catford where his father was groundsman. At thirteen, he took 7-3 including four in four balls for Victoria *v.* Sydenham Comet and for Mid-Kent in 1879 he demonstrated all-round ability with 9-9 *v.* Woolwich Ordnance Stores and 112 *v.* Royal School of Mines. In 1882 he became professional to his father's employers and next year played for Kent colts. In 1884 he made his county debut and when he retired in 1906 he had more runs and more wickets to his credit than any other Kent cricketer. Only one other Kent cricketer, Frank Woolley, has scored more than 10,000 runs and taken more than 1,000 wickets.

Born: Ealing, Middlesex. 22 July 1863
Died: Beckenham, 16 May 1952
County Cap: 1885

Batting

M	I	NO	Runs	Av	50	100
403	687	63	13598	21.79	11	63

Bowling

Balls	Runs	Wkts	Av
54,261	20,323	1,018	19.96

5wI	10wM	ct/st
46	9	352

Best Performances
162* *v.* Nottinghamshire (Nottingham) 1899
8-15 *v.* Gloucestershire (Tonbridge) 1903
13-48 *v.* Yorkshire (Sheffield) 1885
Tests: 1 for England
Wisden **Cricketer of the Year:** 1894

Alec started as a leg spinner, bowling quicker than most, varied with a slower, flighted off break. Finding that the leg break strained his elbow, he reversed the process, using the off spinner as his stock ball with the occasional leg break and a faster, straight ball. As a batsman he was defensively inclined, adept at pushing for ones and twos, with the square cut, a short-arm hook and an upper cut over the slips off the full face of the bat as his most productive strokes. Fame came in Canterbury Week 1884 when Kent became the only county to beat the Australians. Hearne had just two unsuccessful first-team appearances behind him and Lord Harris's decision to pick him largely on the strength of some good performances for the Second XI attracted much pre-match criticism. To play unknown professionals in the Week was simply 'not done' but 5-36 and 2-30 was ample vindication. There followed 6-33 *v.* Derbyshire, 5-27 *v.* Somerset and an end of season tally of 41 wickets at 16.48. By 1889 Alec was established as all-rounder and reliable opening batsman. Of his twenty century opening partnerships, nine were with Jack Mason. In 1899 for the third wicket they scored 321 together *v.* Nottinghamshire at Trent Bridge (Hearne 162★, Mason 181★). Three times he passed a thousand runs in a season; six times he carried his bat through a completed innings. Hearne took 50 or more wickets in a season eleven times with 1893 his best year when he picked up 82 at 18.01. He had match figures of 13-48 *v.* Yorkshire at Sheffield in 1885 and four times took eight wickets in an innings including 8-15 *v.* Gloucestershire at Tonbridge in 1903. He performed two hat-tricks, for Kent *v.* Gloucestershire at Clifton in 1900 and for MCC *v.* Yorkshire at Lord's in 1888. His only Test appearance was in 1891/92 in South

Africa. Against Australian touring teams he took 51 wickets at 16.17 and hit two centuries, 120 for the South of England at The Oval in 1893 and 168 for W.G. Grace's XI at Crystal Palace in 1899. He was chosen four times for Players *v.* Gentlemen.

From 1888 to 1910 he was on the staff of MCC for whom he made his highest score, 194 *v.* Leicestershire in 1902. He was coach at the Tonbridge Nursery 1920-24 and county scorer from 1925 to 1939.

George Gibbons (Young George) Hearne ———— 100 GREATS

LHB & LF/LM 1875-95

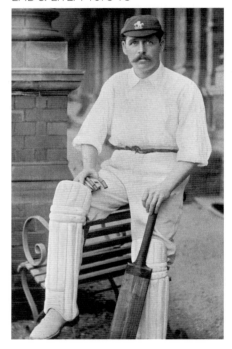

Born: Ealing, Middlesex, 7 July 1856
Died: Denmark Hill, London, 13 February 1932
County Cap: 1885

Batting

M	I	NO	Runs	Av	100	50
252	444	44	7,151	17.87	4	32

Bowling

Balls	Runs	Wkts	Av
26,781	9,390	570	16.47

5wI	10wM	ct/st
36	10	175

Best Performances
126 *v.* Middlesex (Gravesend) 1886
8-20 (14-45) *v.* MCC (Lord's) 1879
Test: 1 for England

At net practice on the Private Banks Ground, Catford in 1875, Lord Harris, newly appointed captain, had his stumps disarranged by George Hearne junior, son of the groundsman. Impressed, his Lordship immediately drafted young George into the Colts team for the forthcoming match against the County, followed within six weeks by a first-team debut at Derby. Kent thus not only gained a valuable all-rounder, within a few years they had also recruited brothers Frank and Alec plus second cousins Herbert and Walter. These five would contribute 24,892 runs and 1,958 wickets to Kent cricket. In Harris's own words 'I found a gold-mine.'

In truth, it looks like claim jumping. The Walker family virtually ran Middlesex cricket and prior to coming to Catford, George senior, a former Middlesex cricketer, had been in charge of their ground at Southgate. Young George and Frank had learned their cricket at Southgate and George had already played for Young Players of Middlesex. Now qualified for Kent by residence, George junior finished his first season with 28 wickets at 9.75. He was particularly severe on Lancashire – 8-46 (including a hat-trick) at Old Trafford, 6-51 at Catford. For a few seasons George was the cutting edge of the Kent attack with 105 wickets at 11.76 in 1877 and 97 at 12.10 in 1878. Bowling fast-medium, he took 14-130 at Derby in 1877, 14-45 *v.* MCC at Lord's and 13-75 *v.* Hampshire at Southampton in 1879. Four times he captured eight wickets in an innings. In the early 1880s Kent were well endowed with left-arm bowlers and after 1881 George bowled less while remaining a useful change. As a batsman his method was primarily defensive, one writer describing him as 'uninteresting to watch', but he cut well and was difficult to get out. In 1886, when he hit a thousand runs in all matches, he participated in two long partnerships, 226 for the second wicket with brother Frank *v.* Middlesex at Gravesend (George 126, Frank 142) and 215 for the third wicket with Cecil Wilson (127) *v.* Yorkshire at Canterbury when he batted five hours for his 117. In 1889 *v.* Sussex at Gravesend he hit 103 in a partnership of 249 for the fourth wicket with Frank Marchant (176). In the same year on a 'diabolical' pitch at Beckenham he batted 105 minutes for 14 to give Kent a narrow victory and deprive Nottinghamshire of the Championship.

George played once for Players *v.* Gentlemen at Lord's and three times for the Players *v.* the Australians. On the MCC staff from 1877 to 1919, he was twice bowled for nought in the famous MCC *v.* Australians match in 1878 when the tourists won in a day. Like brother Alec, his only Test Match was in South Africa in 1891/92. Known as one of the first of the 'gentlemen professionals', George was always immaculately turned out except presumably in the winter when he worked as a contractor laying out cricket grounds. Examples of his handiwork include Rectory Field, Blackheath and the Crabble, Dover.

100 GREATS — William Richard (Topper) Hillyer

RHB & RM (round-arm) 1835-53

'And with five such mighty cricketers, 'twas but natural to win – as Felix, Wenman, Hillyer, Fuller Pilch and Alfred Mynn.' Of the five 'mighty cricketers' in Prowse's often quoted poem, William Hillyer is the odd man out. The others have been much written about – full biographies in the case of Mynn and Felix – but Hillyer remains an almost anonymous figure and it is tempting to think he was included so the line would scan. 'Topper' was in fact one of the finest bowlers of his day and one of the best slip catchers of his era.

Concerning his early cricket, facts are scarce but he was in the Kent team against Benenden in 1834 and next year played his first 'important' match, Kent *v.* England at Lord's, when he opened the batting but did not bowl. Hillyer took at least five wickets in the return at Chislehurst when Kent won by an innings, but the full bowling analysis has not survived. By the end of his career Hillyer had taken 255 wickets in Kent *v.* England encounters, eight times capturing ten or more wickets in a match and four times bowling unchanged through both innings, a feat he achieved

| Born: Leybourne, 5 March 1813 |
| Died: Maidstone, 8 January 1861 |

Batting

M	I	NO	Runs	Av	100	50
82	145	27	687	5.82	–	–

Bowling

Runs	Wkts	Av	Other Wkts
1,475	124	11.89	373

5wI	10wM	ct/st
49	18	73

Best Performances

29 *v.* Nottinghamshire (Nottingham) 1841
8-? *v.* Surrey (Aylesford) 1847 and *v.* Sussex (Hove) 1849
14-? *v.* Surrey (Aylesford) 1847

six times in all. In 1841 he captured nine England wickets at Lord's and thirteen at Town Malling. He took 14 wickets for Kent *v.* Surrey at Aylesford in 1847, thirteen for Kent *v.* Sussex at Hove in 1848.

Allegedly able to pitch the ball on the proverbial sixpence, Hillyer bowled round-arm with his arm below shoulder level, normally aiming to pitch leg stump and move away towards the slips. He had a deceptive flight, many of his wickets coming as a result of batsmen playing forward to short balls. From a shuffling run up 'like a waiter carrying a lot of hot plates and anxious to put them down' according to one source, he bowled genuine medium-pace. Or so we can surmise. In 1840 he played for Fast Bowlers *v.* Slow Bowlers at Lord's; in 1842 for Slow Bowlers *v.* Fast.

Many of his 72 catches for Kent were taken at slip from the fast bowling of Alfred Mynn, whose natural movement was away from the bat. As a batsman, he was said to be an 'obstinate, clumsy sticker'. Although scoring few runs for Kent, he hit – or possibly prodded – 83 for MCC *v.* Oxford University at Oxford in 1847. He appeared 13 times for Players *v.* Gentlemen, captured 71 wickets and in the 1843 match dismissed the distinguished Sussex amateur C.G. Taylor 'hat knocked on wicket'. He was a founder member of William Clarke's itinerant All England XI.

When professional cricket commitments allowed he worked as a gamekeeper. For much of his career he was troubled by rheumatism, gave up cricket earlier than most of his contemporaries and died relatively young from a combination of a liver disease and tuberculosis.

Simon Graham Hinks

LHB & RM 1982-91

Born: Northfleet, 12 October 1960
County Cap: 1985

Batting

M	I	NO	Runs	Av	100	50
154	267	15	7,569	30.03	11	35
134	133	9	3,206	25.85	–	21

Bowling

Balls	Runs	Wkts	Av
580	367	8	45.87
414	360	9	40.00

5wI	10wM	ct/st
–	–	96
–	–	39

Best Performances
234 *v.* Middlesex (Canterbury) 1990
99 v. Glamorgan (Maidstone) 1986 (SL)

Simon Hinks's qualification to play for Kent ultimately derived from a great-great grandfather who in the 1880s walked from the poverty of rural Northamptonshire to find work in the developing cement industry in Northfleet. Following his first-class debut early in the 1983 season during which he played in just one match, he became a prolific scorer in the Second XI with 1,165 runs at 52.95 including three hundreds and a further three scores in the nineties. That early promise however was not initially fulfilled for he was in and out of the Championship side for three years, until winning a regular place in 1985 during which he scored more than 1,000 runs, the first of three seasons when he did so. In that season he also recorded his maiden first-class century. Although recognised as a number one or two batsman, he did not appear as an opener on a regular basis after his first three seasons. Nevertheless, he shared in eighteen century opening stands with various partners and occasionally scored heavily whether opening the innings or going in at three or four.

An aggressive left-handed batsman, when in the mood he was capable of dominating the bowling but was often dismissed when apparently well set. On ten occasions in his first full season he reached a half century but failed to convert it to three figures. And three times in that same season he reached the nineties, once being 99 not out! Throughout his career he passed the half century on no fewer than thirty-five occasions. His career-best score was reached out of a total of 449-2 declared. It was the only double century of his career and formed part of a then-record 366 partnership for any Kent wicket, shared with Neil Taylor. It remains a record for the second wicket.

Hinks was a useful member of the County's one day side. After three early seasons when nothing went right, he played against Surrey in the National Westminster Bank Trophy, scored 95 in a match-winning total of 296-6 and won the Man of the Match award. Of the matches which he played in that competition, he has the best batting average (46.00) of all who played on more than ten occasions. He won the Gold Award for his innings of 78* in the victory over Sussex in the 1988 Benson & Hedges competition, while in the John Player League he just missed out on a maiden limited-overs century, being run out on 99 against Glamorgan at Maidstone in 1986. He had an outstanding season in 1991 when in 21 matches he scored 627 runs at 29.86. Only Neil Taylor scored more. Given that he had only six seasons of regular first-class cricket with the County his aggregate runs show him to have been a reliable batsman who perhaps did not realise his full potential. He was not retained after the 1991 season and joined Gloucestershire, for whom he played from 1992 to 1994.

Carl Llewellyn Hooper

RHB & OB 1992-98

For proof of the contribution made by West Indian Carl Hooper during his time as Kent's overseas player, one needs only a glance at the statistics. He had five years with the County: 1992-94, 1996 and 1998, confirming and probably surpassing all expectations. He missed the seasons of 1995 and 1997 because of international commitments, and refused a contract for 1999 because he wanted to concentrate on preparations for the West Indies' World Cup campaign. It was, therefore a shock to his country's cricket authorities, and to the whole cricketing world, when he suddenly announced his retirement from the game before the competition started. That retirement, however, proved to be short-lived. He returned to play domestic cricket in 2000/01 for his native Guyana, and resumed the captaincy of the West Indies. In 2003 he was part of the World Cup side and in the English season came into the Lancashire side as a replacement for one of their overseas players. He had one further season with the northern county in 2004.

Tall, powerfully built and a superbly elegant batsman who hit the ball extremely hard, Carl Hooper's record for his adopted County places him firmly at the top. His batting average exceeds that of Leslie Ames, who holds second place, by more than six runs an innings. He had a penchant for hitting sixes, doing so 139 times in first-class matches. In two seasons he averaged more than 50 runs per innings and his lowest, in his final season, was still 45.00. His twenty-two first-class hundreds represent one in every four matches. It was not only the runs that he scored, but the speed and style with which he scored them, that made him such an attractive batsman. In 1998 he was joint winner of the Walter Lawrence Trophy for the fastest hundred of the season, scored off 72 balls against Worcestershire at Canterbury. His maiden first-class appearance for Kent was against Durham at Canterbury. He marked the occasion with a second innings of 115 not out in 82

Born: Georgetown, Guyana,
   15 December 1966
County Cap: 1992

Batting

M	I	NO	Runs	Av	100	50
85	142	9	6,714	50.48	22	30
113	106	11	4,158	43.76	6	30

Bowling

Balls	Runs	Wkts	Av
13,007	5,389	154	34.99
5,056	3,393	91	37.28

5wI	10wM	ct/st
2	–	121
1	–	59

Best Performances
236* v. Glamorgan (Canterbury) 1993
145 v. Leicestershire (Leicester) 1996 (SL)
7-93 v. Surrey (Oval) 1998
5-41 v. Essex (Maidstone) 1993 (NL)
Tests: 102 for West Indies (22 as captain)
Limited-Overs Internationals: 227 for West Indies (49 as captain)

balls. This century included thirteen fours and five sixes, one of which cleared the famous lime tree, believed to be only the third batsman ever to do so. His performances gave an early message to supporters and opponents of what was to come. In that first season he scored 1,329 runs at 47.46, including five hundreds, although somewhat surprisingly, only one of those hundreds and 484 of the runs, were scored on home grounds. He bowled 500 first-class overs, the second highest among Kent's bowlers and took 35 wickets with his off breaks. His batting and bowling, added to his 25 catches, mainly at slip where he was outstanding, confirmed his all-round value to the side.

The promise of his first season was fulfilled even more so in 1993. He stood head and shoulders above all the other batsmen with 1,304 first-class runs, the only one to exceed 1,000 runs, at an average of 59.27. He hit three hundreds, including a career-first double-hundred, 236* against Glamorgan at Canterbury, and recorded six scores of more than 50, including two in the nineties. He bowled more overs than anyone else, and his 33 wickets plus his 22 catches were again of immense value in a season when the side was dogged by injury.

In his next three seasons with the County he maintained that consistency. 1994 saw him score a further five centuries among his 1,579 runs with a highest score of 183 and an average of 54.44. He again topped the averages. It was in his innings of 183 at Maidstone, scored off just 151 deliveries that, he established the Kent record

Few batsmen hit the ball harder than Carl Hooper, seen here playing a typical shot during his innings of 96 against Gloucestershire at Tunbridge Wells in 1993 when he added 206 for the second wicket with Mark Benson (103). Jack Russell is behind the stumps.

of ten sixes in an innings, made more remarkable by the fact that he had to retire with his score on 38 due to a dizzy spell. After his absence in 1995 he returned the following year to score 1,287 first-class runs, the most by Kent batsmen, and took a further 26 wickets. He also took 33 catches. His contribution played a major part in the County's rise from bottom place in 1995 to fourth in the County Championship. In his final season, he was again the only batsman to exceed 1,000 runs. His 1,215 included five centuries and a double-hundred against Lancashire at Canterbury, while his 154 against Worcestershire, also at Canterbury, was the innings which won him the coveted Walter Lawrence Trophy. His haul of wickets was 31, including a return of 7-94 against Surrey at The Oval.

His value to the side in the limited-overs game was enormous, his outstanding talent being equally suited to that form of the game. If quick runs were needed he could deliver; if a spell of defensive bowling was required he was invariably the one called on, and he was a key close-to-the-wicket fielder. His Sunday League innings of 145 against Leicestershire in 1996 was a County record in all limited-overs competitions until beaten by Andrew Symonds in 2004, while his innings of 136 not out against Berkshire at Finchampstead in 1994 is a record in the NatWest Trophy. That innings included what remains as a record third-wicket stand of 160, he shared with Trevor Ward. In the Norwich Union League he shared a record third-wicket stand of 208 with Alan Wells. The warmth of the reception he received when he left the field after his final appearance for the County: a standing ovation at the end of an innings that guaranteed Kent's first division status in the Sunday League, demonstrated the depth of feeling supporters had for him. He returned to the St Lawrence ground as Lancashire's overseas player in 2003 when the affection in which he was held was further demonstrated.

100 GREATS

John Charlton (Jack) Hubble
RHB & WK 1904-29

Born: Wateringbury, 10 February 1881
Died: St Leonard's-on-Sea, Sussex, 26 February 1965
County Cup: 1906

Batting

M	I	NO	Runs	Av	50	100
343	496	61	10,229	23.51	5	55

Bowling

Balls	Runs	Wkts	Avge	ct/st
6	1	0	–	411/217

Best Performances
189 v. Sussex (Tunbridge Wells) 1911
6 dismissals (ct 5 st 1) in an innings (10 dismissals (ct 9 st 1) in a match) v. Gloucestershire (Cheltenham) 1923

It is not easy to determine where Jack Hubble ranks in Kent's wicketkeeping hierarchy. *Wisden's* obituarist had no doubts; with Huish and Ames he was 'one of a trio of great wicketkeepers'. All sources agree he was utterly reliable, with a sound, unfussy technique, yet he was never picked for England, the Players or a Test Trial. Pelham Warner, among others, considered he should have gone to Australia in 1920/21 and again in 1924/25 and he was certainly unlucky not to be picked against Armstrong's all-conquering side in 1921. Throughout that series England were troubled by fast bowlers Gregory and McDonald. Hubble was at his best against fast bowling and had batted well against the tourists for MCC. When the selectors were looking for a class wicketkeeper who could also stiffen the batting, from this distance, he looks the logical choice.

After trials at Tonbridge in 1897 Hubble was judged a promising wicketkeeper but only a 'moderate' batsman. Nevertheless, by 1914 when Fred Huish retired, of Hubble's 133 first-team appearances, all but ten were as a batsman. He kept in his debut match *v.* Gloucestershire at Tonbridge in 1904 but with his second appearance, *v.* Yorkshire at Harrogate, came disappointment. He hit 33★ and 43 and held two catches but the pitch was illegally repaired overnight and the match declared void. He did not get another chance to keep for the first team until 1906.

As a batsman, he was strong on the offside with a wristy variant of the off-drive which, played late, sent the ball to or past third man, a favourite shot. His first hundred was 112 *v.* Leicestershire at Dover in 1911 and he followed up shortly afterwards with his career best, 189 in under three hours *v.* Sussex at Tunbridge Wells. In company with Colin Blythe, he added 134 for the ninth wicket. Although only once passing 1,000 runs (in 1914), he hit over 900 in 1926 and over 800 in 1913 and 1920. In 1921 he scored 99 in a partnership of 200 in 105 minutes with Frank Woolley (149) *v.* Warwickshire at Birmingham, one of six occasions when he was dismissed in the nineties. At Bournemouth in 1914 he was 99★ when Kent's last wicket fell. As a 'keeper, he was a model of consistency, with 78 dismissals in 1926 and 60 or more every season from 1920 to 1925. Against Gloucestershire at Cheltenham in 1923 he caught nine and stumped one. He twice accounted for eight in a match, once six in an innings.

Jack Hubble had known the Ames family for many years and he gave his young successor a great deal of help in his early career, not least by providing the security denied to many fledgling professionals by taking Ames into partnership in his sports goods business. He joined the Lord's staff in 1907 and continued to umpire and coach for MCC long after he retired from Kent. He also coached in South Africa.

Frederick Henry (Fred) Huish ———————————— 100

GREATS

RHB & WK 1895-1914

Although Fred Huish was considered one of the best wicketkeepers in the country he never scored sufficient runs to get a selectors' nod and his only representative match was Players *v.* Gentlemen at Lord's in 1902. Pelham Warner, his judgement unclouded by county allegiance, considered him 'one of the greatest wicketkeepers we have ever had' while to *Wisden* he was 'one of the ablest and least demonstrative of his generation'.

Huish played club cricket for Honor Oak and learned the basics of his craft from the Kent, Surrey and England wicketkeeper Harry Wood. With impeccable timing he made his debut against Warwickshire at Edgbaston in June 1895 when Kent had no regular wicketkeeper apart from Manley Kemp, who was seldom available before August. Huish caught one and stumped one, but in his second match, *v.* Lancashire at Old Trafford, he tripped over his bat attempting a short single and was run out without scoring. Worse, he dislocated his shoulder and did not play again until August. Kent used nine wicketkeepers that season. Huish was picked for the opening fixture in 1896 and retained his place as first choice until the outbreak of war in 1914. Despite occasional bouts of lumbago and the bumps and bruises wicketkeepers are heir to − not to mention competition from 'Joe' Murrell and later from the

96

Born: Clapham, 15 November 1869	
Died: Northiam, Sussex, 16 March 1957	
County Cap: 1896	

Batting

M	I	NO	Runs	Av	100	50
469	686	122	7,247	12.84	–	1

Bowling

Balls	Runs	Wkts	Av	ct/st
101	87	0	–	901/352

Best Performances

93 *v.* Somerset (Gravesend) 1906
6 dismissals (ct 1 st 5) in an innings (10
dismissals (ct 1 st 9) in a match) *v.* Surrey
(Oval) 1911

much-younger Jack Hubble – he missed only eighteen games between 1896 and 1914. From 1910 to 1914 he missed only one. He toured the USA with Kent in 1903. His career total of 1,253 dismissals is a Kent record. In 1911 at the age of forty-one, his 101 victims made him the first wicketkeeper to pass three figures. In 1913 he dismissed 99, 81 in 1908, 77 in 1899 and 1905. His nine stumpings and one catch at The Oval in 1911 is a world record. Seven times he accounted for eight batsmen in a match, once six in an innings.

Huish was a competent late-order batsman. In 1906 against Middlesex at Tonbridge, he batted two hours for 17★ although suffering severely from sciatica, sharing a ninth-wicket partnership of 105 with Kenneth Hutchings (125). Hardly able to move, he came in again in the second innings with a runner and batted out an over to help Kent achieve a draw. He finished the season with a total of 562 runs at 18.73 including his career-best 93. Against Somerset at Taunton in 1900 he hit 78 of an eighth-wicket partnership of 140 with T.N. Perkins (62).

When Alec Hearne retired in 1906 Huish became senior professional. He ran a tight ship, insisting on smart appearance and good behaviour on and off the field. It was said that nobody dared shout for a catch at the wicket unless Fred appealed first. On retirement, Huish was Secretary of Sundridge Golf Club. His elder brother Francis, a left-arm medium-pace bowler, played five times for Kent in 1895 and was later registrar to the Football Association before emigrating to the United States.

Edward (Ted/Punter) Humphreys

RHB & SLA 1899-1920

Born: Ditton, 24 August 1881
Died: Maidstone, 6 November 1949
County Cap: 1901

Batting

M	I	NO	Runs	Av	100	50
366	590	44	15,308	28.03	19	81

Bowling

Balls	Runs	Wkts	Av
17,350	8,122	306	26.54
5wI	10wM	ct/st	
5	–	212	

Best Performances
208 *v.* Gloucestershire (Catford) 1909
7-33 *v.* Middlesex (Tonbridge) 1906

Ted 'Punter' Humphreys was among the most dependable of Kent's batsman before the First World War. Quick on his feet and strong off the back foot, he was at his best against the spinners and was said to positively relish batting on the numerous turning wickets encountered when pitches were open to the elements. At a time when it was customary to put the weakest fielder at mid on 'Punter' made a speciality of the position, taking most of his catches there or at short leg. Never chosen for England, he played with success in three Test Trials and appeared three times for the Players *v.* Gentlemen. He hit 111 for the Rest of England in the 1914 MCC Centenary Match.

Arriving with his pads strapped round his bat, 'Punter' came for a trial at Tonbridge at the age of sixteen, primarily as a slow left-arm bowler. In a Club & Ground match early in his career Humphreys bowled a no-ball whereupon his captain, none other than Lord Harris, sent him off the field 'for his own good'. 'Punter' failed to benefit from his punishment. He was apt to overstep throughout his career. On his debut at The Oval in 1899 Humphreys dismissed two Test cricketers, Bill Brockwell and Bill Lockwood, and in 1901 opened the batting for the first time but up to 1903 he was some way off gaining a regular place. Improvement was sudden and dramatic. In 1904 he hit 1,528 runs at 34.72 with three hundreds and took 30 wickets at 16.73. He went on to score a thousand runs in all matches in every season from 1908 to 1914. From 1909 he was virtually a fixture at number one, generally in company with Wally Hardinge or Ted Dillon. In all he shared in twenty-one century opening partnerships. He hit two double-hundreds, 208 *v.* Gloucestershire at Catford in 1909 and 200★ *v.* Lancashire at Tunbridge Wells in

1908. His partnership of 248 with A.P. Day at Taunton in 1908 (Humphreys 149, Day 118) remains the Kent seventh-wicket record.

The presence of Blythe and Woolley meant that 'Punter' was usually relegated to the role of change bowler but he made the ball go with his arm and could swing it in the right conditions. Against Middlesex at Tonbridge in 1906 he excelled himself with 7-33 in the second innings. In 1911/12 Humphreys toured the West Indies with MCC and spent five winters coaching in Jamaica. He had previously coached in New Zealand. One of the truly great coaches, in 1921 he went to Uppingham but such was his reputation that Lord Harris negotiated his return to Kent before the end of his contract. In charge of the Nursery from 1929 to 1948 he soon restored the old standards which had slipped somewhat since the days of McCanlis.

During the First World War 'Punter' served in coastal motor boats and took part in the raid on Zeebrugge, one of the fiercest actions of the war.

100 GREATS — Kenneth Lotherington (Hutch) Hutchings

RHB & RF 1902-12

Born: Southborough, 7 December 1882
Died: Ginchy, France, 3 September 1916
County Cap: 1903

Batting

M	I	NO	Runs	Av	100	50
163	238	12	7,977	35.29	19	43

Bowling

Balls	Runs	Wkts	Av
828	493	15	32.86

5wI	10wM	ct/st
–	–	141

Best Performances
176 v. Lancashire (Canterbury) 1906
4-73 v. West Indies (Catford) 1906
Tests: 7 for England
Wisden **Cricketer of the Year:** 1907

K.L. HUTCHINGS. (KENT.)

From 1906 to 1910 everyone wanted to see Kenneth Hutchings bat. Exceptionally strong in the forearms and wrists, he played the ball very late and few hit it harder or scored faster. In his *annus mirabilis*, 1906, he broke three bats hitting 131 against Yorkshire at Sheffield and demolished another three when he took the Lancashire bowling apart at Canterbury for his career-best 176. Such was the power of his driving and cutting that even the best mid offs stood metres deeper when he was at the wicket and it was not unusual to find five outfielders when he was in full cry. Good-length balls pitching middle and leg were despatched to the boundary between square leg and wide mid-on with a flick of the wrists. A near-infallible catcher with the ability to throw using wrist alone, he excelled at slip, cover or in the deep. Reclining in a deck chair, he once threw to the far wicket at Canterbury without getting up. On another occasion, from a standing position at the Nackington Road wicket, he threw into the top floor of the pavilion six times in succession and, taking a short run, threw over the pavilion for an encore.

Captain in two of his four years in the XI at Tonbridge School, Hutchings played his first game for Kent in 1902 *v.* Worcestershire at Tonbridge. In the following year he hit 106 in 89 minutes *v.* Somerset at Taunton and toured the USA with Kent that autumn, but his achievements in 1906 were unexpected. Joining the side halfway through June he scored 1,454 runs at 60.58 including four hundreds. Possibly his finest performance was *v.* Middlesex at Tonbridge. In the first innings he hit 125 in 135 minutes, putting on 106 for the ninth wicket with the sciatica-smitten Fred Huish (17★). At the end Kent, needing 292, finished 253-9. With the by-now almost totally immobile Huish at the other end, Hutchings, 97★, spurned a deliberate last-ball full toss.

Although never quite matching his 1906 form, he scored over 900 runs in 1907 and 1908 and exceeded a thousand in 1909 and 1910. In 1909 he hit 100 in fifty minutes against Gloucestershire at Catford and his four hundreds in 1910 were 104 in under 100 minutes at Northampton 122 in two hours at Derby, 109 in 100 minutes *v.* Leicestershire at Tonbridge and 144 in 140 minutes at Hastings. When he hit 126 (1 six, 25 fours) in the Second Test at Melbourne on the 1907/08 MCC tour Hutchings became the first Kent cricketer to score a Test match century although two Kent-born players did so before him. He appeared seven times for Gentlemen *v.* Players.

Business and declining form ended his career in 1912. A lieutenant in the King's Liverpool Regiment, he was killed between Guillemont and Ginchy in 1916. His name is on the memorial at Thiepval, one of more than 71,000 with no known grave. Two of his elder brothers also played for Kent.

Alan Paul Igglesden

RHB & RFM 1986-98

In his early days with Kent, Alan Igglesden was considered to be one of the most promising English-qualified fast bowlers on the County circuit. At his best he was a cut above County standard, recognised by his selection for the Sixth Test against Australia at The Oval in 1989 and his inclusion in the England 'A' party that toured Kenya and Zimbabwe the following winter. Against a strong Australian batting line-up he took three wickets, including Mark Taylor and Steve Waugh. He played in just two further Tests against the West Indies in 1993/94, when he took three rather expensive wickets. He also played in four of the five One-Day Internationals, taking 2-12 in the first.

Born: Farnborough, Kent, 8 October 1964
County Cap: 1989

Batting

M	I	NO	Runs	Av	50	100
135	147	59	773	8.78	–	–
139	46	31	164	10.93	–	–

Bowling

Balls	Runs	Wkts	Av
22,446	11,599	409	28.35
6,715	4,346	178	24.41

5wI	10wM	ct/st
17	2	34
2	–	27

Best Performances
41 *v.* Surrey (Canterbury) 1988
26* *v.* Worcestershire *(Worcester) 1991 (B & H)*
7-37 *v.* Zimbabwe B (Harare) 1993
10-91 *v.* Hampshire (Bournemouth) 1988
5-13 *v. Sussex (Hove) 1989 (SL)*
Tests: 3 for England
Limited-Overs Internationals: 4 for England

A succession of injuries restricted his career with Kent, often coming at times when he was in serious contention for an England call. In twelve seasons with the County he averaged just eleven first-class matches per season. He missed the whole of 1996 with a succession of back, ankle and hamstring problems. The injuries which he suffered probably resulted from his vigorous approach and high action, forcing him to adapt his run-up and revert to fast-medium pace. There was a joke that circulated around the Kent grounds that when either he or Martin McCague were missing, they must be one and the same player!

His best bowling performance in the pre-season tour of Zimbabwe was followed by his best season when, although playing in just thirteen matches, he took 54 wickets at 19.77 with a best Championship performance of 6-58 against Durham at Darlington and topped the bowling averages. In 1987 he was the second-highest wicket-taker and second in the averages. His 53 wickets in 1989 was the most by any of the County's bowlers while in 1991 his 50 wickets placed him third in the averages. On just two occasions did he take ten wickets in a match. 1988 against Hampshire was the first, with five in each innings. It was not again achieved until the aforementioned Durham match when he added a further four in the second innings to his six in the first. His best first-class performances were in South Africa where he played for Western Province in 1987/88 and Boland in 1992/93, in which season he topped the South African bowling averages and achieved his career-best return of 7-28 and 12-66 in the match. A regular number ten or eleven right-hand batsman, his average in all but three seasons was in single figures, and his highest aggregate for a season was 115. In 1988 when he achieved his best score, he finished with a creditable average of 17.16.

Injury and ill health (a brain tumour) forced his retirement in 1998 after which he was appointed Master in Charge of Cricket at Sutton Valence School.

Kevin Bertram Sidney Jarvis

RHB & RFM 1975-87

Born: Dartford, 23 April 1953
County Cap: 1977

Batting

M	I	NO	Runs	Av	100	50
237	180	79	321	3.17	–	–
222	83	49	90	2.64	–	–

Bowling

Balls	Runs	Wkts	Av
35,117	18,525	631	29.35
10,500	6,865	298	23.03

5wI	10wM	ct/st	
19	3	55	
1	–	29	

Best Performances
19 v. Derbyshire (Maidstone) 1984
8* v. Essex (Canterbury) 1982 (SL)
8-97 v. Worcestershire (Worcester) 1978
12-146 v. Surrey (Oval) 1981
5-24 v. Nottinghamshire (Nottingham) 1985 (SL)

Kevin Jarvis was one of those bowlers who took more wickets than he scored runs. His haul of wickets was almost double his number of runs. He was the most genuine of number eleven batsmen who in thirteen seasons never once reached 100 runs. In only four seasons did he achieve a highest score in double figures. Few players have attained such a poor batting record. Of the 148 occasions that he was called on to bat, he failed to bother the scorers on 95 of them. But with a score of 19 against Derbyshire at Maidstone in 1984 and sharing a tenth-wicket partnership of 42 with Terry Alderman, he can claim to have played a significant part as a batsman in a Kent victory. That was in marked contrast to his right-arm fast-medium bowling. At his best he looked an England prospect and was included in the England squad for part of the 1982 Test series but was not selected. At times he had problems with his line and length and with run-up difficulties that brought periods of uncertainty. But he was capable of bursts of real pace, particularly when coming down a slope. He threw himself wholeheartedly into his bowling, finishing with a pronounced grunt. His final years with Kent were marred by injury.

Although not always a first choice, he made a mark in his early seasons, taking 134 wickets in his first three when he played in 51 matches. In 1977 he took 55 wickets at 23.70 including 7-58 in Northamptonshire's second innings at Northampton. The following season he took 80 at 22.37 with a season's best of 8-97 against Worcestershire at Worcester. His two second-innings wickets gave him ten in a match for the first time in his career while three times that season he took five in an innings. In five further seasons he exceeded 50 wickets, his career best coming in 1981 with 81 at 23.27. He was the leading wicket taker and second in the averages to Derek Underwood. He twice took ten in a match, with 12-146 against Surrey at The Oval and 11-147 against Leicestershire at Leicester. Five times that season he took five in an innings. Among his career achievements, he can lay claim to being the only Kent bowler to have taken a hat-trick at Lord's for Kent, performed in the 1987 Championship match. His 631 first-class wickets for Kent put him in ninth place among the County's post-war bowlers. He was a key member of the side in the Championship and in the limited-overs successes of the mid to late 1970s. His haul of wickets in the shorter game and his economy rate of 3.92 runs per over place him comfortably in the County's top ten bowlers. On eight occasions he took four or more wickets in an innings.

Kevin Jarvis toured Sri Lanka with a Robins XI in 1977/78 and went with an International XI to Jamaica in 1982/83. Following his departure from Kent he played in 18 first-class matches for Gloucestershire between 1988 and 1990.

100 —————————————————————— **Graham William Johnson**
GREATS

RHB & OB 1965-85

An outstanding all-rounder who was pivotal to Kent's successes in the 'Glory Years', his runs and wickets put him in the top flight of those who appeared for the County in the post-war period. A correct, attractive right-hand batsman who for a period was a successful opener, he was sufficiently versatile to perform there or lower down the order, scoring quick runs as required, or anchoring an innings. He was a fine off-spinner and a superb all-round fielder, confirmed by his 303 catches. He was thought close to international recognition, but probably did not score sufficient runs or take the number of wickets necessary to justify selection. While his record is outstanding, it is possible that by batting down the order as an out and out all-rounder, rather than as a batsman who could bowl, he

Born: Penge, 8 November 1946
County Cap: 1970

Batting:

M	I	NO	Runs	Av	100	50
376	581	76	12,509	24.77	11	53
300	274	43	5,666	24.52	1	25

Bowling

Balls	Runs	Wkts	Av
40,425	17,326	560	30.93
3,513	2,400	104	23.07

5wI	10wM	ct/st
23	2	303
1	–	114

Best Performances
168 *v.* Surrey (Oval) 1976
120* *v. Buckinghamshire (Canterbury) 1974 (GC)*
7-76 *v.* Northamptonshire (Canterbury) 1983
12-151 *v.* Surrey (Blackheath) 1970
5-24 *v. Surrey (Oval) 1974 (SL)*

jeopardised his career. He may have made the England side had he been able to concentrate on opening the batting.

Graham Johnson's first XI debut was against Northamptonshire at Gravesend in 1965, a match in which he took his first Championship wicket. But his first four seasons were not especially encouraging. He managed only 860 runs in that period and took just 14 wickets. The following year, 1970, saw a considerable improvement, with 927 runs including three hundreds. His maiden century was against Sussex at Tunbridge Wells when he opened the innings for the first time and shared a third-wicket partnership of 165 with Colin Cowdrey. His second, against Hampshire at Maidstone was also as an opener, while his third that season was at first wicket down. His 26 wickets included 6-35 in the first innings and 6-116 in the second against Surrey at Blackheath. That performance was a major factor in achieving a victory that confirmed the County as Championship favourites. With 24 catches, his all-round contribution did much to achieve Kent's first Championship success since 1913.

Despite the promise shown, his next two seasons were disappointing with both bat and ball, but then in each of the three years 1973 to 1975 he scored in excess of 1,000 runs, the best being 1975 with 1,366 at 37.94, including three more hundreds. In the first of those seasons he shared with Brian Luckhurst what was then the second-highest opening partnership for the County of 256. In his highest first-class score he shared a second-wicket stand of 208 with Asif Iqbal.

His all-round talents were equally suited to the one-day game in which he had many outstanding performances. His 5,666 runs place him sixth while his 104 wickets put him among the top all-rounders. He has taken more catches than any other player apart from the wicketkeepers and could justly lay claim to be about the best all-round fielder of his generation. He won the Man of the Match Award in the 1972 Gillette Cup match against Gloucestershire and three times won Benson & Hedges Gold Awards. He has a good brain for both cricket and business and in recent years has served on Kent's General and Cricket Committees and is currently Chairman of cricket.

Manley Colchester (Bishop) Kemp

RHB & WK 1880-95

Born: Forest Hill, 7 September 1861
Died: Aylesbury, Buckinghamshire, 30 June 1951
County Cap: 1882

M	I	NO	Runs	Av	100	50
88	141	24	1,522	13.00	–	1

Fielding
ct/st
110/58

Best Performances
51 v. Gloucestershire (Canterbury) 1889
4 dismissals in an innings four times
6 dismissals (ct 6) in a match v. Yorkshire (Maidstone) 1888

When modern cricket historians refer to Kent's great wicketkeeping traditions, 'Bishop' Kemp seldom gets a mention. In the 1880s many would have found this odd. Although perhaps ranked below Kent's Tylecote and Alfred Lyttelton among amateur wicketkeepers of the period, he was certainly in the top half-dozen, amateur or professional. Throughout his career there were only 17 home Test matches and England caps were not plentiful but four times he kept wicket for the Gentlemen v. Players and twice for the Gentlemen against the Australians.

The son of a chartered accountant (and JP), Kemp was in the XI at Harrow between 1879 and 1880 and made his first-class debut while still at school – as wicketkeeper for the Gentlemen of the South v. Gentlemen of the North at Scarborough in 1879. Next year he played in Canterbury Week, for Thirteen of Kent v. England and for the Gentlemen of Kent v. Gentlemen of England, as well as in two county fixtures. Going up to Oxford he played against Cambridge from 1881 to

1884, the last two years as a highly rated captain. In 1884 he contributed 63★ to his side's six-wicket victory over the Australians. While at University he played for Kent in July and August and the pattern continued when he took up teaching, first at Winchester then from 1888 at Harrow. In 1881 and 1882 he played for Kent as a batsman, even opening on occasions, with Tylecote behind the stumps but, although only available during the latter half of the season, he was Kent's first-choice wicketkeeper from 1883, when Tylecote made his last appearance, to 1896 when Fred Huish became established.

Behind the stumps he exuded high spirits with a vociferous appeal often accompanied by a tossing-up of the ball and a leap in the air. Some critics described him as a 'clown cricketer' but he appears to have missed very little. He also had a chivalrous streak. Although he stumped 73 batsmen during his career for the teams he played for, he considered stumping a batsman who raised his foot in playing forward 'a poor way to get anyone out'. With the bat he lacked defence but could hit well, particularly to leg and was adept at squeezing runs from the lower order. By reputation he was a daring, even reckless runner, but in fact he was run out only seven times in his career. How many of his partners suffered is another matter. His habit of pretending to run often brought useful runs in overthrows. His top score for Kent was only 51 but in 1886 he hit 175 (21 fours) for the Gentlemen of England v. Cambridge University at Fenner's. At a lower level he scored 219 for Hertford College v. Trinity College in 1884 and 211 for Tonbridge v. Sevenoaks Vine in 1886.

He won a football Blue in 1883/84 and distinguished himself on the athletics track. He also won the public schools rackets for Harrow two years running. His brothers A.F. and C.W.M. both played for the County. For most of his long life, Kemp was synonymous with his old school Harrow, ruling his form, house and cricket XIs with what his *Times* obituarist called 'affectionate and vivacious tyranny'.

Alan Philip Eric Knott

RHB, OB & WK 1964-85

Alan Knott was in the finest tradition of Kent wicketkeeper-batsmen. During twenty-one years in the game, almost all at the top level, he gave outstanding service to County and country. His record of dismissals for Kent put him in second place behind Fred Huish and when he retired a sequence of some fifty years of Kent providing the England wicketkeeper came to an end. The then-County coach, Claude Lewis and the great Leslie Ames, first witnessed Alan Knott in the nets at Eltham to which he had been encouraged to go by his father, a club cricketer. However it was not as a wicketkeeper, but as a slow bowler bowling both leg-breaks and off breaks. When he was advised to specialise, Knott felt that his natural talent and promise was as a wicketkeeper and left no doubt in the mind of Leslie Ames after he was seen in the Kent Schools' XI against Essex Schools stumping the first three batsmen.

He made his debut as an eighteen-year-old and was awarded his cap the following year when he won the accolade of Best Young Cricketer of the Year. In that season,

Born: Belvedere, 9 April 1946
County Cap: 1965

Batting

M	I	NO	Runs	Av	100	50
349	505	94	11,339	27.58	9	54
286	223	39	2,988	16.23	–	5

Bowling and Fielding Record:

Balls	Runs	Wkts	Av	ct/st
32	13	1	13.00	828/87
–	–	–	–	321/52

Best Performances
144 v. Sussex (Canterbury) 1976
65 v. Oxford and Cambridge Universities
(Oxford) 1976 (B & H)
6 dismissals in an innings six times
9 dismissals (ct 9) in a match v. Leicestershire
(Maidstone) 1977
5 dismissals in an innings four times
Tests: 95 for England
Limited-Overs Internationals: 20 for England
(1 as captain)
Wisden **Cricketer of the Year:** 1970

and the following two, he dismissed 80 or more batsmen for Kent. His career best season was in 1967 when, just twenty-three years old, and in only his third season, he achieved 98 dismissals in all matches. He dismissed six batsmen in an innings on seven occasions, six times for Kent, and against Leicestershire at Maidstone in 1977 he achieved nine in the match, all caught. In that same match he scored 109 in Kent's second innings.

Alan Knott was meticulous in his approach to the game and in his preparation. Descriptions of him as a genius and a great professional are not exaggerated. He always sought the highest standards of physical fitness and his array of exercises on the field whether batting or keeping wicket, were themselves an added entertainment for spectators. He had firm theories about his dietary requirements. His amazing agility resulted in many spectacular catches and stumpings and he rarely missed the opportunity for practice. Even towards the end of his career he could be found in the indoor school in mid-winter, either batting or fielding. Like the Evans/Wright and Ames/Freeman partnerships of previous generations, it was inevitable that another would develop given the unique talents of Knott and the emergence of Derek Underwood. They played together on no fewer than 443 occasions for Kent and in representative matches, combining to dismiss 198 batsmen. Knott was more concerned for his side rather than his personal reputation, standing back to medium pacers such as John

England v. West Indies, Fifth Test match at The Oval 1976. Laurence Rowe was stumped Knott bowled Underwood for 70 during the West Indies innings of 687-8 declared.

Shepherd and Richard Hills, not because he could not stand up to them but because he firmly believed that by standing back he would pick up more catches. Of course, he stood up to Derek Underwood, which must have been far more difficult. While never quite achieving 1,000 runs in a season for the County he did it twice in all matches. As a dashing, sometimes quirky middle-order batsman, he played many memorable and valuable innings, on occasions in crisis situations. Improvising against fast bowling and using his feet effectively against the spinners, he could take bowlers to the height of frustration. His aggregate of runs for Kent put him high on the all-time list of the County's batsmen. His maiden hundred was scored in 1969 against Nottinghamshire on the unglamorous works ground of Ransome & Marles at Newark-on-Trent. It was to be followed by a further eight for the County, two of which were scored in the match against Surrey at Maidstone in 1972. Both of those were not out innings, as were a further three of his nine hundreds for the County. Against Sussex at Canterbury in 1976 he recorded his highest score for Kent, an innings of 144 scored in 102 minutes. He reached his hundred in 70 minutes, the fastest Championship century of the season, which won him the Walter Lawrence Trophy. Another of his hundreds came in a match-saving innings against Essex at Chelmsford in 1982, when with Chris Tavaré he added 256 for the sixth wicket.

He was an automatic selection for England for ten years, winning 95 caps between 1965 and 1981. He would certainly have passed the 100 mark had he not chosen, in 1977, to join Packer's World Series Cricket and then forfeiting further opportunities after opting for the unofficial tour to South Africa in 1981/82, thus incurring a three-year ban. His 4,389 Test runs included a highest of 135 against Australia at Trent Bridge, the first England wicketkeeper since Leslie Ames to score a century against the Australians. Of the five countries he played Tests against he scored hundreds against four and had a highest score of 90 against India. His 269 dismissals make him the top England wicketkeeper in all Tests and place him highly among the world's greatest.

His outstanding wicketkeeping and possibly more so his improvisation as a batsman, made him an automatic selection for limited-overs cricket. He played in 20 internationals, including all four of England's matches in the 1975 Prudential World Cup, but with little batting success. For Kent, although his wicketkeeping was outstanding, his batting record was disappointing. Nevertheless he was a vital part of the team in the seasons of success, winning the Gillette Cup Man of the Match Awards in the victorious semi-final and final in 1974 and a Benson & Hedges Gold Award in 1976.

For a time Knott was part of the England coaching team before retiring to live in Cyprus.

100
Stuart Edward Leary

RHB & LB 1951-71

Stuart Leary, who was born in Cape Town, was an accomplished soccer player for Charlton Athletic and Queen's Park Rangers. For most of his time with Charlton he played as a deep-lying centre forward, one of the pioneers in that position. He was a prolific scorer of goals, averaging twenty a season with Charlton, for whom he scored more than 170. He came to this country primarily to pursue his football career and was a sportsman who could have successfully played both at the highest level. He was probably the smartest and best-looking cricketer of his time, always immaculately turned out.

In Kent cricketing circles he will be best remembered as an outstanding all-rounder who excelled in both the first-class and limited-overs games. Consistent as a free-scoring right-hand batsman, a more than useful leg-break bowler, and a brilliant close-to-the-wicket fielder, he arrived here in 1949 as a sixteen-year-old and made his debut for the Second XI in 1951. His initial first-class appearance was in that same season against Essex at Ilford, but for five years he played in only sixteen first-class matches without distinction. The delay in his development was due to his concentrating on his career in football and two years of national service in the RAF. He established himself in 1957 and from that year until the end of his career in 1971 he scored 1,000 runs in a season on nine occasions. His best season was 1961 when he scored 1,440 runs at 38.91 including three hundreds. His highest was 121* against

Born: Green Point, Cape Town, South Africa, 30 April 1933

Died: Table Mountain, Cape Town, South Africa, 21 August 1988

Batting

M	I	NO	Runs	Av	100	50
381	617	92	16,169	30.79	18	84
60	55	8	1,051	22.36	–	5

Bowling

Balls	Runs	Wkts	Av
9,354	4,714	160	33.67
86	66	4	16.50

5wI	10wM	ct/st
2	–	362
–	–	23

Best Performances

158 v. Northamptonshire (Kettering) 1963

80 v. Pakistan (Canterbury) 1967

5-22 v. Glamorgan (Swansea) 1961

Yorkshire at Scarborough out of a total of 273. The next highest score was 45. When hitting his personal best of 158 he shared a third-wicket partnership of 283 with Bob Wilson (159★).

Leary was particularly strong on the leg side, and his ability to hit the ball very hard made him especially valuable in the limited-overs game in its early years. His sweep brought him lots of sixes and recognition in a national Sunday newspaper six-hitting competition. With 32 sixes in 55 innings, his ratio of almost sixty per cent is second only to Carl Hooper. As he developed, he extended his repertoire of pushes, nudges and deflections to a point where he could get almost anything through on the leg side regardless of where it pitched. He was a brilliant close-to-the-wicket fielder especially at short leg, where he took many catches. His 362 puts him in sixth place in the all-time list of Kent players. He compares well with his great contemporaries: Tony Lock, Micky Stewart, Stuart Surridge, etc. He equalled the Kent record of most catches in an innings, with six against Cambridge University in 1958.

Football kept him fit, and it is said that he did not take net practice seriously, being apt to turn up in his Jaguar, already changed, indulging in a little catching practice, hitting a few balls and then driving off! Following his retirement in 1971 he returned to Cape Town, taking up a number of coaching appointments. It was a troubled retirement and when he was found dead on Table Mountain in 1988 it was believed that he had taken his own life, although the official verdict was open.

William Howard Vincent (Hopper) Levett

RHB & WK 1930-47

Born: Goudhurst, 25 January 1908
Died: Hastings, 1 December 1995
County Cap: 1931

Batting

M	I	NO	Runs	Av	50	100
142	214	44	2,054	12.08	–	1

Bowling

Balls	Runs	Wkts	Av	ct/st
3	6	0	–	228/169

Best Performances
76 *v.* Hampshire (Portsmouth) 1935
6 dismissals (ct 4 st 2) in an innings
v. Northamptonshire (Northampton) 1934
6 dismissals (ct 5 st 1) in an innings
v. Glamorgan (Neath) 1939
9 dismissals (ct 7 st 2) in a match
v. Northamptonshire (Northampton) 1933
9 dismissals (ct 5 st 4) in a match
v. Northamptonshire (Northampton) 1934
Tests: 1 for England

Leslie Ames in his *Close of Play* rates 'Hopper' Levett as 'for two or three years the best 'keeper in England on the leg side.' To Robertson-Glasgow he was 'the most brilliant of English 'keepers'.

He was also one of the best-loved and most widely respected figures in the history of Kent cricket.

'Hopper' – the nickname derives not from the club of which he was a founder member, but probably from his family's involvement in hop-growing – kept wicket for Brighton College from 1924 to 1926 and in his final year for representative public schools sides against the Army and against the Australian tourists. Already his wicketkeeping had received favourable comment in *Wisden*. After occasional appearances for Kent Second XI between 1927 and 1929, he made his first-class debut *v.* Worcestershire at Tunbridge Wells in 1930 (stumped two caught one) and in his only other appearance that season, *v.* Lancashire at Dover, attracted wider attention by catching three and stumping five. One of the latter was from the lively medium-pace in-swing of Bill Ashdown. He thus became Kent's regular second wicketkeeper but one who played more often than most deputies. By 1933 he was no longer merely taking over when Ames was on Test Match duty. Increasingly both played, with Levett keeping wicket and Ames at slip or in the outfield. Sometimes the purpose was to rest Ames' suspect back but often it was to allow the senior man to concentrate on his batting. On occasions the two switched duties during a match.

Ames missed most of the 1936 season with a displaced vertebra, broke a finger in the Lord's Test in 1938 and did not keep at all in 1939, so Levett was as experienced as most regular county stumpers. Three times he achieved more than 50 dismissals in a season, 62 in 1939. Twice he dismissed six batsmen in an innings, three times nine in a match. His dismissal average of 2.89 per match is the highest of any regular Kent stumper. He made a further 13 appearances after the Second World War, during which he served in the Army and reached the rank of Captain.

'Hopper' toured India and Ceylon (as it then was) with the MCC under Douglas Jardine in 1933/34 and played one Test Match. He appeared four times in Gentlemen *v.* Players at Lord's, twice with Ames on the opposing side. In 1931 Ames was 'c Levett b Robins', Levett 'st Ames b Verity'. As a batsman, he had a sound defence and occasionally opened. When hitting his top score of 76 at Portsmouth in 1935 he put on 133 for the seventh wicket with Doug Wright.

Nevertheless, it is 'Hopper' the man whose memory lingers. According to *Wisden* 'probably the most popular man in Kent', he would talk to anyone about cricket or life, regardless of age, social status, sex, creed, occupation, state of mind, or anything else and without always bothering to finish one sentence before starting the next. Robertson-Glasgow lauds his sense of fun and 'invincible conversation'. He was President of Kent in 1974 and President of the Kent County Cricket Supporters Club.

Claude Lewis BEM

LHB & SLA 1933-53

As player, coach and scorer Claude Lewis gave sixty years' service to his County but looking back it is hard to avoid the feeling that as a player he was unlucky. In only three seasons did he appear in more than 20 games. At a time when a left-arm spinner was considered *de rigueur* by most counties, Kent tended to rely on two leg-break bowlers and with Freeman, Marriott and, from 1933, Doug Wright available, a third specialist spinner was something of a luxury. Consequently, as soon as Marriott appeared Lewis generally found himself twelfth man or back in the Second XI. Even when there was only one leg spinner, Lewis was sometimes dropped – particularly for home games – in favour of amateur all-rounders such as Jack Davies, T.C. Longfield or P.M. Whitehouse.

Lewis made his first appearance for the Second XI in 1929 and headed the averages in 1931 with 36 wickets at 12.63. In 1933 he was picked *v.* MCC at Lord's where he claimed his first wicket, Patsy Hendren, but he was taken ill during the match and played only once more that season. In the following year after 8-58 and 2-52 *v.* Essex at Gravesend, he failed to take a wicket in the next match and was promptly dropped in favour of Doug Wright. Later, 12-117 against the eventual Champions Lancashire at Old Trafford gave him a run of eight matches but another left-arm spinner, the Cambridge Blue James Grimshaw, was preferred against Yorkshire at Maidstone. He ended the season with 55 wickets at 30.25. 1935 began

Born: Sittingbourne, 27 July 1908
Died: Borstal, Rochester, 27 April 1993

Batting

M	I	NO	Runs	Av	100	50
128	187	72	738	6.41	—	—

Bowling

Balls	Runs	Wkts	Av
18,333	8,198	301	27.23

5wI	10wM	ct/st
14	4	61

Best Performances

27 *v.* Surrey (Oval) 1939
8-58 *v.* Essex (Gravesend) 1934
12-117 *v.* Lancashire (Manchester) 1934

well with 5-13 *v.* Leicestershire at Gravesend and he held his place for most of the season but again he lost his place immediately after 4-41 and 5-57 against Somerset at Mote Park. His 56 wickets cost 26.41. He was picked less often in the next three seasons but returned to form in the wet summer of 1939 when 56 wickets at 17.12 put him eighth in the national averages. His figures included 11-103 *v.* Worcestershire at Gillingham and 10-124 including a hat-trick *v.* Nottinghamshire at Trent Bridge. During the Second World War he worked in Chatham Dockyard, and when cricket resumed played for about half a season, acquiring a further 29 wickets. He made occasional appearances up to 1953 but his primary concern was now with coaching, and it was here that he made an outstanding contribution. Epitomising all that was best about the pre-war professional cricketer, he had a rare gift for developing strengths and eradicating or compensating for faults in cricketers of all grades and levels of ability. Most of the great Kent players of the 1970s are indebted to him.

As Kent's scorer from 1959 to 1988 he was much liked around the circuit for his quiet efficiency and gentle humour, although those not well versed in British films of the 1940s were often puzzled by his habit of referring to wicket maidens as 'Margaret Lockwoods'. His BEM was for services to cricket. He was expert at restoring antique furniture.

Brian William (Lucky) Luckhurst

RHB & SLA 1958-85

Born: Sittingbourne, 5 February 1939
Died: Alkham, 1 March 2005
County Cap: 1963

Batting

M	I	NO	Runs	Av	100	150
336	568	65	19,096	37.96	39	100
146	144	16	5348	41.78	7	38

Bowling

Balls	Runs	Wkts	Av
5,313	2,617	61	42.90
178	131	7	18.71

5wI	10wM	ct/st
–	–	350
–	–	62

Best Performances
215 v. Derbyshire (Derby) 1973
142 v. Somerset (Weston-super-Mare) 1970 (SL)
4-32 v. Somerset (Gravesend) 1962
3-22 v. Hampshire (Portsmouth) 1965 (GC)
Tests: 21 for England
Limited-Overs Internationals: 3 for England
Wisden **Cricketer of the Year:** 1971

From Boot Boy to President, the title of his autobiography published in 2004, reflected perfectly Brian Luckhurst's fifty-year association with Kent Cricket. He started as a fifteen-year-old, playing his first Second XI match at that age and spending time cleaning the boots of the senior professionals. His formal association with the Club reached its zenith when he was invited to accept the Presidency in 2004. That lifetime's journey took him through the ranks of county cricket where he grew into an outstanding batsman, then on to international honours with England. On retiring from the game he had periods with Kent as cricket coach, cricket manager, cricket administrator, manager of the Ames-Levett Sports Centre and in his final years, as a member of the Club's successful commercial team. His warm and outgoing personality made him a popular figure on Kent grounds throughout his career as a player and beyond.

Brian Luckhurst was a reliable and consistent right-hand opening batsman, fleet of foot, and particularly strong on the leg side, but scoring a lot of his runs square on the off. When first engaged by the County it was as a slow left-arm bowler, although early in his career doubt was expressed about his bowling action. It was on the recommendation of his Sittingbourne schoolmaster that he was offered a trial. There followed regular coaching and the offer of a contract. The family, however, urged caution and insisted he should have the security of a 'trade' before committing himself to cricket. He passed the apprenticeship entrance examination for Chatham Dockyard but the offer of a six-month contract with Kent was too tempting to turn down. He made his first-class debut in 1958 against Worcestershire at Worcester and played his final match twenty-seven years later, when he was called up in an emergency to face the 1985 Australian tourists at Canterbury. His career had gone full circle as he batted at number ten in that match!

His early years were interrupted by national service and although he played for the Army and the Combined Services as an all-rounder, he struggled for a time on his return and was fearful for his future, not confident of being re-engaged. But in 1962 he was to justify the faith shown in him. After a 'pair' in the Second XI match at Northampton, he was unexpectedly called up for the Championship match against Somerset at Gravesend. He batted at number seven, scored 17 in the first innings, and saved the game with a not out 71 in the second. In the Somerset first innings he took 4-32, which was his career-best bowling performance. That season he scored 1,096 runs in 22 matches at 35.35, finishing fourth behind Cowdrey, Richardson and Leary in the averages. Throughout that season he batted in the middle or lower-middle order. The following year he was an ever-present, scoring 1,501 runs – only Peter Richardson scored more – at 33.35. He scored his maiden hundred, 126 not out against Surrey at Blackheath. In the third match he opened the innings for the first time with fellow Sittingbourne man Bob Wilson. But this initial experiment

Playing for England v. Rest of the World at Edgbaston in 1970, Brian Luckhurst hits Intikhab Alam for four, watched by Eddie Barlow and Deryck Murray.

met with mixed fortunes, so that by late July he had dropped back down to the middle order. At this point his bowling had effectively been abandoned. By the late 1960s he had fully established himself as a top-class opener and was being strongly tipped for international honours. From 1962 until 1975, the year before his enforced retirement, he scored 1,000 or more runs in every season, with a top aggregate for the County of 1,914 in 1969, including four hundreds.

In 1970 he was called up by England for all five 'Test' Matches against the Rest of the World XI. He scored 408 runs, including a not out 113 in the second. Nonetheless, he still appeared in 17 of the County's matches, playing a leading part in the County's success with over 1,000 Championship runs. He played a key role against Nottinghamshire at Folkestone in a match that Kent had to win to keep their Championship hopes alive, scoring 156★ in a first innings of 310 and a further 58 in the second. That season also saw his first double-hundred, against Cambridge University, an undefeated 203. He was to repeat this feat three years later against Derbyshire, with his career-best of 215 as part of an opening partnership of 256 with Graham Johnson, scored in 200 minutes.

His performances in the Rest of the World series guaranteed him a place on the 1970/71 tour of Australia and New Zealand when he had passed his thirtieth birthday. He was one of four Kent players on that tour. He played in five of the six Test matches in the Ashes winning side, scoring 455 runs at 56.87 including hundreds at Perth and Melbourne. During the Melbourne innings he carried on batting with the little finger of his left hand broken, causing him to miss the Sixth Test. He was third in the Test match averages, and in all first-class matches he scored 954 runs at 56.11, including another three hundreds. He returned to Australia and New Zealand in 1974/75, but in the side led by Mike Denness he was unable to repeat his previous success, scoring just 54 runs in two Tests against much stronger opposition which included Lillee, Thomson and Max Walker. At home, he played four times against the 1972 Australians with a highest score of 96 in the drawn Trent Bridge match, and then twice in the three-Test series against the West Indies in 1973. Throughout his career he was an outstanding fielder, especially on the leg side. For Kent he took 350 catches, 43 in 1966 alone. Among his contemporaries only Colin Cowdrey and Stuart Leary took more.

In the limited-overs game, in which he was involved from its inception, he was outstanding. His complete career record gives him an average which is the highest of any Kent player apart from Peter Richardson (who played in only three matches). His total of seven hundreds is the second best among Kent players and his 54 sixes place him comfortably in the top ten. He was Gillette Cup Man of the Match on four occasions and won two Gold Awards in the Benson & Hedges Cup.

Luckhurst's elevation to the Kent Presidency in 2004 was universally welcomed. Tragically early in his term of office, he was stricken with cancer. Yet, dispite the obvious ravages of the disease and the treatment, he proved to be a hugely popular and hard-working president displaying the same battling and courageous characteristics that had marked his career. He died just a few days before he was due to give up his reins of office.

Martin John McCague

RHB & RF 1991-2001

Born: Larne, Co. Antrim, Northern Ireland,
24 May 1969
County Cap: 1992

Batting

M	I	NO	Runs	Av	100	50
112	159	41	2,100	17.79	–	6
157	95	31	770	12.03	–	1

Bowling

Balls	Runs	Wkts	Av
18,501	9,960	388	25.67
6,624	5,426	200	27.13

5wI	10wM	ct/st
23	2	60
3	–	28

Best Performances

72 v. Yorkshire (Canterbury) 2000
56 v. Leicestershire (Canterbury) 2000 (NL)
9-86 (15-147) v. Derbyshire (Derby) 1994
5-26 v. Middlesex (Canterbury) 1993 (NWT)
Tests: 3 for England

Born in Northern Ireland, Martin McCague emigrated to Australia with his parents when just one year old, spending his early years 'down under'. He was a product of the Australian Cricket Academy and played for Western Australia for two seasons at the start of the 1990s. He returned to the UK and was engaged by Kent in 1991. A tall, well-built fast bowler, he could turn in devastating spells even on the flattest of wickets. He formed effective partnerships with Dean Headley and Alan Igglesden. His career was, however, marred by injury and loss of confidence, particularly after being withdrawn from the attack in a match against Somerset at Taunton in 1997 when he was adjudged to have bowled too many bouncers and a beamer. As his career progressed he improved as a batsman, occasionally playing valuable lower-order innings with lusty hitting, particularly in limited-overs matches. In all but one season from 1994 to 2000 he recorded a highest score in excess of 50.

In four seasons he exceeded 50 wickets, his best being in 1996 when he took 76 at 24.96 including a hat-trick – one of two by Kent bowlers – in the match against Hampshire at Canterbury. It was in a sustained spell of high-speed bowling in their second innings when, chasing 299 to win and progressing comfortably at 143-1, McCague made the breakthrough which was to turn the match on its head. He took five wickets in succession including the hat-trick and Hampshire were all out for 150 inside a further seven overs. It was the second time that Hampshire he been on the receiving end of his hostile bowling. Four years earlier, again at Canterbury, he took 8-26 in just 12.2 overs, the best analysis by any bowler that season. In his career-best performance, against Derbyshire in 1994, his nine wickets in the first innings was followed by a further six in the second, giving him a match return of 15-147 and equalling John Shepherd's 15-147 against Sussex at Maidstone in 1975. His first ten-wicket haul came in the match against Gloucestershire at Canterbury in 1992. As with Hampshire four years later he was responsible for a second-innings collapse, taking a wicket in five successive overs at a cost of 12 runs. Although his wickets in limited-overs matches were expensively won, he could be a match-winner. His record includes five in an innings in all three competitions. In the 1992 Sunday League match against Glamorgan at Swansea, he performed the hat-trick. Along with Richard Ellison, he is the only Kent player to achieve this in the limited-overs game. His three Test matches were all against Australia. His debut match was at Trent Bridge in the 1993 Ashes series and he played in one on the 1994/5 Australian tour from which he returned home early with a stress fracture. He took six rather expensive wickets.

Martin McCague retired from the first-class game in 2002, subsequently playing for Herefordshire and for Gore Court in the Kent League.

Captain William McCanlis

RHB & RSM (round-arm) 1862-77

Although a useful cricketer, William McCanlis's fame rests on his twelve years in charge of Kent's Tonbridge Nursery. His approach to coaching may seem primitive today but by the yardstick of practical results he must rank as one of the greatest of all time. Blythe, Collins, Fairservice, Fielder, Freeman, Hardinge, Hubble, Humphreys, Jennings, Preston, Seymour and Woolley all graduated under his influence. By the time the last of them (Woolley) retired in 1938 they had contributed a combined total of 155,300 runs, 276 centuries and 10,396 wickets to Kent cricket. So abundant was the crop that Kent were able to pass some to other counties, including Woolley's elder brother Claud to Northamptonshire and Alan Peach to Surrey.

While serving with the Royal Artillery, he learned his cricket on Woolwich Common, a ground devoid of boundaries where all hits had to be run out. On one occasion with a rather portly partner, he ran six only to hear the opposition's umpire call 'five short'. As Sergeant McCanlis, he made his debut for Fourteen of Kent *v.* England in the 1862 Canterbury Week against an attack including John 'Foghorn' Jackson and George 'Tear 'Em' Tarrant, the two fastest bowlers in the game. He managed only two singles and was not picked again until 1864, but from then on played as often as Army duties allowed, frequently appearing under the pseudonym 'Willis'. What this achieved is unclear. Scorecards in most of the sporting press listed

| Born: Woolwich, 30 October 1840 |
| Died: Westcombe Park, 19 November 1925 |

Batting

M	I	NO	Runs	Av	100	50
45	86	4	1,113	13.57	–	3

Bowling:

Balls	Runs	Wkts	Av
867	496	18	27.55

5wI	10wM	ct/st
–	–	19

Best Performances

67 v. Lancashire (Gravesend) 1873
4-67 v. Yorkshire (Middlesbrough) 1864

him as 'Willis' (William McCanlis)'. In 1871 against Lancashire at Old Trafford, he hit 52 out of a team total of 116 and later that season against Surrey at Canterbury he shared an opening partnership of 115 with Edward White. He scored 26 in the only match staged in the Champion County Challenge Cup in 1873, Kent v. Sussex, played on 'perhaps the worst wicket ever seen at Lord's'. He batted prolifically for the Royal Artillery and for Charlton Park, for whom he played until well into his seventies.

McCanlis, promoted to honorary captain in 1886, took over the Nursery in 1900. Almost certainly Lord Harris, who had worked with him at the War Office, had always earmarked him for the job. Although a believer in basic principles, McCanlis's methods did not breed stereotypes. Woolley, Seymour, Humphreys and Hardinge, all technically orthodox, played very much their own way. His success in producing top-class bowlers is even more remarkable. When McCanlis came into the game it was still illegal to raise the arm above shoulder level and Law changes brought changes in technique. Whether developing 'natural' talents such as Blythe and Woolley or getting the best from the less gifted such as Collins, he was ahead of his time. Not the least of his contributions was that he protected his young hopefuls from the drudgery of long hours bowling in the nets to members and their friends. While not underestimating the value of net practice, he believed there was no substitute for time in the middle. Nobody did more to make Kent a power in the game and few coaches have been so highly regarded by former pupils. Younger brother George made 17 appearances for the County.

Francis (Frank) Marchant

RHB, RM 1883-1905

| Born: Matfield, 22 May 1864 |
| Died: Roehampton, 13 April 1946 |
| County Cap: 1885 |
| County Captain: 1890-93 (joint) & 1894-97 |

Batting

M	I	NO	Runs	Av	100	50
226	382	10	7,779	20.91	7	33

Bowling

Balls	Runs	Wkts	Av
598	373	11	33.90
5wI	10wM	ct/st	
–	–	112	

Best Performances

176 v. Sussex (Gravesend) 1889

Wisden considered that had Frank Marchant 'exercised a little more restraint on first going in, he must, with his gifts, have attained the highest honours'. *Wisden* was probably right but Test matches were rare events and 'honours' were less plentiful then. He was highly regarded by his contemporaries, appeared for Gentlemen *v.* Players at Lord's in 1887 and played four times for Cambridge against Oxford (captain in 1887). In 1893 he hit 103 in 105 minutes for MCC against the Australians at Lord's.

Born into a farming family, Marchant was in the XI at Eton where an innings of 93 against Harrow in 1883, scored out of 115, caught the eye of Lord Harris. In August he was picked for Kent against Lancashire at Gravesend where his 24 was top score in Kent's first innings. Over six feet (180cm), Marchant had a penchant for straight drives, cuts and square-leg hits, supplemented by a stroke of his own in which he 'leant' on a good-length ball outside off stump and sent it to the boundary between cover and point. Against Sussex at Tonbridge in 1891 he hit 123 out of 177 in two hours, at Sheffield in 1901 111 out of 150 in 95 minutes against Yorkshire and on a treacherous wicket at Lord's in the same year 100 out of 141 in 75 minutes. His highest score, 176 *v.* Sussex at Gravesend in 1889, might have been a double hundred but on the small Bat and Ball ground when the ball cleared the ropes, the straight boundaries only counted three. Even so, he hit 20 fours, adding 249 for the fourth wicket with George Hearne (103). Things did not always go so well. In 1886 he finished his season with 0, 0, 36, 0, 0, 0, 0.

Good in a crisis, against Gloucestershire at Blackheath in 1888 he came in with the score 51-5 and was last out for 84 scored out of 107. He participated in a number of notable late-order partnerships including 128 for the eighth wicket *v.* Sussex at Hastings in 1896 (Marchant 128, Martin 70★) and 158 for the ninth *v.* Warwickshire at Tonbridge in 1897 (Marchant 144★, Shine 41). Following Lord Harris's departure for Bombay in 1890, Marchant shared the captaincy with 'Harry Pat' Patterson from 1890 to 1893, taking over as sole captain from 1894 to 1897. Under the sharing arrangement, Patterson led the side at Whitsun and in August but, in the absence of a manager, off-field duties – raising teams, travel arrangements and paying bills – devolved on Marchant. Thanks to tolerant business partners, he found time but it could be a nightmare. When Kent played at York in his first season due to, among other things, a telegraph clerk transmitting 'can' instead of 'can't do without you', Kent had only eight batsmen in their first innings and were dismissed for 46. In his own account, Marchant's relief on giving up the captaincy is almost palpable. Ironically, Kent appointed a manager the same year. He was President of Kent in 1934.

100 GREATS — Charles Stowell (Father) Marriott

RHB & LBG 1924-37

Born: Heaton Moor, Lancashire, 14 September 1895
Died: Dollis Hill, London, 13 October 1966
County Cap: 1924

Batting

M	I	NO	Runs	Av	100	50
101	105	31	356	4.81	–	–

Bowling

Balls	Runs	Wkts	Av
24,788	9,391	463	20.28

5wI	10wM	ct/st
32	8	26

Best Performances
21 *v.* Sussex (Maidstone) 1937
7-52 *v.* Sussex (Tunbridge Wells) 1928
12-160 *v.* New Zealand (Canterbury) 1931
Tests: 1 for England

Between the wars 'Father' Marriott was in the top flight of English leg-spinners. Tall, with long fingers, Marriott relied largely on accurate leg-breaks and top-spinners, bowled at near medium-pace and varied with a well-disguised faster ball. Starting from the direction of mid off, he took a short, prancing, slightly comic run and immediately before delivery whipped his right arm behind his back, hitting himself between the shoulder blades with a thump often audible to the expectant batsman. He seldom bowled the googly but made use of the orthodox finger-spun off break. His book *The Complete Leg-Break Bowler* is a minor masterpiece.

The least athletic of cricketers, he had a reputation as one of the worst batsmen and fielders ever to grace the first-class game. Nevertheless he had his moments. At The Oval in 1934 he helped Gerry Chalk (62★) save the match, batting for half an hour against Alf Gover, Freddie Brown, Percy Fender etc. He also held 47 catches in 159 matches, not bad considering that captains tended to send him wherever they thought the ball least likely to go. 'Father' came to Kent with an established reputation. Educated at St Columba's College, Dublin, where, somewhat improbably, he learned to bowl leg breaks, he made his debut for Lancashire in 1919 after war service with the Lancashire Fusiliers. In the same year he played for the Gentlemen *v.* the Australian Imperial Forces and against the Players two years later. He won Blues at Cambridge in 1920 and 1921 where in two seasons he captured 107 wickets at 16.28. Chosen for the Fourth Test match at Manchester in 1921, he was left out of the final XI.

A cultured man of quiet humour and wide interests, he joined Kent on taking up the post of English master at Dulwich College but when first approached by Lord Harris he said he preferred to play for his native Lancashire. Fortunately he changed his mind. He made an immediate impact in 1924, topping the Kent averages and taking 10-110 against Hampshire in Canterbury Week and 11-79 at the expense of his former county at Dover. Although normally confined to matches in August, for the next decade he gave the Kent attack an additional cutting edge and welcome relief for the over-burdened Freeman. The pair complimented each other, providing the spectacle, rare then in county cricket, unthinkable now, of two leg spinners working in tandem. At Canterbury in 1933 they bowled unchanged through the West Indies' first innings and finished with ten wickets each in the match (Marriott 10-90, Freeman 10-122). At Maidstone in 1931 they were unchanged for all but three overs, dismissing Middlesex for 110 and 83 (Freeman 11-102, Marriott 7-76). 1931 was 'Father's' best season with 73 wickets at 14.89. Next year he claimed 66 wickets at 16.66.

On his only Test appearance, *v.* the West Indies at The Oval in 1933, Marriott had match figures of 11-83. He toured South Africa with Lionel Tennyson in 1923/24 and India with the MCC in 1932/33. He also appeared twice more for Gentlemen *v.* Players. During the Second World War he served with the Home Guard as an anti-aircraft gunner.

Steven Andrew (Steve) Marsh

RHB & WK 1982-2000

Born: Westminster, 27 January 1961
County Cap: 1986
County Captain: 1996-98

Batting

M	I	NO	Runs	Av	100	50
291	429	69	10,098	28.05	9	55
310	223	63	2,929	18.30	–	6

Bowling

Balls	Runs	Wkts	Av	ct/st
202	240	2	120.00	688/61
9	14	1	14.00	315/34

Best Performances

142 v. Sussex (Horsham) 1997
71 v. Lancashire (Manchester) 1991 (B & H)
8 dismissals (ct 8) in an innings (9 dismissals (ct 9) in a match v. Middlesex (Lord's) 1991
9 dismissals (ct 8 st 1) in a match v. Durham (Canterbury) 1994
5 dismissals in an innings three times in limited overs

It cannot have been easy for Steve Marsh in his early days: joining Kent in 1981 at a time when Alan Knott was still in his prime, and with another promising young wicketkeeper-batsman on the staff. He nevertheless developed his talent to bear comparison with the great Kent wicketkeeper-batsmen of previous generations. He proved himself to be as good as any of his contemporaries and was unlucky not to have won Test recognition, although he made two appearances for England 'A' in limited-overs internationals in 1991.

Steve Marsh holds the Kent record for the number of wicketkeeping dismissals in an innings, taking eight catches against Middlesex at Lord's in 1991, which equalled the world record. Uniquely, in that same match, he also scored a not out century in Kent's second innings. He also recorded seven dismissals against Durham at Canterbury in 1994, which is the only other instance of more than six dismissals in an innings for Kent. Spanning the years 1996 to 1998, he successfully combined the roles of captain and wicketkeeper, the only Kent player to officially do so. For the previous five years he served as vice-captain. Despite all the additional pressures and responsibilities, his three years as captain compare favourably with any other period in his career. He averaged 28.50 with the bat and recorded 143 dismissals. He also led the County to runners-up position in the County Championship, the Sunday League and the Benson & Hedges Cup in 1997. His all-round career record places him fourth among Kent's wicketkeeper-batsmen. He was a versatile right-hand batsman, reliable in a crisis and able to score runs quickly when the situation demanded. Although never scoring 1,000 runs in a season, he was close to it on a number of occasions and in six seasons finished with an average in excess of 30. His best with the gloves was 1994 with 74 dismissals. His highest first-class score was his final century for the County and embraced a tenth-wicket stand of 183 with Ben Phillips (the sixth-highest in Championship history). It turned an expected Sussex win into an outstanding Kent victory.

Steve Marsh's style of batting was equally well suited to the limited-overs game, while his ability to stand up to all but the fastest of bowlers restricted the most attacking of batsmen. His record with both bat and ball compares well with Alan Knott, the only other regular Kent wicketkeeper during the lifetime of this form of cricket. He recorded five dismissals in an innings on three occasions and his 223 dismissals in the National (Sunday) League is the County record.

At the end of the 2000 season he announced his retirement after captaining the Second XI and playing just as a batsman. He also appeared in a handful of limited-overs matches that year.

Cloudesley Henry Bullock (Slug) Marsham

RHB, RM 1900-22

Born: Stoke Lyne, Bicester, Oxfordshire, 10 February 1879
Died: Wrotham Heath, 19 July 1928
County Cap: 1902
County Captain: 1904-08

Batting

M	I	NO	Runs	Av	100	50
141	224	14	4397	20.93	4	23

Bowling

Balls	Runs	Wkts	Av	ct/st
177	162	2	81.00	74

Best Performances
128 v. Essex (Tonbridge) 1908

Cloudesley Marsham, known as 'Slug', captained Kent to their first ever Championship. While there is no evidence of tactical genius, he was popular with both amateurs and professionals, possessing a gift for extracting the best from a team of many talents, diverse personalities and widely varying social backgrounds. Leading by example and always striving for a positive result, only Dillon and Troughton bettered his record of 51.7 per cent of victories to matches played. In the Championship year his side won 16 and lost only two out of 22 county matches, finishing with 11 wins in succession. One aspect of his personality might not be admired in the modern game. According to *Wisden* his 'charming and courteous disposition endeared him to all opponents'.

The son of the Rev. C.D. Marsham, one of the best amateur bowlers of his day and nephew of George Marsham, a pillar of the Kent cricket establishment, 'Slug' was in the Eton XI in 1897 and 1898 and won Blues at Oxford between 1900 and 1902, being captain in his final year. In the 1901 University Match he opened in the second innings with his side needing 326 and was 100★ at stumps with the score 177-7. In 1906 Kent were well provided with batsmen and at times players of the quality of Alec Hearne, Woolley and 'Happy' Day could not get in the side. This led sections of the sporting press to question Marsham's position, but figures do not perhaps reflect his true worth. He was particularly skilled in unselfishly adapting his game to the needs of the side, equally capable of opening or shepherding the tail from the lower-middle order. Batting number eight with quick runs needed against Sussex at Canterbury in 1906, he scored 119, adding 74 with Huish (30) in half an hour and 111 with Blythe (53) in 35 minutes. Earlier in the season, a steady 73 against Essex at Leyton forced a draw after following-on. In 1908 Marsham and 'Wally' Hardinge put on 219 in 165 minutes for the first wicket against the formidable Derbyshire pace attack at Derby (Marsham 91, Hardinge 127). His last year as captain, 1908, was his best with 963 runs at 26.75. He continued to play the odd game, his last in 1922. Prominent in club cricket, he was captain of the Mote in 1914 and from 1919 to 1928, the year of his death. Although a director of a major insurance company, he frequently cycled to the ground from his home in Chart Sutton, distinctly unusual then, unheard of now.

In 1907 'Slug' became the first Kent cricketer to be appointed to the panel of Test Selectors and in fact the only one until Les Ames in 1950. He began the First World War with the West Kent Yeomanry, was later attached to the Buffs and subsequently transferred to the RAF with the rank of captain. He served in Egypt, Gallipoli and Palestine. He died of heat stroke while still relatively young. His son, A.J.B. Marsham, played six games for Kent in 1946 and 1947.

100 GREATS — Frederick (Fred/Nutty) Martin

LHB & LM 1885-99

Fred 'Nutty' Martin is one of cricket's forgotten men. Figures of 12-102 in your first (and only) Test against Australia and 1,317 first-class wickets ought to be enough for lasting fame but most histories ignore him or grant him a couple of lines at most. For a few years Fred was one of the best medium-pace bowlers in the country. Bowling a tight line and length, his stock ball moved away from the bat but he also had an 'arm ball', an occasional out-swinger as well as a slower ball that 'hung in the air'.

Fred's early cricket was on Dartford Brent where his tendency to play when he should have been working more than once pitched him back among the unemployed. In 1882 his half-brother Arthur Blackman, an amateur who had played for Surrey, Kent and Sussex, arranged for a trial with Kent colts. Only moderately successful, he did better in 1883, appeared for Kent Seconds in 1884 and meanwhile

Born: Dartford, 12 October 1861
Died: Dartford, 13 December 1921
County Cap: 1887

Batting

M	I	NO	Runs	Av	100	50
229	362	78	3,375	11.88	–	6

Bowling

Balls	Runs	Wkts	Av
51,262	17,201	947	18.16

5wI	10wM	ct/st
64	15	84

Best Performances
90 *v.* Nottinghamshire (Gravesend) 1897
8-45 *v.* Lancashire (Tonbridge) 1894
13-48 *v.* Middlesex (Lord's) 1891
Tests: 2 for England
***Wisden* Cricketer of the Year:** 1892

played as professional, for Yalding, Chilham Castle and finally St Lawrence. At this level he ranked as an all-rounder, hitting several hundreds and twice taking 100 wickets. His first-class debut, against Sussex at Gravesend, was undistinguished but in 1886 he finished top of the averages with 29 wickets at 10.44 in six matches, including 12-86 against Surrey at The Oval. He also joined the MCC staff which, although hard work, provided extra income. In 1888 he claimed 65 wickets for Kent at 11.24 and in 1889 took a hundred wickets in all matches, an achievement he was to repeat five times – 190 at 10.11 in 1890. Among his best performances were 7-18 *v.* Nottinghamshire at Beckenham in 1889, 6-18 *v.* Surrey at Catford in 1896 and match figures of 13-48 *v.* Middlesex at Lord's in 1891. In 1888 he began his partnership with Walter Wright. Three times the pair bowled unchanged through a match, ten times through a complete innings. Together they assumed an awesome workload – between 1888 and 1891 they bowled 31,961 balls for the county. Martin holds the Kent record for the most balls bowled in an innings, 490 *v.* Nottinghamshire at Trent Bridge in 1891. 'Nutty' performed a hat-trick against Surrey at The Oval in 1890 and four in four balls for the MCC *v.* Derbyshire at Lord's in 1895. Although at county level he was encouraged to concentrate on his bowling, he was a more than useful batsman.

His England call-up was on a rain-affected wicket at The Oval in 1890 when first-choices Peel and Briggs were unavailable. In ideal conditions, he took 6-50 and 6-52 and in all matches against the Australians that year claimed 56 wickets at 11.30. His only other Test match was in South Africa in 1891/92.

Although never losing his accuracy, 'Nutty' became less effective towards the end of the 1890s due perhaps to better wickets, increasing weight and sheer wear and tear. Troubled with injury in his final season, he still finished seventeenth in the national averages with 46 wickets at 20.43. In 1894/95 he ran an indoor cricket school in Canterbury with his teammate Walter Hearne.

John Richard (Jack) Mason

RHB & RFM 1893-1914

Born: Blackheath, 26 March 1874
Died: Cooden Beach, Sussex, 15 October 1958
County Cap: 1893
County Captain: 1898-1902

Batting

M	I	NO	Runs	Av	100	50
300	491	33	15,563	33.98	31	77

Bowling

Balls	Runs	Wkts	Av
37,688	16,969	769	22.06

5wI	10wM	ct/st
31	9	360

Best Performances
183 *v.* Somerset (Blackheath) 1897
8-29 (12-55) *v.* Somerset (Taunton) 1901
Tests: 5 for England
Wisden Cricketer of the Year: 1898

Although never selected for a Test match in England, Jack Mason was one of cricket's great all-rounders. A batsman in the highest class, even if he had batted immediately above the extras he would have been worth his place as a bowler alone. To cap it he was one of the best slip fielders of his generation. A close student of the game, he was, in the opinion of many, the best captain Kent ever had. Frank Woolley was a great admirer and he had been captained by distinguished names such as Marsham, Dillon, Chapman and Valentine.

Mason learned the basics of the game at the Abbey School, Beckenham, before going on to Winchester where he was in the XI from 1890 to 1893 and captained the side in his final year. Against Eton in 1892 he scored 147 and 71, took eight wickets and held three catches. At the age of nineteen he made his first appearance for Kent, *v.* Sussex at Beckenham in July of his final school year, contributing 31 to

Jack Mason at practice before start of play at Tonbridge in June 1899. That season he hit 1,113 runs for Kent, claimed 82 wickets and held 25 catches.

an opening partnership of 65 with Alec Hearne. A month later he hit 49 and 50 against Nottinghamshire at Canterbury and 48 and 52 against Sussex at Hove. In 1894, his first full season, he found it hard to adjust to regular county cricket, averaging only 18, but he achieved his first hundred, 102 against Lancashire at Tonbridge, and was selected for Gentlemen *v.* Players at Lord's and The Oval. In 1895 he graduated as a first-class cricketer. He hit three hundreds, shared five century opening partnerships with Hearne and scored over a thousand runs as he subsequently did in every season until 1902. His best years were 1900, when he finished fifth in the national averages with 1,828 runs at 53.76; 1898, 1,531 runs at 39.25 and 1901, 1,561 runs at 36.30. In the latter year he also claimed 118 wickets at 20.44, thus becoming the first Kent cricketer to perform the double (in all matches). In 1902 he took 89 wickets at 16.79.

When Mason scored 72 and 46★ and took 4-23 and 6-34 against Middlesex at Tonbridge in 1900 he became the first Kent cricketer to score a hundred runs and take ten wickets in a match; he did so on four further occasions. Kent have rarely been without at least one good all-rounder but only Woolley has emulated him since. In 1904 he hit three hundreds in succession, 138 *v.* Yorkshire at Tunbridge Wells, 126 *v.* Somerset at Beckenham and 123 *v.* Essex at Canterbury. At The Oval against Surrey in 1900 he narrowly missed two hundreds in a match, 98 and 147. During his career he shared 63 century partnerships, four over 200 and nine for the first wicket with Alec Hearne. The pair still hold the Kent record for the third wicket, 321 (unfinished) *v.* Nottinghamshire at Trent Bridge in 1899 (Hearne 162★,

Mason 181*). He tended to do well against Nottinghamshire, hitting 1,309 runs at 46.75 including five centuries. He was even more severe on Somerset – 2,002 runs at 47.66 with eight centuries and 110 wickets at 14.65. At Taunton in 1901 he hit 145 and bowled unchanged with Blythe through both innings for match figures of 12-55. A near infallible slip fielder, he twice held six catches in an innings.

When Frank Marchant relinquished the captaincy in 1897 and the relatively inexperienced Mason was appointed in his place, Kent had just finished twelfth (out of fourteen). Although when he took over Martin and Wright, the backbone of the attack, were approaching the end of their careers and the products of the Nursery were only just beginning to emerge, he took the side to third place in 1900 and finished seventh three times and eighth once. When he gave up the leadership at the end of 1902 to concentrate on his practice as a solicitor, he had won 34 county games, drawn 37 and lost 33, not in themselves startling figures but better than what had gone before. Above all, Blythe, Humphreys, Seymour, Burnup, Dillon, S.H. Day etc were established and foundations had been laid for the triumphs to come.

Playing as often as his practice allowed, Mason scored 853 runs at 40.61 in 1904 including four hundreds, averaged 40 again in 1906 and as late as 1909 headed the national averages with 783 runs at 65.25. Between 1904 and 1912 he hit 12 centuries and claimed a further 155 wickets, 55 of them in 1904. Mason was first-choice as captain whenever the regular skipper was unavailable – which was not infrequently as Kent captains of the time were genuine amateurs rather than ' assistant secretaries' or similar euphemisms for paid amateur. He finished with an overall record of thirty-seven per cent of wins to matches played.

Mason toured Australia with Stoddart in 1897/98. With a top score of 32 he did little in the Test matches but hit 128* v. Victoria, caught everything that came his way and finished top of the bowling averages. He was among thirteen chosen for England at Birmingham in 1902 but did not make the final eleven, subsequently widely considered the strongest ever to represent England. He headed the batting averages when Kent toured the USA in 1903 and played eight times for the Gentlemen v. Players at Lord's, once at The Oval.

When Mason started, the bulk of his runs came from drives off the front foot and square cuts. Reputedly few batsmen hit the half-volley harder. Over six feet (180cm), he used his height to drive almost everything except rank long hops but following experience in Australia, he refined his technique, tightening his defence, scoring more runs off the back foot, off his legs and in the arc between wide mid on and square leg. He bowled a lively fast-medium with a high action, attacking off stump and moving the ball off the seam. Mason served for many years on the Kent Committee and was President in 1938.

Alfred Mynn

RHB & RF (round-arm) 1834-59

Born: Twisden, Goudhurst, 19 January 1807
Died: Newington, Southwark,
    1 November 1861

Batting

M	I	NO	Runs	Av	50	100
90	167	12	1,971	12.71	4	—

Bowling

Runs	Wkts	Av	Other Wkts
1,156	114	10.14	303

5wI	10wM	ct/st	
38	14	56	

Best Performances
92 v. Sussex (Hove) 1849
9-? v. Sussex (Brighton) 1842
12-88 v. England (Canterbury) 1844

Alfred Mynn, 'the Lion of Kent' was the most famous cricketer who ever lived until the advent of W.G. Grace. At six foot one (185cm), weight varying between eighteen and twenty stone (114-127 kg) and shoulders 'like an ox', he was difficult to overlook. Born into a yeoman farming family, Mynn began serious cricket around 1825 when the household moved to Harrietsham, a centre of cricket in the County. Here he was spotted by John Willes, a pioneer of round-arm bowling who lived nearby at Sutton Valence. When delivering round-arm at pace, it is difficult to bowl wicket to wicket and, with wicketkeepers invariably standing up, long stop was one of the most important positions in the field. He was also the busiest in the case of young Alfred, who took a long run and sprayed the ball about. At Willes' persuasion, Mynn changed his action to six gradually accelerated, walking paces, relying on physical strength and an action 'smooth as a piston rod' to generate pace. Clearly Mynn was not fast by modern standards but what he lost in pace he gained in accuracy. For the pad-less, gloveless and otherwise unprotected batsman, facing a big, strong countryman, trained on beef and beer, aiming at leg stump and banging the ball into the rough, scythe-cut turf would not have been a comfortable proposition. Nor was it much fun for the similarly unprotected wicketkeeper or for the long stop on the sheep-cropped, generally unrolled outfield. Mynn's favoured long stop was his elder brother Walter who, on hard wickets, wore a chest protector. Even so, he is reputed to have more than once gone home spitting blood. Some sources suggest that Mynn swung the ball; all agree it passed the batsman with a distinct buzz. At the crease Mynn relied largely on the drive, square cut and full-blooded front-foot leg hit but he also employed the risky looking under-leg shot which must have taken courage without any form of protection. Although hardly a greyhound in the field, with his huge hands he was a reliable slip.

Mynn's first recorded match was for Leeds *v.* Meopham and Gravesend in 1829 but he did not make any real impact until 1832 when his performances in local cricket came to the notice of London's sporting press. He does not at this stage seem to have done anything extraordinary but it was enough to gain selection for Gentlemen *v.* Players at Lord's where his four wickets included his future teammate Fuller Pilch. Mynn took seven wickets on his first-class debut, for Gentlemen of Kent *v.* Gentlemen of England at Chislehurst in 1832, and two years later appeared for Kent *v.* England at Lord's. This was the first match Kent had played as a county for five years and the beginning of a golden age. Within three years the 'Grand Old Kent XI' was one of the strongest county sides in the history of the game. Against England between 1837 and 1849 they won 16 and lost 12; in County cricket over the same period they won 24, tied one, drew two and lost six. Some of Mynn's best bowling performances were in Kent *v.* England encounters – ten times ten or more wickets in a match, three times bowling unchanged through a completed match with 'Topper' Hillyer. They did so twice in 1841 when England were dismissed for 31 and 44 at Lord's and 119 and 110 at Town Malling. In all Kent *v.* England

Photographed late in life, 'kind and manly' Alfred Mynn continued to play cricket up to within a few weeks of his death despite ill health and an expanding waistline.

matches Mynn took at least 214 wickets. In July 1842 he picked up 66 wickets in six matches, including nine in an innings for the Gentlemen of Kent *v.* Gentlemen of England at Lord's and nine again for Kent *v.* Sussex at Brighton.

Mynn's runs normally came quickly but when scoring his 92 for Kent *v.* Sussex at Brighton in 1849, his partnership of 135 for the second wicket with Tom Adams (78) lasted four hours. His best year was 1836, when he hit 45 and 92 for MCC *v.* Sussex followed a week later by 21★ and 125★ for South *v.* North at Leicester, his only first-class hundred. During this innings his (unpadded) leg was so badly battered by Nottinghamshire's Sam Redgate that for several weeks amputation looked inevitable. A return to London strapped to the roof of a coach could hardly have helped.

Despite dubious amateur status Mynn played 20 times for Gentlemen *v.* Players at Lord's and his all-round ability did much to reduce the long-standing disparity between the two sides. He was also a founder member of William Clarke's commercially orientated All-England XI for whom he made 13 appearances, ostensibly as an amateur. He probably needed the money. For most of his life Mynn existed with little visible means of support other than what he made from cricket and the generosity of patrons. At one time he described himself as a farmer but he seems to have done little farming. Later he called himself a hop merchant but, although he kept a tankard of bitter beside his bed, any involvement with hops in their dry state seems to have been confined to the closing years of his life. He was imprisoned for debt more than once; in 1845 he was declared bankrupt. A series of single-wicket matches played for the 'Championship of England' boosted his finances. Mynn won all six, beating Thomas Hills of Town Malling, his friend Felix and Yorkshireman James Dearman twice each. The two latter games were played for £100 each in front of crowds estimated at 5,000.

Although the archetypal gentle giant, 'kind and manly' Alfred Mynn could be aroused. On one occasion he threatened to flatten a member of the aristocracy who tried to bribe him. A man 'with countless friends and no enemies', he played his last match in 1861 and died of diabetes the same year, deeply mourned and one of the few cricketers to have a poem written about him.

John Colin Theodore Page

RHB & RFM/OB 1950-63

The name of Colin Page will go down in the annals of Kent cricket as one of the twin architects of Kent's great team of the 1970s. Along with Leslie Ames he was responsible for spotting and developing young talent, playing a crucial role in the distinguished careers of Derek Underwood, Alan Knott, Graham Johnson, Alan Ealham, Bob Woolmer and many others who went on to achieve great success. When his first-class career came to an end, he had already been captaining the Second XI for two years, a responsibility he had until 1973. During that time he led the side to three Second XI Championships. He took over from Leslie Ames as team manager in 1974 and as Cricket Manager in 1975, in which post he served until 1980.

Born: Mereworth, 20 May 1930
Died: Sevenoaks, 14 December 1990
County Cap: 1957

Batting

M	I	NO	Runs	Av	100	50
198	273	124	818	5.48	–	–

Bowling

Balls	Runs	Wkts	Av
30,340	14,967	521	28.72

5wI	10wM	ct/st
22	2	74

Best Performances
23 v. Glamorgan (Neath) 1957
8-117 v. Warwickshire (Birmingham) 1957
12-169 v. Northamptonshire (Northampton) 1954

In his years as manager the team won the County Championship in 1978 (having shared it the previous year), the Gillette Cup, the Sunday League and the Benson & Hedges Cup twice. His final ten years were as the Club's Director of Youth Coaching. Ill health forced his retirement and he died just weeks later.

Colin Page came to Kent initially as a fast-medium bowler. His first-team debut against Northamptonshire in 1950 was not a great success, neither was his second match as he was wicket-less in both (although in the second he did score 20 runs, which proved to be his second-best score). But his first victim came in his third match: fellow pace bowler Brian Statham. In that season and the next he took only ten wickets in all, but from the latter half of the 1952 season he gained a regular first-team place. His 61 wickets that year included a number of notable batsmen including Cyril Washbrook, Peter May and the Indian Test players Panakaj Roy and Pahlan Umrigar. He continued to show consistency and reliability, taking in excess of 50 wickets a season in all but 1956. In 1957 he switched to off spinners, bewildering many a batsman by clicking the fingers of his left hand as he delivered the ball with his right. The change gave immediate success and his best return to date with 69 wickets. The following season proved to be his best, with 86 wickets at 18.34 including match figures of 10-63 in the opening match at Fenner's (five in each innings) . On three further occasions that season he took five in an innings, including 7-37 against Hampshire at Southampton. This was a golden spell for Page. In the early matches of the season he bowled 129 overs for 264 runs and took 28 wickets. In his career-best performance he bowled 39 overs in a Warwickshire total of 443. A genuine number eleven batsman, not once did his average reach double figures and in only three seasons did he exceed 100 runs. In 1953-54 he had eight successive scoreless innings.

Perhaps not an outstanding technical coach, Colin Page was, beneath a somewhat stern exterior, a good psychologist with a rare gift for building up a player's confidence. He died suddenly on his way home from a coaching engagement in Sevenoaks.

William Harry (Harry Pat) Patterson

RHB & SRA(lobs)/RM 1880-1900

Born: Royal Military College, Sandhurst, Berkshire, 11 March 1859
Died: Hove, Sussex, 3 May 1946

Batting

M	I	NO	Runs	Av	100	50
152	264	18	6,646	27.01	9	27

Bowling

Balls	Runs	Wkts	Av
1,439	865	23	37.60

5wI	10wM	ct/st
–	–	106

Best Performances
181 v. Somerset (Taunton) 1896
4-13 v. Yorkshire (Maidstone) 1888

A solicitor by profession, Harry Patterson was normally only available at Whitsun and in August but for nearly twenty years he upheld his reputation as one of the best batsmen in the country with minimal practice – generally little more than a perfunctory net. When the ball was turning Charles Fry considered him 'almost without a superior'. Son of an Army officer, Patterson followed the orthodox route of Harrow and Oxford University but, unlike most public school/Oxbridge batsmen, his method was very much his own. Strong in defence, he played mainly off the back foot with a variety of wristy strokes between fine leg and wide mid on. He was particularly adept at turning good-length straight balls past square leg's left hand. On the off side he cut well and pushed, rather than drove, through the covers. He was an enthusiastic seeker after short singles.

At Oxford he won Blues in 1880 and 1881 and in the latter year played a key role in Oxford's victory, carrying his bat for 107*, scored in five hours, much of the time with a broken finger. On his debut for Kent against Lancashire at Old Trafford he opened the batting and finished top scorer with 31, meriting a 'Well played my boy' from his captain, Lord Harris. Youthful euphoria was dampened when he discovered the press had credited his score to his near namesake W.B. Pattison who was not playing.

Although rarely managing more than half a season, Patterson three times averaged over 40. His best year was 1885 when he headed the Kent averages with 539 runs at 49.00. He took part in three double-century partnerships, 220 (Patterson 181, Lord Harris 119) for the fourth wicket *v.* Somerset at Taunton 1896; 220 (A. Hearne 112, Patterson 111) for the second wicket *v.* Somerset at Tonbridge 1898 and 213 for the third wicket (Patterson 91, Mason 152) *v.* Gloucestershire, Gravesend 1898. Against Middlesex at Canterbury in 1887 he became the first Kent batsman to be dismissed for 99.

Patterson took over the captaincy on a shared basis with Frank Marchant in 1890. Inability to field a settled team and the need to give too much work to too few bowlers made this a difficult period for Kent, and the dual captaincy experiment only lasted three seasons. Even so, Patterson has a respectable record as a captain, 44.4 per cent of wins to matches played. This includes a number of later matches when he captained in emergencies.

Patterson was an excellent outfielder and kept wicket occasionally. As a bowler he could be a useful partnership breaker. He appeared four times for Gentlemen *v.* Players at Lord's. A man of quiet humour, 'Harry Pat', as he was known to his intimates, gave many years' service to Kent as right-hand man and general 'fixer upper' to Lord Harris on the Kent Committee. He was President in 1922, Vice-President and Trustee up to the time of his death. His firm acted for the Club in the purchase of the St Lawrence ground. He served on the Committee of MCC and for many years captained the Butterflies.

100 GREATS ——————— Henry Anthony (Tony) Pawson OBE

RHB & OB 1946-53

Some of the most entertaining moments during the Canterbury Weeks of the early post-war years were when Godfrey Evans and Tony Pawson were batting together. Both fleet of foot, their running between the wickets could at times be breathtaking. A right-hand batsman with a very crouched stance, Pawson was a magnificent cutter and an excellent outfielder but his appearances were restricted mainly to the month of August. He bowled occasional off breaks, his best performance for Kent being 2-26 in seven overs in the match in which he also achieved his highest score for the County.

In his debut match in Canterbury Week against Hampshire he scored a quick-fire 90 in Kent's total of 477 before being run out. That first season he scored 327 runs in 11 innings at 32.70. It was not until his final season of any significance, 1950, that he scored his two centuries. His first, scored in 90 minutes was his highest and was the third of three hundreds scored by batsmen three, four and five, in an innings total of 532. For Kent he played on only six further occasions, four in 1951 and two in 1952. In his autobiography *Runs and Catches* he describes how, when chasing 232 for

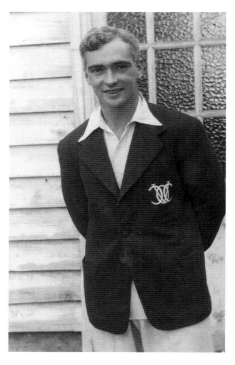

Born: Chertsey, Surrey, 22 August 1921

Batting

M	I	NO	Runs	Av	100	50
43	70	7	2,100	33.33	2	13

Bowling

Balls	Runs	Wkts	Av
194	131	4	32.75

5wI	10wM	ct/st
—	—	16

Best Performances
137 v. Essex (Maidstone) 1950

victory against Middlesex at Canterbury in 1947 and with Kent at 30-4, he and Bryan Valentine decided to take up the challenge, adding 95 in 37 minutes. Only when they were both out in quick succession did Kent settle for a draw. Although he thrilled with his running between the wickets, he was run out on an above average number of occasions and against Middlesex at Lord's in his first season he was dismissed 'hit wicket' when smashing the ball to the boundary and sitting on his stumps, demolishing all three!

Tony Pawson began his cricket career as a fifteen-year-old Winchester schoolboy in sensational fashion, scoring a brilliant 237 at Lord's for the Public Schools XI. A double Oxford Blue, in his first season for the University he scored 774 runs at 43.00 including a career-best 150 against Worcestershire at Worcester when he opened the innings, and a debut hundred against Gloucestershire. This was at a time when the counties fielded strong sides against the universities. In the first of his Varsity matches he scored 135 in the drawn match. The following year he captained the side to an innings victory. His year as captain saw him top the batting averages with 653 runs at 50.23 including a second-innings not out 103 against Sussex. For the second season in succession he exceeded 1,000 runs. He was selected for the Lord's Gentlemen v. Players match in 1947 and opened both innings, in neither of which did he reach double figures.

An outstanding all-round sportsman, Pawson played in the Corinthian spirit. He was an amateur international association footballer and twice won Amateur Cup winners' medals with Pegasus, a team made up of ex-Oxford and Cambridge players, as well as playing three games as an amateur for Charlton Athletic. He was selected for Britain's Olympic soccer team in 1948 and added to his sporting achievements by becoming world fly-fishing champion. His OBE was for services to angling. For almost thirty years he wrote on cricket and football for the *Observer*. Tony Pawson can also boast a distinguished war record, serving with the Rifle Brigade throughout the Tunisian and Italian campaigns, ending up as a Major and being mentioned in dispatches. He also had a notable career in public service in sports-related areas.

Frank Penn

RHB & SRA (round-arm) 1875-81

Born: Lewisham, 7 March 1851
Died: Patrixbourne, 26 December 1916

Batting

M	I	NO	Runs	Av	100	50
62	109	10	2,906	29.35	5	11

Bowling

Balls	Runs	Wkts	Av
770	312	8	39.00

5wI	10wM	ct/st
–	–	31

Best Performances
158 *v.* Surrey (Maidstone) 1878
3-36 *v.* Lancashire (Maidstone) 1877
Tests: 1 for England

*W*isden described Frank Penn as 'among the finest batsmen in England'. He was at the wicket when Grace made the winning hit in the first ever Test match on English soil and had his career not been cut short by illness he might be better known. Apart from Harris himself, few did more to re-establish the County side when most of the best amateurs were reluctant to play outside the upper-crust milieu of Canterbury Week.

Penn's father was the engineer John Penn, who designed and built marine engines at works in Deptford and Greenwich. The company ran their own cricket team (Ravensbourne CC) and two other sons also played for the County. William had a short career, joining his elder brother John in running the business on the death of their father but Alfred, a left-arm bowler with the ability to swing the new ball, took 197 wickets between 1875 and 1884.

Strong in defence, Frank Penn drove hard and was considered among the most powerful leg hitters of his time. On debut against Sussex at Catford in 1875 he was run out for 20 when going well. But 79 against Derbyshire at Derby and a Canterbury Week during which he took 48 from a formidable England attack and hit 101 against the Gentlemen of MCC established him as a batsman of consequence. In 1876 he was picked for Gentlemen *v.* Players at both Lord's and

The Oval, the first of eight appearances in what was then the most prestigious fixture of the season. In 1877 he headed the Kent averages with 857 runs at 40.80, including 148★ *v.* Surrey at The Oval and 135 against England in Canterbury Week. Next year he led the averages again with 515 runs at 34.33 and hit his career best, 160 *v.* Surrey at Maidstone. He was less consistent for Kent in 1879 but scored 135 for the MCC *v.* Cambridge University at Lord's, an innings considered his best by the *cognoscenti*.

In Kent's first game of the 1881 season, *v.* MCC at Lord's he hit 102 but sunstroke, later diagnosed as a heart condition, prevented him from taking any further part in the match. He never played for Kent again but later in the season he appeared for the Gentlemen at Lord's and The Oval and for South *v.* North when, in scoring 68★ he hit the metronomically accurate Alfred Shaw over The Oval pavilion. He played occasional minor cricket and as late as 1895 hit 60 in a club match.

Penn joined Lord Harris's team in Australia in 1878/79 after the first (and only) Test match but he hit 56 against New South Wales at Sydney. Brought into the side for The Oval Test match in 1880 when A.N. Hornby, still miffed over the infamous Sydney riot, declined the invitation. Penn hit 23 and in the second innings, with England needing only 57, he came in at 10-2 and saw his side home with 27★.

He was President of Kent in 1905. The white scoreboard at Canterbury, which stood for over seventy years on the site now occupied by its electronic successor, was presented to Kent in his memory.

Arthur Henry Phebey

RHB 1946-61

After serving as a wartime pilot in the Fleet Air Arm, Arthur Phebey became one of Kent's early post-war players. An all-round sportsman, he played Association Football with Dulwich Hamlet, having been a schoolboy international prior to the war. He began his cricketing career as an amateur, but turned professional in 1948. He had an excellent technique especially against the new ball, although in his first few years he was played as a middle-order batsman. He graduated to opening the innings and throughout his career he was partner to Leslie Todd, Arthur Fagg, Peter Richardson, Colin Cowdrey and Bob Wilson, with whom he forged what was considered one of the best opening partnerships in county cricket. With his various opening partners, he shared fourteen century stands, including the matches against the Indian tourists of 1952 and the South Africans of 1955. On four occasions he carried his bat as opener, including an innings of 85 out of 181 against the 1953 Australian tourists with Lindwall, Miller and Benaud in their attack. In 1960, Phebey and Bob Wilson came within eighteen runs of beating Kent's third-wicket partnership of 321 which has stood since 1899. In that innings he just failed to improve on what was to be his best score.

His career started slowly and it was some seasons before he was able to command a regular spot in the team. Even then there were occasions when he had to give way

Born: Catford, 1 October 1924
Died: Kingswood, Surrey, 28 June 1998
County Cap: 1952

Batting

M	I	NO	Runs	Av	100	50
320	585	33	14,299	25.90	12	69

Bowling

Balls	Runs	Wkts	Av
20	4	0	—

5wI	10wM	ct/st
—	—	202

Best Performances
157 v. Gloucestershire (Bristol) 1958

during August to Tony Pawson. In his first season he scored 354 runs at 19.66 but did not play at all in 1947. The following year he was selected for just two matches and it was not until 1951, during which he was promoted to opener, that he became a regular choice. He had to wait until 1952 to score 1,000 runs in a season for the first time, and a further year before he scored his maiden hundred. He went on to score in excess of 1,000 runs in nine consecutive seasons, his best being in 1959 with 1,737 at 33.40. Compared with some, he has a fairly indifferent batting average. But his career was centred on the 1950s when the pitches were uncovered and the summers invariably wet. He was a good gully fielder but apt to make things look a little more difficult than they were and was reluctant to chase the ball when it got past him. Only five of his contemporaries took more catches, and all but one of those played in substantially more matches. He frequently led the side as vice-captain to Colin Cowdrey during the early years of his captaincy.

His final first class appearance was for the MCC against Ireland in 1964. He served on Kent's general committee from 1977-93, was Chairman of the Cricket Committee and a Vice-President from 1990 until his death.

100
GREATS

Roy Francois Pienaar

RHB & RM 1987-89

South African-born Roy Pienaar, who came to Kent as a replacement overseas player in 1987 primarily as a right-arm medium-fast bowling all-rounder, enjoyed greater success as a batsman. Because of injuries to his knees, his bowling in 1989, which was his final season with the County, was restricted to just 11 overs. Despite that, his batting more than justified his selection.

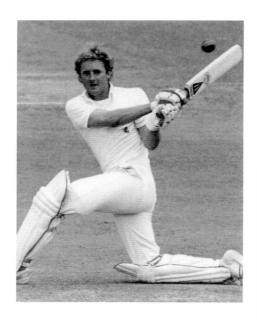

Born: Johannesburg, South Africa,
17 July 1961

County Cap: 1988

Batting

M	I	NO	Runs	Av	100	50
45	72	6	2,876	43.57	8	15
29	25	2	745	32.39	1	3

Bowling

Balls	Runs	Wkts	Av
3,306	1,632	51	32.00
750	503	23	21.86

5wI	10wM	ct/st
1	–	15
–	–	9

Best Performances

153 *v. Derbyshire (Derby)* 1987

119 v. Glamorgan (Canterbury) 1989 (SL)

5-27 *v. Middlesex (Tunbridge Wells)* 1988

4-34 v. Middlesex (Canterbury) 1988 (SL)

Born in Johannesburg, he was a high-class attractive batsman of impeccable technique who made his first-class debut as a sixteen-year-old playing for Transvaal and Western Province. He appeared for Worcestershire Second XI in 1987 and made his First XI debut for Kent against Essex in the same season, scoring 41 runs in his only innings and taking 5-134 in the match. Four weeks later, and on his twenty-sixth birthday, he scored his maiden century in England – an innings of 153 that proved to be his highest score. That was his only century in his first season but in eight innings he finished with an average of more than 40, placing him second to Mark Benson, a position he was to hold for his two further seasons with the County. In 1988, his first full season, he scored 1,228 stylish runs at 37.21, a total only exceeded by Chris Tavaré. This performance was an important contribution towards Kent's second place in the Championship that season. In his final year he averaged 52.84 and was again second in the total number of runs scored.

Kent had a poor season in 1989. It would have been far worse but for two important innings played by Pienaar in successive victories. Against Yorkshire at Scarborough he scored a magnificent second-innings 125 off 183 balls in a chase to get 277 for victory, a target reached with just ten balls remaining. Then the following week at Canterbury his first-innings 132 out of 372 and off 144 balls (the next best score was 57) was another vital knock in a match where victory was achieved with just three balls remaining. While he probably did not perform as hoped with the ball, he often took wickets when most needed. His 5-27 from 16 overs in the Middlesex second innings at Tunbridge Wells in 1988 was the decisive factor in a Kent victory by five wickets in a low-scoring match.

Roy Pienaar was no less effective in the limited-overs game. In his relatively short time with the County he had a more than creditable batting and bowling average with a bowling economy rate of 4.02 runs per over, putting him among the best. His top score of 119 was scored off 113 balls. He won two successive Man of the Match awards in the 1988 National Westminster Bank Cup competition.

Because of injury problems he did not return to England after 1989, but continued playing first-class cricket in South Africa up to 1999/2000.

100 GREATS — Fuller Pilch

RHB & SRA (round-arm) 1836-54

Born: Horningtoft, Norfolk, 17 March 1804
Died: Canterbury, 1 May 1870

Batting

M	I	NO	Runs	Av	100	50
84	156	11	2,844	19.61	–	11

Bowling

Runs	Wkts	Av	Other Wkts
72	2	36.00	13

5wI	10wM	ct/st
–	–	45

Best Performances
98 v. England (Canterbury) 1842
4-? v. Sussex (Canterbury) 1844

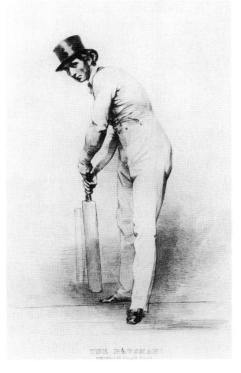

THE BATSMAN
PORTRAIT OF FULLER PILCH

Fuller Pilch was already hailed as the best batsman in England when he came to Kent in 1835. To the cricket historian Rowland Bowen, Pilch 'stood head and shoulders above his contemporaries'. Lured from his native Norfolk by a salary of £100 to manage the ground at Town Malling (now West Malling), he came at the instigation of a consortium headed by prominent residents of the town and carrying the stamp of approval of the Second Lord Harris. An additional carrot was dangled in the form of proprietorship of the adjoining tavern. Once settled, only perhaps Mynn did as much to create the 'Grand Old Kent XI'.

Kent had abundant evidence of his ability. In the previous year he had hit 551 runs at 61.22 including two centuries, as well as 60 for Players v. Gentlemen. For England at Lord's in 1835, the year of his move, he hit the Kent bowlers for 59 and in the following year, scored 107 against Kent as 'given man' for Benenden. This was one

Although burdened with money worries, Fuller Pilch's final years were brightened by visits from old cricketing friends to his pub, the Saracen's Head.

of ten centuries hit during his career, three of them now ranked first-class. The consortium began to see a return on their investment when later in the season Pilch hit 44 for Kent *v.* Sussex at Town Malling and next year when he achieved his personal best, 160 for Town Malling *v.* Reigate against an attack including the redoubtable Frederick William 'I bowl the best ball in England' Lillywhite.

One remarkable aspect of Pilch's batting was the ease with which he handled the transition from under-arm to round-arm. He learned his game when round-arm, although by no means unknown, was nevertheless illegal. In 1827 he had played in the three 'experimental' England *v.* Sussex matches staged to evaluate what was known as 'Sussex' (i.e. round-arm) bowling of which Lillywhite and James Broadbridge were the prime exponents. There was much ill-feeling. After the second match, Pilch was one of eight England players who signed a declaration refusing to play in the third unless the Sussex bowlers 'play fair – that is abstain from throwing'. In the end he played and quickly became one of the first to learn to cope with the new bowling and, by common consent, handled it better than anyone.

Pilch batted mainly off the front foot although, unlike almost all of his contemporaries, he was equally comfortable playing back. He used his height, over six feet (180cm), and 'seemed to crush the bowling with his long forward lunge' colloquially known as 'Pilch's poke'. With right-arm bowlers operating almost exclusively from round the wicket he developed the full range of off-side strokes from off drive to late cut, with a penchant for scoring from good-length balls on or outside off stump. On the on side he played the then-fashionable leg hit off the front foot as well as the draw, a strange, happily obsolete, stroke in which the ball was steered between the batsman's legs and the leg stump. At the time most batsmen took guard clear of leg stump which made it easier but even so, on rough wickets and without pads or other safeguards, the shot seems to carry more than its fair share of risk.

Of his 11 fifties for Kent, four were against England, six against Sussex and one against Nottinghamshire. He also passed 40 thirteen times in Kent matches. His highest for Kent, 98 *v.* England in the first ever Canterbury Week, was hit from an attack including Lillywhite, 'Jemmy' Dean and Tom Barker. One of his best efforts was at Brighton against Sussex (with Lillywhite and Broadbridge) in 1837 when, with Kent needing 152, the highest total of the match, he came in at number seven to steer them to victory with 69★. He was top scorer in twenty-eight per cent of his innings for Kent and the County's leading scorer in twelve seasons, 1837 to 1844, 1847 to 1848 and 1850 to 1851.

Off the field Pilch also contributed. He managed the team, acted as chief selector cum talent scout and captained whenever Ned Wenman was not available. With its small population, Town Malling was never viable as a centre for Kent cricket and in 1841 the project was wound up although for many years the ground still carried Pilch's name. Pilch himself moved to Canterbury, initially to run the Beverley Ground in Sturry Road. In 1847, he moved again to St Lawrence where his wickets quickly gained a reputation for excellence.

Pads, sometimes worn beneath the trousers like shin guards, were coming into use in Pilch's time and he was one of the first to adopt them. In his early days he played in the conventional top hat but later switched to the white cap then becoming fashionable. The Players *v.* Gentlemen match of 1837 when he was dismissed 'hat knocked on wicket' may have made his mind up for him.

In 1833, before coming to Kent, Pilch played Tom Marsden of Sheffield at single-wicket for the Championship of England and beat him twice. Pilch and Mynn were friends and like two wary old tom cats they avoided playing each other for the title. As well as twenty-two appearances for Players *v.* Gentlemen, Pilch played twice as given man for Gentlemen *v.* Players. Like Mynn and Felix he was a founder member of William Clarke's All-England XI. He played his last game for Kent in 1854.

A tailor by profession, he started a tailoring business in Canterbury with brother Walter as well as becoming landlord of the Saracen's Head, which stood at the junction of Lower Bridge Street and Burgate until it fell victim to road widening in 1969. A bachelor, he ran the business with his sister but although it was a popular meeting place for the cricketing fraternity he went bankrupt in the 1860s. He died in 1870 from a heart condition, known at the time as dropsy. His pedestal tombstone with memorial plaque based on the G.F. Watts lithograph was moved to the St Lawrence ground in 1978 when St Gregory's church was declared redundant.

Canon William Rashleigh

RHB & SRA 1885-1901

Born: Farningham, 7 March 1867
Died: Balcombe, Sussex, 13 February 1937
County Cap: 1887

Batting

M	I	NO	Runs	Av	100	50
96	165	3	4,003	24.70	7	14

Bowling

Balls	Runs	Wkts	Av
29	29	0	–

5wl	10wM	ct/st	
–	–	35	

Best Performances
163 v. Middlesex (Tonbridge) 1896

Cricketing fame can be fickle. Stoddart's 1894/95 team to Australia is generally considered the closest to a full-strength England side ever to tour up to that point. Rashleigh was invited but had to decline. In 1895 the editor of *Wisden* wrote that if an England team had been chosen that year 'it is practically certain that Mr Rashleigh would have been asked to play'. According to the *Wisden* obituarist, 'Rashleigh, as nearly as anyone has done, deserved the description of the perfect batsman'. Charles Fry considered him 'as fine a punishing bat as there is', but twenty-five years later, to another *Wisden* contributor, he was 'relatively little known'. In subsequent histories he rarely rates a mention.

Rashleigh's father played for the Gentlemen of Kent, as did his uncle and young William was encouraged to play from infancy. At Tonbridge he was in the XI from 1882 to 1885, averaging over 60 in each of his final two years and hitting a double-hundred against Dulwich. In August 1885, his final year at school, he was invited to play for Kent v. Hampshire at Tonbridge and responded with 54. Commenting favourably, *Wisden* labelled him 'the famous Tonbridge schoolboy'. Ten days later he hit 59 against Middlesex at Mote Park. At Oxford in 1886, he played several useful innings but W.G. Grace advised the Oxford captain not to pick him against Cambridge, advice fortunately ignored, The upshot was an innings of 107 and a 243-run first-wicket partnership with the future Surrey captain Kingsmill Key. Rashleigh was in the Oxford XI for four years, captain in 1888 and also won a Rugby Blue at full-back. In 1887 he hit his first century for Kent, 108 v. Gloucestershire at Clifton.

After Oxford, he returned to Tonbridge as assistant master, giving valuable service to Kent in Tonbridge Week and in the holidays. Possibly inspired by ordination in 1892, his best seasons were 1893, when he led the Kent averages with 482 runs at 37.07, 1894, when he topped the averages again with 620 at 36.47 and 1896, 528 runs at 35.20. Among his best displays were 163 in 150 minutes *v.* Middlesex at Tonbridge in 1896 when he hit a hundred before lunch; 109 in 100 minutes *v.* Lancashire at Canterbury in the same year; and 120 *v.* Warwickshire at Catford in 1899 during which, with Mason, 182 was added for the fifth wicket in 105 minutes.

With strong wrists – Fry termed his cutting 'perfection' – Rashleigh was equally at ease off front or back foot, placed well on the leg side, played the pull on slow wickets and 'was a fine driver, especially to the on'. There were weaknesses. He was an uncertain starter and, in the early days, unreliable in the field. In his own words 'I was always in a mortal funk until recently' (1895) which probably explains Grace's advice. Hard work and possibly understanding captaincy seem to have brought improvement.

He was a Minor Canon of Canterbury Cathedral from 1903 to 1912 and subsequently Vicar of Horton Kirby and Ridgemount, Bedfordshire.

100 ———————————————————— Peter Edward Richardson

GREATS

LHB & RM 1959-65

After serving Worcestershire for ten years from 1949 to 1958 including a three-year stint as captain, Peter Richardson – one of three brothers to play county cricket – joined Kent in 1959 and qualified to play championship cricket the following season. He came to the County as a professional, (having played for Worcestershire as an amateur) and as an established Test player, with 25 caps up to then.

A patient but highly effective left-hand opening batsman with strong forearms, he pushed and deflected the ball with little backlift and was expert in taking quick singles. He had a record of consistency that served Kent well during his seven seasons with the hop county. His wide experience was of special value to a group of promising emerging players, especially Brian Luckhurst, with whom he was to share the top-order batting positions for a number of seasons. Throughout his career he topped 1,000 runs on 11 occasions, reaching 2,000 four times including twice for Kent. While serving his year's qualification he played for Kent against Cambridge University, but failed on his first appearance with the bat. However, his six seasons with Kent yielded him in excess of 1,000 runs five times, missing out only in his final season. Once back into the first-class game he quickly found his form with over 1,600 runs in 1960, over 2,000 in each of the next two (2,119 at 38.52 and 2,081 at 38.53). He missed the 2,000 mark in 1963 by just 23 runs but topped the Kent averages with 42.06 – his best for the County. In those three seasons he scored 13 hundreds with his highest coming in the Canterbury Week match against Hampshire in 1963, when he shared in a third-wicket stand of 204 with Stuart Leary. In all, he scored 18 hundreds for his adopted county, the first

Born: Hereford, 4 July 1931
County Cap: 1960

Batting

M	I	NO	Runs	Av	100	50
162	290	12	9,975	35.88	18	52
3	3	–	168	56.00	1	–

Bowling

Balls	Runs	Wkts	Av
226	164	4	41.00

5wI	10wM	ct/st
–	–	96

Best Performances
172 *v.* Hampshire (Canterbury) 1963
127 *v. Sussex (Tunbridge Wells)* 1963 *(GC)*
Tests: 34 for England
***Wisden* Cricketer of the Year:** 1957 (for Worcestershire & England)

being against Cambridge University in 1961, a match remembered for a mere 54-run second innings total by the students after scoring 382 in their first.

Altogether he played in 34 Test matches with considerable success, including an outstanding tour to India, Pakistan and Ceylon in 1961/62, during which he scored more than 1,000 runs. He shared fruitful opening partnerships for England with Colin Cowdrey. He failed completely on the 1958/59 tour to Australia, but would have got much satisfaction from his performance for Kent against the 1964 Australians when he scored a century in each innings, emulating Colin Cowdrey's achievement at Canterbury three years earlier.

Peter Richardson had a reputation as a humorist, specialising allegedly in sending faked cricket records to E.W. Swanton for publication in the *Daily Telegraph* and apparently on one occasion complaining about excessive noise from Mr Swanton in the commentary box. On an occasion at Trent Bridge he provided the scorers with a totally fictitious batting order made up of double-barrelled and otherwise unlikely names and he also persuaded Brian Johnston that Mike Denness was the son of a crofter!

He announced his retirement from the game in 1965 after a disappointing mid-season spell.

Frederick (Fred) Ridgway

RHB & RFM 1946-61

Born: Stockport, Cheshire, 10 August 1923
County Cap: 1947

Batting

M	I	NO	Runs	Av	100	50
298	442	100	3,812	11.14	–	9

Bowling

Balls	Runs	Wkts	Av
50,432	22,740	955	23.81

5wI	10wM	ct/st
38	6	203

Best Performances
94 v. Sussex (Tunbridge Wells) 1953
8-39 v. Nottinghamshire (Dover) 1950 and
v. Lancashire (Dartford) 1960
12-86 v. Yorkshire (Hull) 1947
Tests: 5 for England

A right-arm fast medium bowler, Fred Ridgway's career probably suffered from the lack of a regular new-ball partner. Despite being quite short for a fast bowler, he combined hostility with accuracy and was able to move the ball sufficiently to worry the best of batsmen. Although many of his contemporaries were faster, he could keep going for long periods and was often the workhorse of the team. In his years with the County only Doug Wright and Ray Dovey consistently bowled more overs and only Wright was marginally more economic. Only seven Kent bowlers have taken more wickets for the County and in the post-1945 period, Derek Underwood is the only bowler to have exceeded Ridgway's haul. Although he never reached 100 wickets in a season for Kent he came close on two occasions with 97 in 1949 and 98 in 1958, but with additional first-class wickets in other matches he reached 105 in 1949 at an average of 23.32. In 1951 at Folkestone, he equalled a record for Kent first set in 1862 by Joseph Wells, father of H.G., when he took four wickets with successive balls against Derbyshire and although he had eight in the match, he finished up on the losing side. That four in four was the first of his two hat-tricks, the second being against Oxford University in 1958. Three times he took eight in an innings.

As a hard-hitting tail-end batsman he often scored useful runs and came close to a maiden century on two occasions. In 1949 in the match against Sussex at Tunbridge Wells he shared a then-record ninth-wicket partnership of 161 with Brian Edrich, making his then-highest score of 89. That record stood until 1997. His best season with the bat was 1953 when he scored 679 runs at an average of 18.35. A fine all-round fielder, he was especially fast and terrier-like in the deep, and had a safe pair of hands. His 203 catches were not exceeded by anyone over the same period.

Throughout the early post-war years, he was on the fringes of England selection, unluckily having to compete for international recognition at a time when England possessed a number of outstanding bowlers of similar type. He was selected for the five Tests on the 1951/52 tour to India and Pakistan in a team that performed under the handicap of being termed 'England's second string'. He had a disappointing time, taking just seven wickets and scoring few runs.

Fred Ridgway was a popular footballer in the Kent League, playing a number of seasons on the wing for Ramsgate. He saw wartime service with the Royal Marines.

David Michael Sayer

RHB & RF 1955-76

Born: Romford, 19 September 1936
County Cap: 1962

Batting

M	I	NO	Runs	Av	100	50
154	173	64	835	7.66	–	–
8	4	–	0	0.00	–	–

Bowling

Balls	Runs	Wkts	Av
24,375	10,587	441	24.00
465	271	14	19.35

5wI	10wM	ct/st
11	1	57
–	–	4

Best Performances

39 v. Middlesex (Gravesend) 1966
7-37 (10-67) v. Leicestershire (Leicester) 1958
3-24 v. Suffolk (Ipswich) 1966 (GC)

A graduate of Brasenose College, David Sayer played for Oxford University from 1958 to 1960 and won a Blue each year. A right-arm fast bowler, he was considered possibly the fastest in the country during his time at the University. However, he had problems with his technique and in resolving those he lessened his pace. He was probably the fastest bowler to wear spectacles while bowling. In his three years at Oxford he took 146 wickets and had a particularly impressive first season, topping the bowling averages with 62 wickets at 13.40.

He made his first-class debut against Sussex at Tunbridge Wells in 1955 while still at school and after a successful introduction four weeks earlier in the Second XI match against Middlesex in which he had match figures of 7-77. He played in only a couple of matches that season, taking just two wickets. In the following two years he played no first-class cricket, but in his first year at Oxford he returned to play seven matches for the County, in which he took 27 wickets at 13.88, including once achieving ten in a match and twice five in an innings. It was in his opening year at Oxford that he achieved the first half of what was to become a somewhat unique 'double', taking a hat-trick against Kent and returning match figures of 11-91. Six years later against Glamorgan at Maidstone, he performed the feat for Kent! On the first of those occasions his victims were Tony Catt, Fred Ridgway and Alan Brown (with whom he was to strike up an effective fast-bowling partnership and share a benefit).

It was 1961 before he won a regular place and even then his selection was not guaranteed, with Kent being in a position to perm any two from a quartet of Norman Graham, John Dye, Alan Brown and Sayer. In 1963 and 1965 he played in fewer than half the Championship matches, but nevertheless performed well when called upon. In three seasons he exceeded 50 wickets, his best being in 1964 when in 21 matches he took 77 wickets at 21.88 and recorded a best innings performance for the season of 7-54 against Derbyshire at Chesterfield. Although two bowlers took more wickets he topped the averages for the County. He was selected for the Gentlemen v. Players at Lord's in 1959 and 1960, when he took 6-69 in the Players' first innings on the first occasion and 4-36 in the Players' second innings in the thrilling match of 1960 when the scores ended level.

A lower-order right-hand batsman, his highest first-class score of 62 was for the University against Nottinghamshire at Oxford in 1959. He twice toured with MCC: to South America in 1958/59 (not first-class) and to New Zealand in 1960/61. His last first-class match for the County was against Leicestershire in 1976 when he was recalled in an emergency, having retired in 1969.

James Seymour

RHB & OB 1902-26

The historian R.L. Arrowsmith considered Seymour had 'perhaps the widest range of strokes of any batsman in England'. With a slightly open stance – described in a rather stuffy *Times* obituary as 'too modern' – he held the bat low down on the handle, played every shot in the book plus several others. To a ball just short of a length on or outside off stump he employed a flat-batted shot past cover and liked to pull straight balls pitching middle and leg. He used the old-fashioned leg hit played with a vertical bat and was probably the last major batsman to play the even more archaic 'dog' or 'under leg' stroke. Although sometimes inclined to play shots too early, he had a strong defence with an excellent back-foot technique when the

SEYMOUR KENT

PHOTO
B.C. FLEMON
TONBRIDGE

Born: West Hoathly, Sussex, 25 October 1879
Died: Marden, 30 September 1930
County Cap: 1902

Batting

M	I	NO	Runs	Av	100	50
536	881	60	26,818	32.66	53	129

Bowling

Balls	Runs	Wkts	Av
1,080	680	15	45.33

5wI	10wM	ct/st
–	–	659

Best Performances
218* v. Essex (Leyton) 1911
4-62 v. Somerset (Taunton) 1908

ball was turning. In the field there have been few better slip cordons than Seymour, Mason, Hutchings and Blaker.

In 1900, before joining Kent, he made his first-class debut for London County v. Derbyshire at Derby, one of three appearances for Grace's team. Later that year an innings of 66* for Kent Club & Ground v. Gravesend earned him a place at the Tonbridge Nursery. Qualified by living in Pembury, he made his first appearance for Kent at Old Trafford in 1902, finishing the season with 575 runs including two fifties. At Old Trafford next year he hit his first hundred and by 1904 he was a first-team regular. Despite competition in August from Kent's coloured cap and striped blazer fraternity he remained so until he retired. He holds the Kent record for the number of consecutive appearances, 187 in all matches, 196 in the Championship. From 1904 to 1926 he failed only three times to reach 1,000 runs and seven times passed 1,500. He headed the Kent averages in 1907 and 1911 and was leading run scorer in 1907 and 1908. During his career he scored hundreds against all the then-fifteen counties except Sussex – nine against Essex, six each against Somerset and Worcestershire and five each against Lancashire and Surrey. He hit three double-hundreds, two from the long-suffering Essex bowlers. His 204 v. Hampshire at Tonbridge in 1907 included a century before lunch.

Seymour participated in 15 double-century partnerships, the highest 307 in 165 minutes for the second wicket v. Worcestershire at Kidderminster in 1922 (Hardinge 151, Seymour 170). At Derby in 1908 Seymour (171) and Hutchings (102) hit 240 for the third wicket in just over two hours and at Taunton in 1907, Seymour (104) and Mason (119★) added 230 in 100 minutes for the fifth wicket. He also shared two century last-wicket partnerships with Fielder.

Inexplicably, the nearest Seymour got to an England place was a Test Trial in 1912. He appeared twice for the Players at The Oval, never at Lord's.

His benefit in 1920 led to a long drawn out battle between Lord Harris and the Inland Revenue, which ended successfully in the House of Lords. Ever since, cricketers have enjoyed increasingly lucrative tax-free benefits. Sadly Seymour did not live long to enjoy his. His brother John played for Sussex and Northamptonshire.

100 GREATS

John Neil (Shep) Shepherd

RHB & RMF 1966-81

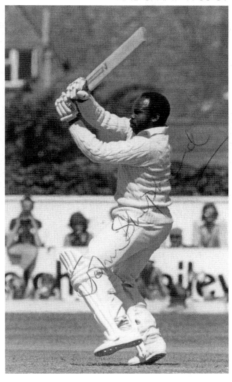

Born: Belleplaine, St. Andrew, Barbados, 9 November 1943
County Cap: 1967

Batting

M	I	NO	Runs	Av	50	100
303	431	74	9,401	26.33	8	49
250	206	43	3,555	21.80	1	12

Bowling

Balls	Runs	Wkts	Av
52,856	22,106	832	26.56
11,734	6,810	332	20.51

5wI	10wM	ct/st
45	2	212
–	–	74

Best Performances
170 v. Northamptonshire (Folkestone) 1968
101 v. Middlesex (Canterbury) 1977 (GC)
8-83 v. Lancashire (Tunbridge Wells) 1977
15-147 v. Sussex (Maidstone) 1975
4-17 v. Middlesex (Lord's) 1978 (SL)
Tests: 5 for West Indies
Wisden Cricketer of the Year: 1979

He was known affectionately as 'Shep' by supporters from his early days with the County, and still referred to as such some forty years on. But for unknown reasons fellow players called him 'Walter'. Whatever, John Shepherd quickly won the hearts of cricket-lovers for his commitment, approachability, his infectious laugh and his irresistible enthusiasm. He came from the island of Barbados as a result of an invitation from Leslie Ames and Colin Cowdrey when they were touring the West Indies in 1964.

John Shepherd bowling against Surrey in a Benson & Hedges zonal match at The Oval in 1980, a game uniquely postponed for twenty-four hours due to a TUC 'Day of Action'.

A fine, natural all-round cricketer John Shepherd was a popular figure on Kent grounds and a significant contributor to Kent's successes from the mid-1960s through to the late 1970s. His record during the sixteen years rates him as one of Kent's finest all-rounders. He is one of only sixteen players who have achieved the double of 5,000 runs and 250 wickets (both of which he comfortably exceeded) and had it not been for his call-up to the West Indies touring side to England in 1969, during which he picked up a back injury that plagued him for much of his career, he almost certainly would have reached 10,000 runs and 900 wickets for Kent. His full career record of 13,359 runs and 1,157 wickets rates him highly among all-rounders. Stockily built and with a large reservoir of stamina, he could always be relied upon to bowl long spells. With Derek Underwood and Bob Woolmer on regular Test duty, he found himself carrying a heavy load as the team's stock bowler. He could move the ball both ways off the seam and was especially difficult to play in overcast or humid conditions. He was consistent and reliable, taking wickets at crucial times, stemming the scoring rate when batsmen were getting on top, and a specialist in breaking stubborn partnerships. Of his contemporaries, only Derek Underwood bowled more overs, making him the second busiest among all of Kent's post-Second World War bowlers. In that same period only four bowlers took more wickets. He was a key player in Kent's 1970 Championship-winning side. Despite his back injury, he took 86 wickets – more than any other bowler – scored 734 runs and took 23 catches.

A fine all-round performance against Sussex at Maidstone in 1975, when he bowled unchanged in both innings, recording what proved to be a career-best bowling performance of 8-93 and 7-54, and scoring 52 runs, epitomises his career. That season he bowled 579 overs, 112 more than any of his colleagues. That margin was even wider two years later, the season when Kent shared the Championship with Middlesex, when he bowled 300 overs more than any other Kent bowler, and had thirty-two wickets more than the next best. Although never taking 100 wickets in a season he twice came close, with 96 in 1968 at 18.72 and 92 in 1973 at 22.32. In the first of those years he recorded five wickets in an innings on eight occasions.

While primarily a bowling all-rounder, expectations of him as a batsman were never completely fulfilled. His 9,400 runs included only eight hundreds, all of which he scored in just five seasons, and only once did he exceed 1,000 runs – a relatively poor return in sixteen years. Given that three of his hundreds came in only his second full season – that in which he reached the 1,000-runs landmark, it was inevitable that much more would be expected of him with the bat. That was possibly his best season, just failing to be the first Kent player since 1936 to achieve the double of 1,000 runs and 100 wickets, which he certainly would have, needing only four more wickets, had he not missed three matches through injury. Nevertheless, as a hard-hitting batsman he made notable contributions on important occasions, able to score his runs at a fast rate when necessary or defending effectively when the situation demanded. Had he not had to bear such a load as a bowler he would undoubtedly have scored more runs. His career-best score of 170 was achieved in 175 minutes. It included five sixes and 24 fours and included a partnership of 164 in one and three-quarter hours with Alan Ealham.

John Shepherd's abilities with bat and ball, and as an outstandingly athletic fielder with one of the best throwing arms in the game, made him an important and indispensable part of Kent's limited-overs sides. His accuracy as a bowler, giving nothing away and frustrating batsmen as Derek Underwood could, was rewarded with the fourth-highest number of dismissals and the third-best economy rate in Kent's one-day history. On eleven occasions he took four wickets in an innings, a record beaten only by Derek Underwood and Bob Woolmer. In Kent's Gillette Cup-winning season of 1967 he played a significant part in the semi-final win against Sussex at Canterbury when, going in to bat with the score at 3-1 after five overs, he scored a brisk 77 runs. In the final he scored 30 runs but had to bowl at a reduced pace having pulled a thigh muscle while fielding.

Nevertheless, he contained the batsmen in a low-scoring match, taking 2-27 in his 12 overs.

He left the County amid some acrimony in 1981 after not being re-engaged. He joined Gloucestershire in 1982, was awarded his Cap the following year and was then appointed coach. As sometimes happens, he played particularly well for his new county against Kent, scoring 112 in the Championship match at Bristol in 1983, having in the previous year recorded a career-best 6-52, also at Bristol in the John Player League.

John Shepherd became a controversial figure in the Caribbean by becoming the first black cricketer to tour South Africa as a member of Derek Robbins' 1973 team. He went on to play for Rhodesia in the Currie Cup in 1975/76. He spent some years coaching at Eastbourne College, before being appointed the International Cricket Council's development officer for the Americas.

Christopher James (Chris) Tavaré ———————— 100

RHB & OB 1974-88

For those outside Kent, Chris Tavaré was something of an enigma – remembered as a batsman disinclined to score runs at an acceptable rate, certainly at Test level. He gained this reputation as the result of some stubborn performances for England under instructions and in the unaccustomed role of opener. He occupied the crease for almost 12 hours for just 147 runs against Australia at Old Trafford in 1981, and for more than five hours for 35 against India in Madras the following winter. Yet Kent followers knew a different Tavaré. While he could get his head down and graft for runs when the situation demanded, he was able to demonstrate an exciting array of attacking shots, particularly in the one-day game in which he was a consistently heavy scorer.

Sevenoaks School and Oxford University educated, he was a correct and determined right-hand batsman with a disciplined approach. He made his first-class debut for Kent at the age of twenty against Cambridge University. The following three years he won Blues at Oxford and in his first full season with the County he scored 1,432 runs at 44.75. For nine seasons he exceeded 1,000 runs for Kent with 1,591 at 54.86 in 1981. His 29 hundreds for the County included a career-best 168 not out against Essex at Chelmsford in 1982 that embraced an undefeated sixth-wicket partnership of 156 with Alan Knott, who scored 115 not out. He was captain in 1983 and 1984 but he lost the leadership in somewhat controversial circumstances at the end of the 1984 season. In both seasons the team were losing finalists in the NatWest Trophy.

A specialist slip fielder and also good in the run-saving positions, his 269 first-class catches included a County record 48 in 1978. His 112 in the limited-overs game puts him second to Graham Johnson, who took 114.

His record as a one-day batsman is outstanding and is exceeded only by Mark Benson and Trevor Ward. His eight centuries is the most by a Kent player while his

Born: Orpington, 27 October 1954
County Cap: 1978
County Captain: 1983-84

Batting

M	I	NO	Runs	Av	100	50
259	425	51	14,201	37.97	29	71
245	242	31	6791	32.18	8	38

Bowling

Balls	Runs	Wkts	Av
630	493	5	98.60
—	—	—	—

5wI	10wM	ct/st
—	—	269
—	—	112

Best Performances
168* v. Essex (Chelmsford) 1982
143 v. Somerset (Taunton) 1985 (B & H)
Tests: 31 for England
Limited-Overs Internationals: 29 for England

38 scores in excess of 50 place him fourth among Kent's best. His top limited-overs score won him the Gold Award for the fourth time. In the NatWest Trophy he was adjudged Man of the Match on three occasions.

Overall, his career record is even more impressive than his record for Kent. He scored 24,278 first-class runs at 39.28 with 47 hundreds, and took 296 catches. He achieved his career-best score of 219 for Somerset against Sussex. He was capped by England on 31 occasions, playing in Test series at home between 1980 and 1989. He also played in the Test series in India and Sri Lanka in 1981/82 and Australia in 1982/83. In all Test matches he scored 1,755 runs at 32.50.

Four years after being deposed as captain he left the County and joined Somerset, for whom he was captain from 1990 to 1992. He is currently a member of Kent's Cricket Sub-Committee.

Neil Royston Taylor

RHB & OB 1979-95

Born: Farnborough, Kent, 21 July 1959
County Cap: 1982

Batting

M	I	NO	Runs	Av	100	50
302	513	68	17,721	39.82	42	84
229	220	17	6,581	32.41	5	36

Bowling

Balls	Runs	Wkts	Av
1,569	891	16	55.68
155	91	6	15.16

5wI	10wM	ct/st
–	–	151
–	–	54

Best Performances
204 v. Surrey (Canterbury) 1991
137 v. Surrey (Oval) 1988 (B & H)
3-29 v. Dorset (Canterbury) 1989 (NWT)

Few batsmen have a better record of consistency for Kent than Neil Taylor. When just nineteen years old, he scored 110 against Sri Lanka on debut and joined what was in 1979 a select band of just five Kent players who scored a century on their first appearance. He went on to score in excess of 1,000 runs in a season in ten of his seventeen years with Kent and in 1990 reached almost 2,000. A remarkably consistent right-hand batsman, who for much of his career opened the innings, he was a determined accumulator of runs with a wide range of strokes. He has the distinction of being the only Kent batsman to have scored a double hundred and a hundred in the same match on two occasions, a feat that he achieved against Surrey at Canterbury in 1990 and in the following season against Sussex at Hove. In the match at Canterbury, he shared a second-wicket partnership of 366 with Simon Hinks which at the time broke the record for the highest Kent partnership for any wicket. It remains the second-highest partnership. At Hove, his second-innings double-hundred was his third successive three-figure innings and was in one of the early four-day Championship matches in which 1,578 runs were scored. Remarkably, the result was a tie!

Neil Taylor scored 14 of his first-class hundreds at Kent's Canterbury headquarters, a record that had been previously held jointly by Frank Woolley and Colin Cowdrey with 12. With Mark Benson, he also holds the record first-wicket partnership of 300, achieved against Derbyshire in 1991. Twice he carried his bat through a completed innings, 123 out of 219 against Northamptonshire at Canterbury in 1987 and 67 out of 121 against Leicestershire at Leicester in 1988. His best season was 1990, when he scored 1,979 runs at an average of 61.84, including six hundreds and one double-hundred.

His consistency in the first-class game was carried into the limited-overs competitions. In 220 innings he scored 6,581 runs, the fourth-highest aggregate of all Kent's batsmen, and averaged 32.41, also the fourth highest of all who played 30 or more innings. He especially enjoyed the Benson & Hedges Cup, in which he scored five hundreds – more than any other batsman – and won eight Gold Awards – the most by a Kent player. In all limited-overs matches he also scored 36 fifties.

An occasional off-break bowler, he took 16 first-class wickets. In 1992 he played one match for the England B side. In the mid-1990s he was unable to hold down a regular first-team place, and spent 1996 captaining the Second XI. The following year he joined Sussex and was capped by them in 1997, when he scored 1,000 runs in the season.

Leslie John (Les/Toddy) Todd
LHB & LM/SLA 1927-50

Born: Catford, 19 June 1907
Died: Buckland, Dover, 20 August 1967
County Cap: 1929

Batting

M	I	NO	Runs	Av	50	100
426	709	93	19,407	31.50	36	96

Bowling

Balls	Runs	Wkts	Av
34,452	15,197	555	27.38

5wI	10wM	ct/st
20	1	226

Best Performances
174 v. Leicestershire (Maidstone) 1949
6-26 (11-64) v. Nottinghamshire (Tonbridge) 1936

Leslie Todd had a wide range of strokes, a strong defence, the ability to hit the ball on the rise, good technique against the new ball and no serious vulnerabilities except occasionally against spinners. Sometimes opening both batting and bowling, he bowled left-arm medium pace with a good late in-swinger, and in 1936 achieved the double, the last Kent cricketer to do so. He was an excellent fielder, 'particularly if he could do something eye catching' in the words of a teammate. He was also one of the game's enigmas – according to a contemporary 'the most infuriating, perverse cricketer of his generation'. If runs were wanted quickly he would defend; with a match to be saved he would get out playing extravagant shots. All depended on personal whim. A remark by a spectator could affect him. Whether his captain was soft or hard on him was immaterial. To make matters worse, when he first appeared he was hailed as 'a second Woolley'. It never helps to be called a second anybody. Playing for much of his career in the great man's shadow, Kent exacerbated the problem by trying to convert him into a Woolley-style left-arm spinner. It was not until 1934 that he was allowed to operate permanently at his more natural medium-pace; from 1935 to the outbreak of war he took 80 or more wickets every season, 102 in 1936, 90 in 1938. Mentioned between the wars as an England prospect, he came no nearer than a Test Trial in 1937 and post-war, when he was more consistent, age and persistent back trouble probably precluded serious consideration.

Given a trial at fifteen, Todd played for the Second XI in 1926 and made his First XI debut in the following season, beginning with a duck at Derby. In 1929 he became a first-team regular, narrowly missing his thousand runs despite batting mostly in the lower-middle order. Apart from 1932 when according to *Wisden* he 'did little more than display style', he progressed steadily, hitting 1,000 runs in every season but one between 1933 and 1949. With a hundred against every county except Yorkshire, his best seasons were 1937, 1,791 runs at 49.75; 1946, 1,864 runs at 44.38 and 1947, 2,057 runs at 44.71.

Despite a preference, he did not get an extended run as opener until after the Second World War. He shared 18 century opening partnerships, 14 of them with Arthur Fagg, three in excess of two hundred: 219 *v.* Middlesex at Lord's (Todd 162, Davies 138) in 1946; 230 *v.* Northamptonshire at Tunbridge Wells (Todd 88, Fagg 167) in 1948 and 251 *v.* Leicestershire at Maidstone (Todd 102, Fagg 137) in 1949.

In 1930 Todd was hit between the eyes by a ball from Harold Larwood and subsequently suffered periodic eye trouble, which probably influenced his retirement mid-season in 1950. With a total lack of concern for his feelings and despite his record, he was abruptly told his services were no longer required while sitting in the dressing room during Gravesend Week. He was briefly on the umpire's list! During the Second World War he served in the RAF. He played Association Football for Dulwich Hamlet and Sheppey United and was a table tennis international. Eccentricities notwithstanding, 'Toddy' had a sense of humour and most people who knew him viewed him with affection albeit tinged with exasperation.

Edward Ferdinando Sutton Tylecote

RHB & WK 1875-83

Born: Marston Moretaine, Bedfordshire,
23 June 1849
Died: New Hunstanton, Norfolk,
15 March 1938
County Cap: 1882

Batting

M	I	NO	Runs	Av	50	100
22	41	1	949	23.72	2	3

Bowling

Balls	Runs	Wkts	Av
24	14	0	–

5wI	10wM	ct/st
–	–	31/11

Best Performances
104 v. Sussex (Maidstone) 1881
3 dismissals in an innings seven times
4 dismissals in a match four times
Tests: 6 for England

Edward Tylecote has several notable firsts to his credit. He was the first in the illustrious line of Kent wicketkeepers to play for England, the first wicketkeeper to score a century for the County and the first Kent cricketer to score a hundred against the Australians – 100★ for Kent at Canterbury in 1882. He was also one of the first wicketkeepers to dispense with long stop. Credit generally goes to Australia's Jack Blackham, but there is evidence that Tylecote, Henry Phillips (Sussex), George Pinder (Yorkshire) and Alfort Smith (Derbyshire) were all on occasions keeping without the additional back-up around the same time or earlier.

The son of a Canon, Tylecote was in the XI at Clifton between 1864 and 1868, captain in 1868. In that year he averaged over 70 and attracted attention by carrying his bat in a Clifton house match for a then record 404★. Spread over three afternoons, the runs were scored out of 630 in six hours. Whatever the quality of the bowling, it was a considerable feat of physical endurance. Apart from one shot out of the ground, all hits were run out! At Oxford, where he distinguished himself academically, he played against Cambridge every year from 1869 to 1872, as captain in 1871, when Oxford won by eight wickets and 1872 when they lost by an innings.

From 1870 to 1877 Tylecote played for his native Bedfordshire. Following appointment as Mathematical Tutor at the Royal Military Academy, Woolwich (1875-95) he appeared once (presumably unqualified) for Kent v. Hampshire at Catford in 1875 and from 1881 to 1883 became first-choice wicketkeeper whenever duties allowed. Unlike his contemporary 'Bishop' Kemp, Tylecote was of the quietly efficient, unobtrusive school, 'with few, if any, superiors ' according to the magazine *Cricket*. As a batsman, he had an equable temperament, played himself in carefully and when set scored quickly. There were 15 fours in his 104 against Sussex in 1881 and 13 in his hundred against the Australians, an innings described as 'perfection'.

Alfred Lyttelton was preferred for the Test match at The Oval in 1882 but Tylecote toured Australia that winter with Ivo Bligh's team pledged to recover the Ashes. Playing in every match, he captained when Bligh was absent and in the decisive Third Test at Sydney his innings of 66 gave England an ultimately vital first-innings lead. In 1886 he kept wicket in the victorious England sides at Lord's and The Oval and made 16 appearances for Gentlemen *v.* Players, 11 at The Oval, three at Lord's and two at Prince's. At Lord's in 1883 he hit a chanceless 107★ in 150 minutes, the first hundred against the Players by a wicketkeeper.

Due to a knee injury, Tylecote played no serious cricket after 1886. He developed an interest in lepidoptera and on his death his extensive collection of specimens passed to the Ashmolean in Oxford. Two brothers, H.G. and C.B.L., both captained Clifton and H.G. won a Blue at Oxford.

Derek Gilbert Ufton

LHB & WK 1949-62

Associated with Kent for not far short of sixty years, Derek Ufton joined the staff in 1946 and became president in 2001, emulating one of his great heroes, Leslie Ames by being one of a very small number of former professional cricketers to win that honour. He had served on committees of the Club for many years and was Chairman of Cricket until he became President. 'His contribution for the Club both as a player and administrator, has been exceptional' was how the late Colin Cowdrey greeted the news of his successor.

Many of his First XI games were as reserve wicketkeeper to Godfrey Evans (whom he regarded as a genius), although he was sometimes picked as a batsman. Following the retirement of Evans in 1959 he became Kent's first choice behind the stumps for two seasons. He was regarded as a better wicketkeeper than Jim Parks of Sussex, who went on to play for England, and he had three offers to move to other counties but stayed loyal to Kent. Several good judges considered that although he may not have been able to match the genius of Evans at his peak, or the great man's flair for the big occasion, he was the more consistent of the two in the hard, unglamorous, day-to-day grind of the county circuit. He kept particularly well to spinners and Doug Wright for one was always happy to have him behind the stumps.

1961 was his best season, when he played in 30 matches and scored 668 runs at 20.24. In his role as wicketkeeper he dismissed 90 batsmen, 76 caught and 14 stumped. Only Fred Huish and Leslie Ames have exceeded that number for Kent in a single season. In the match against Glamorgan at Swansea, he dismissed eight

| Born: Crayford, 31 May 1928 |
| County Cap: 1956 |

Batting

M	I	NO	Runs	Av	100	50
148	242	48	3,915	20.18	1	10

Fielding

5wI	10wM	ct/st
—	—	269/44

Best Performances
119* v. Sussex (Hastings) 1952
5 dismissals in an innings three times
8 dismissals (ct 7 st 1) in a match v. Glamorgan
(Swansea) 1961

batsmen, seven caught and one stumped, including five in Glamorgan's second innings of 73. His one first-class century came in a fifth-wicket partnership of 155 with Brian Edrich. Between them they scored 201 of Kent's 302 first-innings total against Sussex at Hastings in 1952. Following his retirement from the first-class game he spent several seasons as captain of the Second XI and played Kent League cricket for Dartford, his home-town club. He has been a prominent member of the Lord's Taverners and was its chairman for two years.

An exceptionally gifted all-round sportsman, he played professional football for Charlton Athletic from 1949 (on the staff from 1948) to 1960, firstly in the position of left half as it was then known and later as centre half. He made 263 appearances and was captain from 1955. He also won an international cap, playing for England in 1953 in the famous 4-4 draw against the Rest of Europe. He had a four-year stint as manager of Plymouth Argyle and has been a Charlton Athletic director since 1984.

Derek Leslie (Deadly) Underwood MBE

RHB & LSM 1963-87

They called him 'Deadly' – and deadly he could be on even the most placid of wickets, bowling his left-arm slow or medium-pace spinners that he could vary depending on the conditions. For most of his career he had the advantage of uncovered wickets when he would bewilder and torment the most talented of batsmen. At all times he was the model of accuracy. Instantly recognisable by his plodding approach to the stumps and feet pointing at ten to two, he bowled a nagging line and length that could frustrate the best.

Born: Bromley, 8 June 1945
County Cap: 1964

Batting

M	I	NO	Runs	Av	100	50
520	538	154	3,793	9.87	I	2
374	*181*	*76*	*751*	*7.15*	*—*	*—*

Bowling

Balls	Runs	Wkts	Av
104,042	37,482	1,951	19.21
18,023	*10,038*	*530*	*18.93*

5wI	10wM	ct/st
127	38	183
8	*—*	*100*

Best Performances
111 *v. Sussex (Hastings) 1984*
28 v. Sussex (Tunbridge Wells) 1963 (GC)
9-28 v. Sussex (Hastings) 1964
14-82 v. Sussex (Hastings) 1967
8-31 v. Scotland (Edinburgh) 1987 (NWT)
Tests: 86 for England
Limited-Overs Internationals: 26 for England
***Wisden* Cricketer of the Year:** 1969

His career began in sensational fashion when he became the youngest player to take 100 wickets in his debut season. He claimed 100 wickets in a season in all matches ten times. Only Freeman and Blythe have taken more for the County. In his first six seasons he dismissed 744 batsmen and by the age of twenty-five he reached the milestone of 1,000. In 1966 he headed the first-class bowling averages with 157 wickets at 13.80 In the same year he was chosen by the Cricket Writers' Association as the Best Young Cricketer of the Year.

Well before being engaged by Kent he showed a natural and outstanding ability. Playing for Dulwich College Preparatory School under tens he took nine wickets for 10 runs; at the age of sixteen he took all ten wickets for Beckenham and Penge Grammar School against Bromley Grammar School, and for the-then village side, Farnborough, he repeated the feat against Bromley Town. At the same age he played for Kent's Second XI and in his first match he took 5-45 in the first innings and 4-15 in the second. On three occasions he took nine wickets in an innings. The first was in 1964 against Sussex, when on a dry and breaking surface at Hastings he recorded what was one of his most outstanding performances with 9-28 in 14.5 overs, including in one spell six successive wickets for 17 runs. Two years later Essex suffered on a dusty surface at Westcliff. In their second innings he took 9-37 to add to his four wickets in the first innings. It was twelve years on that he repeated the feat. This time it was Surrey at The Oval and the return was 9-32 after again taking four in their first innings, giving him a match return of 13-49. *Wisden* records that 'Surrey fell foul of the best wet wicket bowler in the world.' Remarkably, throughout the whole of his career he only achieved one hat-trick, against Sussex at Hove in 1977. Sussex were on the receiving end again in 1973 at Hastings. On a wicket affected by rain and in bright sunshine, Underwood was unplayable, taking 8-9 in 10.1 overs – the best return by a bowler in the season. He must have licked his lips

Metronomically accurate as ever, Derek Underwood in action for England, watched by umpire Bill Alley.

whenever Kent played Sussex. In 39 matches against them he took 151 wickets at 17.23 apiece, and scored his only first-class hundred at Hastings, a ground on which he particularly enjoyed playing.

His bowling was at its meanest in the limited-overs game to which he was so well suited. His 3,000-plus overs, seventeen per cent of them maidens, in 374 matches is far and away the most by any Kent bowler. His economy rate was 3.34 runs an over and he took a wicket every 34 balls. On 31 occasions he took four or more in an innings and eight times five or more. In his first match in the then John Player League he took 4-26 against Hampshire. His most remarkable performance was his 8-31 against Scotland in the NatWest Trophy match at Edinburgh in 1987. Yet he could be equally effective even when not taking wickets in this form of the game. In a low-scoring Gillette Cup match against Essex in 1972 his contribution to Kent's success by 10 runs was immense, conceding just 10 runs in his 11 overs. But despite his many match-winning performances, he won only two Gold Awards in the Benson & Hedges competition and one Man of the Match in the Gillette Cup. The 374 matches in which he played is by far the highest of any Kent player.

At the age of twenty-one Derek Underwood embarked upon a Test career embracing 86 matches between 1966 and 1981/82, including tours of Australia and New Zealand, India and Pakistan, the West Indies and Sri Lanka. But for his decision to join World Series Cricket in 1977 and a 'rebel' tour to South Africa in 1981/82, he would almost certainly have reached a century of Test caps and considerably increased his haul of 297 Test wickets. On seventeen occasions he took five wickets in an innings and six times ten wickets in a match. Probably best remembered is his second-innings 7-50 against the Australians at The Oval in 1968, on a wicket he exploited to the full, after a thunderstorm appeared to have deprived England of victory. His seven victims were dismissed in 31.3. overs, the last wicket falling with only six minutes remaining, the final four falling in 4.3 overs at a cost of 6 runs. On another wet wicket against Pakistan at Lord's in 1974, following 5-20 in the first innings, he took 8-51 in the second. His second-innings return included a spell of 6-9 in 11.5 overs. In the 1970/71 tour of Australia and New Zealand he topped the bowling averages for all matches. In taking 12-97 against New Zealand at Christchurch he claimed his 100th Test wicket.

Underwood was a more than useful tail-end batsman for both County and country. Although scoring only one first-class hundred, which came in his twenty-second season and his 618th first-class innings, he was effective as a night-watchman, and had the ability to hang around when necessary. In Test matches he scored 937 runs at 11.56 with a top score of 45★.

Derek Underwood continues to be closely involved in the County's affairs as a member of the Cricket Sub-Committee.

Bryan Herbert Valentine, MC

RHB & RM 1927-48

Born: Blackheath, 17 January 1908
Died: Otford, 2 February 1983
County Cap: 1931
County Captain: 1931-37 (joint) & 1946-48

Batting

M	I	NO	Runs	Av	50	100
308	491	28	14,131	30.52	25	73

Bowling

Balls	Runs	Wkts	Av
1,085	648	18	36.00

5wI	10wM	ct/st
–	–	243

Best Performances
242 *v.* Leicestershire (Oakham) 1938
Tests: 7 for England

Bryan Valentine was arguably the best of Kent's amateur batsmen between the wars; or at least the one who made the most of his talent. Many professionals liked bowling at the 'fancy caps' and Valentine began as a typical public school batsman, good to watch but inconsistent if the ball deviated. Around 1932, by applying himself and studying others, he tightened his defence without curbing his natural aggression and learned to watch the turning ball. To quote Robertson-Glasgow he 'schooled gifted abandon into orderly freedom'. Always a superb cutter and driver, he extended his range, especially on the leg side, on-driving with a full swing of the bat and expert at dealing with the large crop of off-spinners and in-swing bowlers spawned by the new lbw law. A personal trademark was a ritual tap on the right thigh as the bowler ran in.

Valentine captained Repton in 1926 and made seven appearances for Kent in the following season, impressing with an innings of 60 against Yorkshire at Tonbridge. Overlooked for a Blue at Cambridge in 1928, he was a belated choice against Oxford in 1929 but justified his selection with an innings of 62. Playing regularly from 1931, he reached his thousand runs in 1932 and hit his maiden century in county cricket, 180 at Leyton, the first of four hundreds against Essex. Next year he hit 1,653 runs at 36.73, including five centuries, and passed his thousand again in 1934, 1938 and 1939. Five centuries again in 1938 included 242 *v.* Leicestershire at Oakham and among four in 1939 was 201 *v.* Nottinghamshire at Trent Bridge.

During the Second World War Valentine was awarded the MC in 1942 while commanding an anti-tank platoon of the Royal West Kents in Tunisia. Later he was severely wounded. In 1946, he picked up where he left off, hitting 1,566 runs at 41.21 with five centuries and reached four figures again in 1947.

Valentine usually scored his runs quickly. At Folkestone against Gloucestershire in 1933 he hit 113 in 100 minutes and during a fourth-wicket partnership of 202 with Leslie Ames against Essex at Gravesend in 1938 (Ames 170, Valentine 151) the scoring rate reached 3 runs a minute. In 1939 the same pair hit 202 in two hours at Worcester.

Deputy captain between 1931 and 1936, joint captain with Ronnie Bryan in 1937, he became captain in his own right from 1946 to 1948. In all he won 58 and lost 40 of his 131 games in charge. A good tactician, always playing to win but never treating cricket as a life or death matter, he aimed to ensure everyone enjoyed cricket as much as he did.

Valentine excelled in the outfield and bowled medium-pace out-swing well enough to open the bowling for the Gentlemen. Never picked for a home Test match, he toured India in 1933/34, South Africa in 1938/39, scored a century on his Test debut and averaged 64.85. He won the Public Schools Lawn Tennis Championship in partnership with H.W. 'Bunny' Austin. A football Blue at Cambridge, he went on to play for the Corinthians and later became a scratch golfer. President in 1967, he served for many years on the Kent Committee.

Trevor Robert Ward

RHB & OB 1986-99

Trevor Ward's career-best innings of 235★ is the highest second-innings score by a Kent batsman. A right-hander with a wide range of attacking shots, he was capable of destroying top-class bowling, although he never quite reached the heights many expected of him. At one time he was close to international recognition and may well have got the call had he been able to curb his natural attacking instincts. Even so, he was selected to play for England 'A' in the two 50-over matches against Sri Lanka in 1991, in the second of which he was top scorer with 78.

He made his Second XI debut in 1983 at the age of fifteen and three years later his first-class debut against Hampshire at Southampton in which he opened the innings with Mark Benson. In the years that followed this became an established opening partnership that laid the foundations for many of Kent's high scores in the 1980s and 1990s. Later in his career he batted at three or four but continued to open in the limited-overs game. In six of his 14 seasons he exceeded 1,000 runs, his best being 1992 with 1,648 at 48.47 including five hundreds. This just exceeded his record of the previous season when he scored 1,493 runs at 46.65, which included his career-best score. Twice he scored two hundreds in a match, on both occasions against Glamorgan: at Maidstone in 1991 and Abergavenny in 1994. He carried his bat through a completed innings against Northamptonshire in 1995, scoring 114★ out of 215. Thirteen counties were on the receiving end of his 24 first-class hundreds, and he seemed to take a particular liking to the Glamorgan bowling, off

Born: Farningham, 18 January 1968
County Cap: 1989

Batting

M	I	NO	Runs	Av	100	50
206	355	19	11,897	35.40	24	70
247	242	10	7,421	31.98	7	50

Bowling

Balls	Runs	Wkts	Av
1,083	647	8	80.87
414	351	10	35.10

5wI	10wM	ct/st
–	–	197
–	–	52

Best Performances
235* v. Middlesex (Canterbury) 1991
131 v. Nottinghamshire (Nottingham) 1993 (SL)
3-20 v. Glamorgan (Canterbury) 1989 (SL)

whom he reached three figures six times. In his career-best score he shared a second-wicket partnership of 226 with Neil Taylor, between them turning to Kent's advantage a match that had been going Middlesex's way.

Trevor Ward's aggressive style of batting was ideal for the limited-overs game. Only Mark Benson has scored more runs, while his career average is up among the first half-dozen. His 4,838 runs in the Sunday (National) League is over 500 more than the next best. His seven hundreds and 50 fifties rank him among the top three, while his 89 sixes puts him in fourth place. In the 1995 Benson & Hedges Cup, he shared with Mark Benson five consecutive century opening partnerships that carried Kent through to the final at Lord's. Twice in that competition he won the Gold Award and was once adjudged Man of the Match in the NatWest Trophy.

His career with Kent ended disappointingly. Declining form in 1998 and 1999, his benefit year, led to his release from the County. He signed a three-year contract with Leicestershire in 2000 and was capped by them the following year. He was not retained after 2003.

RHB & RFM 1929-39

Born: Limpsfield Chart, Surrey, 19 June 1907
Died: Pembury, 3 February 1974
County Cap: 1932

Batting

M	I	NO	Runs	Av	50	100
226	326	37	4,018	13.90	–	9

Bowling

Balls	Runs	Wkts	Av
38,318	17,325	608	28.49

5wI	10wM	ct/st
34	6	130

Best Performances
96 *v.* MCC (Lord's) 1932
8-100 *v.* Leicestershire (Tunbridge Wells) 1937
14-90 *v.* Middlesex (Maidstone) 1938

Even the most sophisticated cricket watcher loves a good hitter and Kentish crowds brought up on the stroke play of Woolley, Ames, Valentine *et al* still welcomed the arrival of Alan Watt at the wicket. Although never in the class of his great contemporary, the Kent-born Arthur Wellard, Watt could be fearsome on his day, especially when he stopped trying to hit everything over square leg and began to drive straight. Nevertheless, his main contribution to Kent was as a fast-medium bowler, ready and willing to bowl for long spells. With a short run and a good sideways action, he hit the pitch hard, bowled a tight line and full length with a lethal late out-swinger. When he first came into the side the primary function of Kent's opening bowlers was to get the shine off for Freeman and Marriott, but he developed. Towards the end of the decade, in Watt and Leslie Todd, later reinforced by Norman Harding, Kent had as good a new-ball attack as most.

Watt had his first trial for Kent at the age of fifteen and made his second XI debut in 1928. He gained first-team selection at Northampton the following year but apart from 4-44 at Tonbridge in 1931 when he bowled unchanged with Freeman (6-26) to dismiss Northants for 79, success was slow in coming and not until 1932 did he become a first-team regular. From 1932 until 1939 he only once failed to take 50 wickets in a season and in 1936 claimed 88 at 23.92, taking 7-37 *v.* Essex at Tunbridge Wells plus match returns of 10-188 *v.* Middlesex at Maidstone and 11-177 *v.* MCC at Folkestone. Next year he improved on this with 108 wickets at 26.63, with seven five-wicket hauls. In Maidstone Week 1938 he had match figures of 9-136 *v.* Glamorgan and 14-90 *v.* Middlesex.

Watt's big-hitting propensities became widely known in 1932 when at Lord's he hit a respectable MCC attack for 96 in 65 minutes. Next year against Leicestershire at Mote Park he smote 89 (4 sixes, 11 fours) out of 124 in 55 minutes and in the same season at Trent Bridge followed 68 in 55 minutes in the first innings with 42 in 17 minutes made up of 4, 6, 6, 6, 6, 4, 6, 4. In the run chase at Dover in 1937 when Kent scored 219 in 77 minutes to beat Gloucestershire, Watt hit 39★ of the last 51 runs in 10 minutes, finishing the match with a straight six out of the ground. The ball was not found until after the Second World War.

In 1946 the Kent Committee offered a contract 'if Watt would explain why he was turned out of the Home Guard'. It is not clear why this was any concern of a cricket club committee but in any case, the offer was declined. Instead he became landlord of the Star at Matfield. There was one post war first-class appearance, for Leyland's XI *v.* the Rest in the Harrogate Festival.

100 ——————————————— Edward Gower (Ned) Wenman

GREATS

RHB, SRA (under-arm) & WK 1825-54

Originating from Benenden, a prolific seedbed for cricketers at the time, Ned Wenman was a key member of the 'Grand Old Kent XI' and the first great Kent wicketkeeper. His figures may hardly seem to justify the title 'wicketkeeper-batsman' but in his day he was highly rated in both departments.

Wicketkeeping was different then. Pads only came in towards the end of Wenman's career. So too did gloves and those worn were no more than unlined leather without padding. To stand back was unheard of and, with most of the bowling delivered round-arm from round the wicket, long stop was a key position. Wicketkeepers made no effort to stop every ball; much of their skill lay in knowing which balls to take and which to leave to long stop. To a fast bowler on a hard wicket (and rough outfield) two long stops were not unknown. Most wicketkeepers left everything on or outside leg stump but Wenman, considered unique in his skill with the left hand, excelled on the leg side, especially in stumping, normally carried out one handed. Fuller Pilch described Wenman in action, 'with his eyes on the batsman's foot and the crease, without pads or gloves; and as sure as a man showed a sign of drawing his foot, he took the ball close to the bails and just broke the wicket'. It is difficult to imagine how this worked in practice but his technique was much admired. So too was his captaincy. It is not clear when he began to captain Kent but much of the team's success was attributed to his leadership and tactical know-how. Interestingly, although there were always amateurs in the side, both Wenman and

Born: Benenden, 18 August 1803
Died: Benenden, 28 December 1879

Batting

M	I	NO	Runs	Av	100	50
61	107	5	1,063	10.42	–	2

Bowling

Other wkts	5wI	10wM	ct/st
10	–	–	54/33

Best Performances
73 v. Surrey (Sevenoaks) 1828
4-? v. Sussex (Sevenoaks) 1828
4 dismissals (ct 2 st 2) in an innings & 6 dismissals (ct 2 st 4) in a match v. Surrey (Sevenoaks) 1828

Pilch, his usual deputy, were professionals. Things had changed dramatically by the final quarter of the nineteenth century.

Over six foot one (185cm) and weighing around fifteen stone (95kg), Wenman, like many batsmen of his time, played almost exclusively off the back foot, scoring the bulk of his runs square on the off side. Although he played relatively few long innings, Wenman was reliable when runs were hard to get. Forty-three of his scores in first-class or 'important' matches were between 20 and 49. He was also a useful bowler.

Wenman played 16 times for the Players and once for the Gentlemen as 'given man'. He was on the committee of the Maidstone-based Kent Club formed in 1859. In 1834, in company with another Benenden cricketer Richard Mills, he played and beat an Isle of Oxney XI. A carpenter and wheelwright as well as a cricketer, he played well into his seventies. In 1875, together with his cousin John (aged seventy-one) and Richard Mills (aged seventy-seven), he offered to play any three of similar age for up to a hundred guineas. There were no takers. His image appears on the sign outside his home village, a rare distinction. Son William and two cousins also played for Kent and great grandson William (Reg) was prominent in Canadian cricket.

Edgar (Ned) Willsher

LHB & LFM (round-arm) 1850-75

Born: Rolvenden, 22 November 1828
Died: Lewisham, 7 October 1885

Batting

M	I	NO	Runs	Av	100	50
145	265	20	3,221	13.14	–	7

Bowling

Runs	Wkts	Av	Other Wkts
9,580	762	12.57	24

5wI	10wM	ct/st
64	19	124

Best Performances
89 *v.* Sussex (Sandgate) 1863
8-16 *v.* England (Canterbury) 1860
13-58 *v.* Derbyshire (Wirksworth) 1874

Ned Willsher's debut for Kent was at The Oval in 1850, alongside Fuller Pilch and Alfred Mynn. When he made his last appearance for the County in 1875, Lord Harris had just taken over as captain. Harris played his final first-class game in 1911; in the side was Frank Woolley, who played *his* last match in 1938, a direct link from the 'Grand Old Kent XI' to relatively modern times.

At his peak Willsher was the best bowler in England; Surrey's William Caffyn considered him 'most difficult of all the bowlers I ever met'. He was also Kent's only professional of class throughout the barren years between the decline in the early 1850s to the establishment of the present Club in 1870. Approaching the crease with a 'quick-march step' he made the ball lift, gained sharp movement from leg to off and was Kent's leading wicket taker in 11 seasons. As evidence of his accuracy, for South *v.* North at Canterbury in 1871 he began with 16 consecutive maidens.

Tall, thin and 'cadaverous in appearance', despite his pivotal role in cricket history, Willsher remains curiously anonymous, best known for his part in the legalisation of over-arm bowling. According to Caffyn, by the 1860s 'nine out of ten' bowlers were raising their hand above shoulder level at times but Willsher was reputedly the most blatant. Matters came to a head in the England *v.* Surrey match at The Oval in 1862 when umpire John Lillywhite no-balled him six times in succession. Throwing down the ball, Willsher left the field followed by all eight of his professional colleagues. Play was resumed next day with a different umpire. There is a whiff of stage management about the affair. The old Law had clearly had its day and Willsher and the umpire were close friends. Within two years bowlers were free to raise their arms as high as they liked. Willsher claimed he was never the same bowler afterwards but in 1868 he captured 78 wickets for Kent at 6.90, 108 in all matches, and in 1870 collected 56 at 9.83. Of his 19 hauls of ten or more wickets in a match for Kent, 12 were after the Law change.

He was a useful batsman, stubborn when necessary. For Kent and Surrey *v.* England at Canterbury in 1855 he batted four hours for 20 and hit 73 for Players *v.* Gentlemen in 1860, one of 21 appearances in the fixture. His 89 *v.* Sussex at Sandgate in 1863 was made out of a team total of 169. He played for the itinerant All-England XI, subsequently becoming secretary/captain of the breakaway United South of England XI. In 1868 he led an all-professional team to North America.

On retirement he umpired and was head bowler at Prince's. Other activities included a sports goods business in Greenwich and management of a billiard hall on Blackheath Hill. Sadly the memorial stone over his grave in Ladywell cemetery subscribed to by 'Lord Harris and one hundred gentlemen and professional cricketers of England' was vandalised by, among others, the Luftwaffe. Only the base remains. Elder brother William played once for the County.

Robert Colin (Bob) Wilson

LHB & OB 1952-67

100
GREATS

There cannot be many players whose career-best season coincided with their benefit, but for Bob Wilson it did. A reliable middle-order left-hand batsman who was also a successful opener, he exceeded 2,000 runs in 1964 at an average of 46.31 including four hundreds. He is one of only five Kent batsmen to have reached 2,000 since the Second World War and is the last to have done so. With the County Championship now restricted to 16 matches there is every chance that this milestone will not again be reached. In that season he also recorded his second-highest score.

Bob Wilson made his debut for both Second and First XIs in 1952. His first senior match was against Yorkshire at Headingley when he batted at number nine. In the next match he scored 52, sharing a fifth-wicket stand of 143 with Richard Mayes. He played only three matches in each of his first two seasons, but showed promise in the Minor Counties Championship. One of the strongest players of his time off the back foot, he was pugnacious and powerful and successfully overcame the difficulties that could beset the left-hander who is short in reach. His 30 hundreds for Kent included four scores in excess of 150 yet he never got close to a double-hundred. In 13 successive seasons between 1954 and the year before his retirement, he scored more than 1,000 with over 1,500 five times. In addition to his hundreds he was dismissed

Born: Bapchild, 18 February 1928
County Cap: 1954

Batting

M	I	NO	Runs	Av	100	50
365	644	38	19,458	32.10	30	109
5	5	–	67	13.40	–	–

Bowling

Balls	Runs	Wkts	Av
109	90	4	22.50

5wI	10wM	ct/st
–	–	200
–	–	2

Best Performances
159* v. Northamptonshire (Kettering) 1963
159 v. Glamorgan (Blackheath) 1960
44 v. Hampshire (Southampton) 1966 (GC)
3-38 v. Glamorgan (Pontypridd) 1962

in the nineties 11 times. His consistency was such that discounting his first two seasons, he scored hundreds in 12 successive seasons. In five of his hundreds he was undefeated. The first of these was against Somerset at Gillingham in 1956 in a match-winning second-wicket partnership with Arthur Phebey of 180 in which Wilson scored 103. He scored hundreds against 12 of the then-sixteen first-class counties and was rated one of the best batsmen of his time without an England cap. His career best was achieved when he shared a third-wicket partnership of 304 with Arthur Phebey, going to the wicket when Kent had lost two wickets for just 10 runs. He equalled that score with a not out 159 against Northamptonshire in 1963. Kent's 356 for 3 declared featured another outstanding partnership of 283 with Stuart Leary. It was his second hundred against Northamptonshire that season, whose attack he obviously took a liking to, as in the following season he scored a further hundred and 67 in the match at Wellingborough. His hundred in the first innings of that match was out of a total of just 213.

He was an outstanding fielder in the deep and those who saw him will remember how he could speed round the boundary, swoop, pick up and throw the ball almost in one movement. Not surprising, as he also had a successful career playing Kent League football on the left wing.

Bob Wilson is the eighth most prolific batsman for the County, and of post-Second World War batsmen, only Colin Cowdrey has scored more runs. Following his retirement, he served for a number of years on the Committee of Kent County Cricket Club.

Frank Edward Woolley

LHB & SLA 1906-38

E.WOOLLEY
KENT.

PHOTO
E.C.FLEMONS
TONBRIDGE.

Born: Tonbridge, 27 May 1887						

Died: Chester, Halifax, Nova Scotia, Canada, 18 October 1978

County Cap: 1906

Batting

M	I	NO	Runs	Av	100	50
764	1,213	67	47,868	41.77	122	239

Bowling

Balls	Runs	Wkts	Av
73,950	31,653	1,680	18.84

5wl	10wM	ct/st
115	24	773

Best Performances

270 *v.* Middlesex (Canterbury) 1923

8-22 *v.* Gloucestershire (Maidstone) 1921

14-90 *v.* Warwickshire (Birmingham) 1922

Tests: 64 for England

***Wisden* Cricketer of the Year:** 1911

It is no coincidence that the largest structure, a substantial concrete stand, on the St Lawrence Ground at Canterbury bears the name of Frank Woolley. For as a player, no one looms larger in the history of Kent cricket than the graceful left-hander who from his debut aged nineteen to his retirement aged fifty-one was an inherent, indeed legendary component of the County side. In that time Woolley played more matches, scored more runs and took more catches for Kent than anyone else has ever done. For good measure, as a bowler, he also stands fifth in the all-time list of Kent wicket-takers. This overall achievement will never be matched. He could arouse Neville Cardus to his most lyrical heights and provide for all who saw him the eternal yardstick for all left-handed batsmen. As much as the scores he made, it was the way he scored them. Time and time again it was a cameo innings of 60 or 70 rather than large hundreds that left an impression. Few players of note can have scored their runs at a greater pace or in a finer style.

Woolley was born conveniently in what was in his developing years the heart of Kent cricket, Tonbridge. Just up the road from his father's garage and repair shop was the Angel Ground, the home from 1897 of the Kent Nursery. The Kent trial book, which survives, confirms an initial interest in his bowling, the assessment made in 1902 being 'medium left [bowler], fair bat'. Indeed it was for the injured Blythe that he made his first-team debut in 1906 in a match of mixed fortunes – three dropped catches, a duck, but the top score in the second innings. With a hundred in his fourth match (at Tonbridge), it was increasingly clear that this element of Woolley's game may have been underestimated. Although he was left out of the side for Canterbury Week a few weeks later to make way for one of Kent's proliferation of amateurs, that was the last time that fate befell him before he retired thirty-two years later. *Wisden* in its report on Kent in 1906 made no truer prediction in its history. 'Good as he already is, Woolley will no doubt… go far ahead of his first season's doings. It is quite possible… he will be the best left-handed bat in England.'

The clue to Woolley's batting success was his height (6ft 3ins, 190cm) and great reach. He could make strokes in a wide range without obvious adjustment of feet or body. He was fundamentally sound, playing with a straight bat with the ability to drive the ball just short of a length. This made him very difficult to pin down. There is a host of innings to illustrate the point. At Bradford in 1931 on a difficult wicket, with two wickets gone early, he hit Hedley Verity, whom he was facing for the first time, for three sixes in the next two overs. He finished with 188 out of 296, leaving his opponent to contemplate figures of 0 for 70 off 12 overs. Even in his final season with a Kent side seemingly easy prey to fast bowling, his indifference to any pace found him at the age of fifty-one promoted to a very effective opener, taking 81 in an hour off the 1938 Australian attack in his last innings at Canterbury.

Kent v. Surrey, 1935. Frank Woolley threatens the trams in Harleyford Road with a majestic six out of The Oval during his innings of 229 in Andy Sandham's benefit match. The runs were scored in 190 minutes out of 344. The wicketkeeper is Ted Brooks.

Until a knee injury restricted him after the 1924/25 tour to Australia, Woolley was also a very fine slow left-arm bowler. His style was not unlike his great mentor, Colin Blythe, beginning his delivery swing from behind his back, although his arm came from the hip pocket rather than the right armpit, as in the latter's case. His height again proved of great assistance, giving him a lively degree of bounce on all pitches and with his great power of spin, lethal on a responsive pitch. The 50 minutes at Tonbridge in 1913 when these two great bowlers removed Warwickshire for just 16 was surely one of the great moments in Kent cricket history. In the immediate post-First World War period, Woolley dominated the Kent side both with bat and ball until the injury and the emergence of the prolific wicket taking of Freeman reduced his bowling to a bit-part status. Yet with Freeman retired after 1936, there came a rejuvenation in Woolley's bowling, and he was still taking ten wickets in a match in his last year.

Woolley was in his time the complete all-rounder, in which his catching played no insignificant part. He will certainly remain the only player to take over a thousand catches in a first-class career. In his early days he was a useful deep fielder, but it is his record as a slip catcher where again his great reach and lively reflexes were a distinct advantage, that is unique. Contemporaries state that immediately before the First World War he had no peer.

On first sight his record may indicate that Frank Woolley should not figure in the front rank of Test cricketers. Yet no Englishman can match his achievement of automatic selection for the national side for a period of seventeen years. His figures may not be exceptional, but in his time nor really were many others. Compare his Test batting average of 36.07 with Fry (32.18), MacLaren (33.87) or Trumper (39.04), and Woolley did take 83 wickets as well. His Test career highlight was probably the Lord's Test of 1921 when he carried the England side single-handed, holding off the ferocious Australian fast bowling attack of Gregory and McDonald in their prime, with two remarkable nineties. McDonald, who subsequently played for Lancashire, also felt the power of Woolley in two notable innings for Kent, 137 in under three hours at Dover in 1926 and 151 out of 277 at Old Trafford in 1928.

In his later years Woolley was still to be seen on Kent grounds, particularly Canterbury during Cricket Week, this even after a second marriage and consequent emigration to Canada. After he died his ashes were returned to Kent and scattered in front of the stand that bears his name.

Robert Andrew (Bob) Woolmer

RHB & RM 1968-84

Born: Kanpur, Uttar Pradesh, India,
14 May 1948
County Cap: 1970

Batting

M	I	NO	Runs	Av	100	50
279	428	68	12,634	35.09	28	58
272	220	35	3,781	20.43	1	15

Bowling

Balls	Runs	Wkts	Av
18,872	7,810	334	23.38
12,543	7,137	349	20.44

5wI	10wM	ct/st
12	1	195/1
3	–	89

Best Performances
203 *v.* Sussex (Tunbridge Wells) 1982
112 v. Nottinghamshire (Nottingham) 1980
(SL)*
7-47 *v.* Sussex (Canterbury) 1969
13-135 *v.* Sussex (Canterbury) 1972
6-9 v. Derbyshire (Chesterfield) 1979 (SL)

Tests: 19 for England
Limited-Overs Internationals: 6 for England
***Wisden* Cricketer of the Year:** 1976

An outstanding cricketer who became a much sought-after international coach, Bob Woolmer, who was born in India, was a key member of Kent's trophy-winning sides of the 1970s. In the County's Championship success of 1970 he was second in the bowling averages; the shared Championship with Middlesex in 1977 saw him top the bowling and take second place in the batting averages. In the following year's successful defence of the title he was second in the bowling and third in the batting averages.

Starting his career in the lower-middle order, he progressed to opening the innings by the mid-seventies, in the process developing into an attractive right-hand batsman. He was a fluent driver on both sides of the wicket and could deflect the ball with an exquisite sense of timing in the style of Colin Cowdrey. A useful medium-pace bowler with a near-perfect action, he was particularly effective in cloudy conditions, able to swing the ball both ways. He was an excellent fielder, particularly close to the wicket. He is one of 16 Kent players to have achieved the double of 5,000 runs and

Technically one of the soundest of Kent's 1970s generation, Bob Woolmer went on to develop into one of the game's most respected coaches.

250 wickets for the County, a record shared by two of his contemporaries, Graham Johnson and John Shepherd.

Educated at Skinner's School, Tunbridge Wells, Woolmer made his Second XI debut in 1966. His first-class debut two years later was not without incident. He scored a maiden not out 50 against Essex at Maidstone, during the course of which Stuart Leary sacrificed his wicket to save Woolmer. He played in six matches that season, finishing with the respectable average of 30.80. But it was some eight years before he really made his mark with the bat when he scored 802 runs at 28.64 in 1974 including his first century. His bowling was showing considerable promise, with 168 wickets in five seasons including what was to prove a career-best second innings 7-47 against Sussex at Canterbury in the opening match of 1969. He had bowled only 15 overs in his previous (debut) season. Sussex were again the victims in the 1972 Canterbury Week when he again took seven wickets after taking six in the first innings. He was equally happy batting against them, scoring five of his centuries including his career best score of 203. In 1974 he had his best season with the ball, with 56 wickets at 18.01, twice taking five in an innings. He was second to Derek Underwood in the County's averages. But in his final years, back problems restricted his bowling in first-class matches.

1974 was also the season in which he recorded the first of his 28 hundreds for Kent. It was in 1976 that Woolmer first opened the batting, and with considerable success. In his first eight innings he scored 561 runs including a top score of 143. This proved to be his best season with the bat, scoring 1,461 runs at 56.19 and topping the averages. In only one season from then until his enforced retirement did his average drop below 30 and in five of his remaining eight seasons he exceeded 40. Three seasons saw him score more than 1,000 runs for Kent (five times in all), his best in all first-class matches being 1,749 at 47.27 in 1976.

Bob Woolmer's all-round abilities made him a key figure in Kent's one-day successes. His career spanned Kent's golden years in limited-overs cricket. His overall career performance in the three competitions compares with the best. Only Derek Underwood and Matthew Fleming took more wickets and his economy rate was of the best. He had an impressive record in the Sunday League, being the County's second-highest wicket-taker in the competition, but he probably enjoyed greater success in the Benson & Hedges in which he took 81 wickets at 20.41 and an economy rate of 2.79 runs per over. He won five Gold Awards, including the 1978 final when Kent beat Derbyshire and in which he scored 79 and took 1-15 in ten overs. He also twice won the Man of the Match Award in the Gillette Cup. In all limited-overs matches he took four wickets in an innings on 29 occasions (only Derek Underwood did it more times) with a best performance of 6-9 against Derbyshire at Chesterfield in 1979.

Woolmer had an impressive introduction to international cricket in 1975. Playing for the MCC against the Australians he enjoyed success with bat and ball, scoring 55 and 85 and taking four Australian first-innings wickets including a hat-trick. This was just days after he had shared in what proved to be a match-winning stand with Colin Cowdrey for a famous Kent victory against the tourists. These performances earned him his first England cap in the Second Test at Lord's. He batted at number eight, scoring 33 and 31 and took 1-31 in Australia's first innings. He played again in the final match of that series, and was influential in saving it, scoring a second-innings 149. His century took 396 minutes, then the slowest by an Englishman against Australia. That season he finished second in the England batting averages with 54.50. Woolmer went on to play in another 17 Tests, during which he scored two further hundreds against Australia. His 1,059 runs gave him a career average of 33.09 but he took only four wickets. Ten of his 19 Test Caps were won against Australia and in addition to a tour there, he also toured India and Sri Lanka but dropped out of international consideration after joining Kerry Packer's World Series Cricket. Although being selected for four further Tests in 1980/81, he was not able to repeat his previous success.

Following his retirement he had a short spell as coach with Kent and then moved to Warwickshire with whom he enjoyed great success in the 1990s. He was appointed the South African coach on that country's return to international cricket and in 2004 was appointed coach to the Pakistan national team.

James (Jimmy) Wootton

LHB & LSM 1880-90

Born: Sutton-at-Hone, 9 March 1860
Died: Leytonstone, Essex, 21 February 1941
County Cap: 1885

Batting

M	I	NO	Runs	Av	100	50
115	187	48	1,021	7.34	–	–

Bowling

Balls	Runs	Wkts	Av
26,671	10,234	597	17.14

5wI	10wM	ct/st
49	15	62

Best Performances
39 v. Hampshire (Gravesend) 1884
8-27 v. Lancashire (Maidstone) 1886
14-162 v. Sussex (Hove) 1886

James Wootton was one of the hard-working professionals who contributed so much to Kent cricket during the difficult years of the 1880s and 1890s. He gave the ball air, bowling a full length, varying the left-hander's stock ball with one that went with his arm and a well-disguised faster delivery. Described by Lord Harris as a 'cheerful little cricketer', he turned the ball a lot but on plumb wickets tended to serve up half-volleys through trying too hard to spin it.

Wootton's early cricket was in his home village and later with Farningham, but on starting work in local stables there was little cricket until 1879 when he was engaged by the Yalding club. Next year he joined Erith, where his 70 wickets cost just over 4 apiece. Already Kent had spotted him and in May that year, following 7-16 in the annual colts match at Mote Park and 5-43 and 2-14 against Surrey colts at The Oval, he was summoned to play against Sussex at Hove. The telegram was late and Wootton arrived to find play already in progress. Backing his own judgement, Lord Harris immediately tossed the ball to the newcomer and saw his faith repaid by 3-46 and 3-57. Left out of the next fixture he returned against Surrey at Tunbridge Wells Common where 4-55 and 8-34 followed by 6-54 for Thirteen of Kent v. England at Canterbury secured his place in the side, a place he was to hold for a decade.

He took 100 wickets in a season (all matches) in 1884, 1886 and 1887, four times led the Kent bowling averages and was the County's leading wicket taker every year from 1882 to 1888. Among his more notable performances were 13-84 v. Lancashire on a good wicket at Gravesend in 1883, 13-64 v. Lancashire at Maidstone in 1886 and 5-8 in the Middlesex second innings at Gravesend in 1888. He played a major part in two of Kent's historic victories over the Australians at Canterbury with match figures of 7-93 in 1884 and 10-100 in 1886.

A fine off-side fielder, Jimmy Wootton contributed rather less with the bat. His 1881 season ended with consecutive innings of 0, 0 ,0, 0*, a pair, 1* and 4. 1882 began with a pair, 0, 0*, a pair, 14, 0, 0*, 0 and another pair.

He joined the MCC staff in 1884 and remained for six years. Although a boost to his finances, with his Kent commitments, the workload was considerable. In 1887 he bowled a total of 1,618 (four ball) overs. In later life he was said to have no biceps on his left arm as a legacy. A blow under the ribs received when playing against Yorkshire at Huddersfield in 1888 affected his bowling and in 1890 he left to become coach at Winchester. Not until 1895 did he regain his old action. Between 1895 and 1900 he made 24 appearances for Hampshire

Thanks to his time as a stable boy he was good on horseback. Lord Harris took him as second horseman when hunting with the South Down.

Albert Charles (Charlie) Wright

RHB & RFM 1921-31

Bowling off a short run, Charlie Wright was big, strong and seemingly tireless. Although dangerous on green pitches, he was more often required to plug away for long spells on the many flat wickets encountered in the 1920s, keeping runs down by bowling just 'back of a length' in the modern jargon. He was also a useful lower-order batsman and a normally reliable mid-off although he once missed three successive catches in that position. Legend has it that Wright himself laughed when catches were dropped off his bowling but the Kent slip fielding was notoriously

Born: Borstal, Rochester, 4 April 1895
Died: Westminster, 26 May 1959
County Cap: 1923

Batting

M	I	NO	Runs	Av	100	50
225	298	49	3,280	13.09	–	9

Bowling

Balls	Runs	Wkts	Av
34,353	14,463	596	24.26

5wI	10wM	ct/st
24	1	127

Best Performances
81 *v.* Essex (Gravesend) 1924
7-31 (12-64) *v.* Somerset (Taunton) 1924

fallible at the time and the joke must have soon worn thin.

Given a trial at Tonbridge Nursery in 1919, he joined the staff in the following year and made his first-class debut *v.* the MCC at Lord's in 1921 where he hit 53 out of 77 in 57 minutes and picked up two good wickets. For the Second XI he distinguished himself with 7-37 *v.* Norfolk at Hythe. Next year he was top of the Second XI averages with 53 wickets at 11.07 including 11-68 *v.* Wiltshire at Blackheath, but three first-team appearances brought only three expensive wickets. Possibly frustrated, he signed for the Lancashire League club Oswaldtwistle, but Kent held him to his five-year contract.

All turned out for the best in 1923 when he became established and finished the season with a respectable 50 wickets at 21.06. He went on to capture 50 or more wickets in every season between 1924 and 1929 – 102 at 18.82 in 1926 when he headed the Kent averages and 107 at.20.38 in 1927. In 1925 he excelled against Warwickshire – at Edgbaston 6-62 and 3-70, at Tunbridge Wells 1-16 and 4-11, including a hat-trick on the last day. Perversely, *Wisden* records a hat-trick on the first day by Warwickshire's Robert Cooke but ignores poor Charlie's moment of glory. He had others. Against Somerset at Taunton that year he had figures of 5-33 and 7-31 and two years later took 6-29 on the same ground when Somerset were dismissed for 55. His successes were not confined to bowler-friendly wickets. On a typical Trent Bridge pitch in 1927 his 5-52 and 4-61 included all but one of the powerful Nottinghamshire top order.

Although not quite a genuine all-rounder Charlie Wright generally played at least one valuable innings a season. In 1924 he hit 68 *v.* Essex at Leyton, sharing an eighth-wicket partnership of 133 with Barry Cumberlege (76) and did even better in the return at Gravesend with 81 and a record partnership of 157, again for the eighth wicket, with Alan Hilder (103★). Curiously the match does not rate a mention in the official history.

Probably due to hard work as much as anything, Charlie Wright had a moderate season in 1930, lost his place in 1931 and retired at the end of the season.

100 GREATS — Douglas Vivian Parson (Doug) Wright

RHB & LBG 1932-57

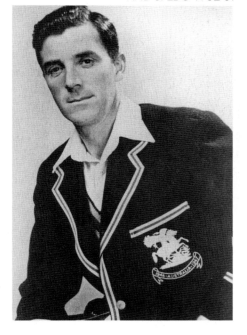

Born: Sidcup, 21 August 1914
Died: Canterbury, 13 November 1998
County Cap: 1936
County Captain: 1954-56

Batting

M	I	NO	Runs	Av	100	50
397	595	188	5,074	12.46	–	15

Bowling

Balls	Runs	Wkts	Av
73,441	38,774	1,709	22.68

5wI	10wM	ct/st
132	38	152

Best Performances
84* v. Hampshire (Southampton) 1939
9-47 v. Gloucestershire (Bristol) 1939
16-80 v. Somerset (Bath) 1939
Tests: 34 for England
Wisden **Cricketer of the Year:** 1940

Kent's first appointed professional captain, Doug Wright was one of cricket's most respected and popular figures. According to Don Bradman he was the greatest leg-break bowler in his time, saying that he would always like to have Wright on his side. Described as the artist who bowled every ball to take a wicket, the man with 'Enigma Variations', he was coached by the distinguished South African exponent of the googly, Aubrey Faulkner. E.W. Swanton wrote of Doug Wright that on his best days he was 'a uniquely dangerous bowler of quick leg-breaks and googlies and on his not-so-good days a generous contributor to the general entertainment'.

That now diminishing band of cricket lovers who saw him before 1952 will remember the long, loping run with a few short steps, followed by a series of longer bounding ones and ending in a leap, arms spread wide and in delivery going full

Doug Wright shortened his run towards the end of his career but at the point of delivery it changed little if at all. He remains by far England's most effective exponent of the leg break and googly at Test level.

circle. He could be inconsistent and his unusual action sometimes led to a glut of no-balls. Even within a single over there could be a couple of such balls, a wicket or maybe two (something he did on numerous occasions) and a couple of balls that would beat batsman and wicketkeeper, resulting in four byes.

His partnership with Godfrey Evans in the early post-war years was especially fruitful for Kent but strangely not so for England. A familiar entry in Kent's score books would show 'c (or st) Evans, b Wright'. In the 118 post-war matches when they were together in the side they combined to dismiss 98 batsmen of whom 61 were caught and 37 stumped. Against Derbyshire at Canterbury in 1947 four batsmen were caught and three stumped. Yet the magic did not work in the Test matches in which they both played, as on only five occasions did they successfully combine to take wickets.

Engaged by Kent in 1932, his opportunities were restricted by the presence in the side of 'Tich' Freeman, who was taking more than 200 wickets a season in Wright's early years, but they did appear together on a number of occasions. On Freeman's retirement in 1936 he became a regular, taking 100 wickets for the first time in 1937. He repeated this feat in the final pre-war season in which he took 131 wickets for the County, including his career-best performance in which the only batsman able to deal with him was the England captain, Walter Hammond. He topped Kent's bowling averages, taking his wickets at 15.65 apiece. Sir Pelham Warner was quoted in the 1940 *Wisden* as not having seen more difficult bowling since the days of S.F. Barnes. In nine seasons for Kent he took more than 100 wickets and three times he topped the bowling averages. His 16 wickets against Somerset in 1939 were taken in 28.4 overs, with eight victims in each innings. He holds the record for the best innings analysis by a Kent bowler against Gloucestershire and Middlesex (8-30) and his performance in that Somerset match is a Kent record against that county. His 15 wickets in the match at Maidstone against Leicestershire in 1949 included a second-innings nine dismissals. Possibly an even more remarkable performance was on the first morning at Maidstone seven years later when his eight wickets routed Middlesex. When Wright took his second-innings 8-31 against Hampshire at Southampton in 1954, he twice took two wickets with successive balls. That was a remarkable match-winning performance, with Hampshire requiring just 113 to win and losing their last eight wickets for 23 runs. He twice had outstanding performances against Worcestershire, at Worcester in 1939 when he took 13 wickets, then at Dover in 1955 when he took a first innings 8-36.

His seven hat-tricks are a world record. One of them, against Sussex at Hastings in 1947 was in a performance when he again took 15 wickets in the match, including his fifth hat-trick. Remarkably, five of his seven came in his early years, including two in the 1937 season against Worcestershire and Nottinghamshire. Six of his seven were for Kent, the other being on the 1938/39 tour of South Africa against Border. On that tour he took more first-class wickets than any other MCC bowler. His final hat-trick was in the traditional Bank Holiday Canterbury Week match against Hampshire in 1949.

Doug Wright was a more than useful tail-end batsman. With the exception of his first season he averaged double figures. In six seasons he averaged more than 15 and seven times had a top score of 50 or more. His career-best score was the second highest in Kent's second innings against Hampshire in 1939, a major contribution in a Kent victory.

In an international career that included two tours of Australia and New Zealand and two to South Africa, his figures do not reveal the ability that made him an integral part of the England team in the early post-war years. On the 1946/47 tour of Australia he took more Test wickets than any other bowler on either side, but expensively. His 23 wickets cost 990 runs. In the Fifth Test at Sydney he recorded his best international return with 7-105, including the wickets of Bradman, Hassett and Miller in Australia's first innings. In all first-class matches on that tour his 54 wickets was more than any other of the ten MCC bowlers used as was his 51 wickets on the 1938/39 tour of South Africa. The 1950/51 tour of Australia and New Zealand yielded 52 wickets in all matches, just one short of Alec Bedser's haul. In the home Test series against South Africa in 1947 his 19 wickets was the best of all England's bowlers. He took ten in the Lord's Test of that series.

Wright played his final match for his County in 1957. In retirement he became a highly successful coach at Charterhouse, King's School Canterbury, St Edmund's Canterbury and the University of Kent. He also maintained his close association with Kent, assisting with coaching and encouraging the emerging players. During the Second World War he served in the Royal Artillery, reaching the rank of lieutenant.

Walter Shooter Wright

RHB & LM 1888-99

A pioneer of swing bowling, one of Walter Wright's claims to fame is that the great Yorkshire all-rounder George Hirst learned to bowl his left-arm in-swingers by watching him. This was at a time when the technique was little practised or understood. Wright came to Kent from his native Nottinghamshire following a dispute over pay. Married and settled in Maidstone, where he was in his second spell as professional at the Mote, he qualified by residence and made his debut in 1888, signalling his arrival with 5-40 v. the MCC at Lord's. He ended the season with 86 wickets at 14.29 including 6-54 against the Australians in Canterbury Week and match figures of 10-102 v. Lancashire at Old Trafford. The year also saw the beginning of his partnership with 'Nutty' Martin, for a few years one of the most destructive pairings on the county circuit. Between 1888 and 1891 they delivered sixty-eight per cent of the overs bowled for the county and accounted for sixty-seven per cent of the wickets. Bowling unchanged at Tonbridge in 1888, they skittled Sussex for 51 (Martin 6-27, Wright 4-16) and again in 1889 when Yorkshire were routed at Mote Park for 71 and 62 (Martin 10-65, Wright 9-51). 1889 was Wright's best season with 114 wickets at 12.98 in all matches and match returns of 10-46 v. Yorkshire at Sheffield and 13-106 v. Middlesex at St Lawrence.

Born: Hucknall Torkard, Nottinghamshire,
   29 February 1856
Died: Leigh, Lancashire, 22 March 1940
County Cap: 1888

Batting

M	I	NO	Runs	Av	100	50
191	307	77	2,751	11.96	–	3

Bowling

Balls	Runs	Wkts	Av
37,757	13,989	696	20.09

5wI	10wM	ct/st
–	7	93

Best Performances
70* v. Sussex (Hove) 1892
9-72 v. MCC (Lord's) 1889
13-106 v. Middlesex (Canterbury) 1889 & v.
Middlesex (Lord's) 1890

Wright claimed 89 wickets in 1890, 84 in 1891 and as late as 1895 took 13-150 against his former county at Maidstone. At The Oval in 1890 he dislocated his left thumb and, although fears of amputation proved groundless, opinion was that he was never the same bowler afterwards. The workload might have contributed. In all first-class cricket between 1888 and 1891 he bowled 17,807 balls; he still holds the Kent record for the most balls bowled in a match – 630 v. Nottinghamshire at Gravesend in 1890.

A useful batsman and excellent fielder, he hit 237 for Mote Park v. Free Foresters in 1887. For Nottinghamshire v. Gloucestershire at Trent Bridge in 1883 he went in as night-watchman at 6.15 p.m. on the first evening and batted over all three days for 415 minutes, finishing with a career best 127*.

Wright's was a varied career. As a professional sprinter, reputedly the second fastest in the world over 130 yards (118.8 metres), he twice won the then-prestigious (and profitable) Sheffield Handicap. Unable to break into the strong Nottinghamshire XI, in 1878 he became professional at Mote Park where he made his mark with 12-97 v. MCC and an innings of 151 against Cobham. In 1880 he made his first appearance for Nottinghamshire and also played for the itinerant All-England XI as well as for a Canadian touring team as replacement for their captain, who had been arrested as a deserter from the Horse Guards. Correctly sensing impending financial disaster,

Wright too deserted after taking 63 wickets. Among numerous other professional engagements were Linton Park, Radley and, briefly, Sussex. In 1904 he played for Buckinghamshire. He was five years on the umpires list and was later trainer to Reading FC. For some years he ran a sports goods business in Maidstone.

William (Bill) Yardley
RHB & SLA (under-arm) 1868-78

Born: Altomont, Bombay, India, 10 June 1849
Died: Kingston-upon-Thames, Surrey, 28 October 1900

Batting

M	I	NO	Runs	Av	100	50
34	63	3	1,473	24.55	1	6

Bowling

Balls	Runs	Wkts	Av
228	126	7	18.00

5wI	10wM	ct/st
–	–	20/1

Best Performances
126* v. W.G. Grace's XI (Maidstone) 1871

Had law and the theatre not occupied so much of his time, Bill Yardley might be better remembered. His cricket was finished by the time he was thirty but for a few years he ranked second only to Grace as the best batsman in England. He sometimes backed himself against the great man for half a crown (12.5p).

The son of a judge, Yardley scored heavily at Rugby School and in 1868, at the end of his final term, hit 51 and 24 in Canterbury Week for Kent v. the Gentlemen of MCC. Despite the presence of regular keeper Edward Henty, he also kept wicket for part of the game and achieved a stumping off George Bennett's 'ground bait'. Further success came with 59 against Cambridgeshire at Gravesend as well as 54★ and 30 at Mote Park for 'Press and Critics' against the touring Australian Aboriginals.

It was at Cambridge, where he was awarded Blues every year from 1869 to 1872 inclusive (captain in 1871), that he attracted attention. In the famous 'Cobden's

Match' of 1870 he scored exactly 100, the first ever century in the University match. Two years later he hit the Dark Blues' bowling for another hundred, 130, a feat unequalled for another sixty years. Throughout his time at Cambridge and afterwards when called to the Bar, he continued to play for Kent, sometimes under an assumed name. In 1870 he hit 96 v. Sussex at Hove out of a team total of 181 and in 1876 92 against Surrey at Mote Park. In 1872 he scored 126* in 140 minutes for Kent v. W.G.Grace's XI at Maidstone. This not only won him his half-crown from W.G., he hit Grace's elder brother Henry clean out of Mote Park.

He represented the Gentlemen against the Players at Lord's every year from 1869 to 1874 but for 'personal reasons' appeared only once in The Oval fixture. Able to bat with minimal practice and always looking to dominate the bowling, he made full use of his height, over six foot one (185cm), excelled in the drive and all the orthodox off-side shots including the then-fashionable forward cut. He was rated without equal as a leg-hitter. Genuinely ambidextrous, he could reputedly throw 100 yards (91.4 metres) with his right arm, 75 yards (68.5 metres) with his left and according to legend once took a wicket by changing arms mid-over.

A noted tennis and racquets player, Yardley led a full life. Always devoted to the theatre – he was a friend of W.S. Gilbert of Gilbert and Sullivan fame – he made a considerable name for himself as amateur actor, playwright and leading light in the Old Stagers. Eventually he turned professional writing farces, burlesques and pantomimes etc, as well as working as a dramatic critic and sporting journalist. His works were performed in the West End and in the USA and he does not seem to have lacked work as a journalist, but when he died his young American wife and four children were unprovided for. Why is unclear. A Yorkshire v. the Rest match was staged at Lord's for their benefit.

BIBLIOGRAPHY

Among numerous sources of information used in the preparation of this book, the following publications were of particular value:

C.W. Alcock, *Famous Cricketers and Cricket Grounds*, 1895.

Leslie Ames, *Close of Play*, 1953.

John Arlott (editor), *The Middle Ages of Cricket*, 1949.

R.L. Arrowsmith, *Kent: A History of County Cricket*, 1971.

Philip Bailey & others, *Who's Who of Cricketers*, Second Edition, 1994.

Gerald Brodribb, *Felix on the Bat*, 1962.

William Caffyn, *Seventy-one Not Out*, 1899.

Stephen Chalke, *Caught in the Memory: County Cricket in the 1960s*, 1999.

Stephen Chalke, *Runs in the Memory: County Cricket in the 1950s*, 1997.

John Evans & others, *Images of Kent Cricket: The County Club in the Twentieth Century*, 2000.

C.B. Fry, *The Book of Cricket: A Gallery of Famous Players*, 1899.

Lord Harris, *A Few Short Runs*, 1921.

Lord Harris & F.S. Ashley-Cooper, *Kent Cricket Matches 1719-1880*, 1929.

Lord Harris & others, *The History of Kent County Cricket* (with appendices A-D), 1907, Appendices E-J, 1910-2003.

J.W. 'Jack' Hearne, *Wheelwrights to Wickets: The Story of the Cricketing Hearnes*, 1996.

David Lemmon, *Percy Chapman: A Biography*, 1985.

David Lemmon, *'Tich' Freeman and the Decline of the Leg-break Bowler*, 1982.

G.D. Martineau, *The Valiant Stumper: A History of Wicketkeeping*, 1957.

Christopher Martin-Jenkins, *World Cricketers: A Biographical Dictionary*, 1996.

Howard Milton, *Cricket Grounds of Kent*, 1992.

Howard Milton, *Kent Cricketers 1834-1983*, 1984.

Howard Milton, *Kent Cricket Records 1815-1993*, 1994.

Dudley Moore, *The History of Kent County Cricket Club*, 1988.

Patrick Morrah, *Alfred Mynn and the Cricketers of his Time*, 1963.

Clive Porter, *Kent Cricket Champions 1906*, 2000.

R.C. Robertson-Glasgow, *Cricket Prints: Some Batsmen and Bowlers 1920-1940*, 1943.

R.C. Robertson-Glasgow, *More Cricket Prints: Some Batsmen and Bowlers 1920-1945*, 1948.

Ric Sissons, *The Players: A Social History of the Professional Cricketer*, 1988.

E.W. Swanton, *Cricketers of my Time: Heroes to Remember*, 1999.

E.W. Swanton (editor), *Barclays World of Cricket: The Game from A to Z*, Third edition, 1986.

Sir Pelham Warner, *Gentlemen v. Players*, 1949.

E.M. Wellings, *Vintage Cricketers*, 1983.

G. Derek West, *The Elevens of England*, 1988.

Frank Woolley, *The King of Games*, 1936.

Relevant issues of the following annuals, periodicals and other continuing works were also of value: *Association of Cricket Statisticians and Historians; Important/First-Class Cricket Matches; Cricket: A Weekly Record of the Game; The Cricketer [International]; The Cricket Field; Cricket Scores and Biographies of Celebrated Cricketers; James Lillywhite's Cricketers' Annual; John Lillywhite's Cricketers' Companion; Kent County Cricket Club 'Blue Book'/Annual/Yearbook; Wisden Cricket Monthly; Wisden Cricketers' Almanack.*

Other cricket titles published by Tempus

Kent County Cricket Club
WILLIAM A. POWELL

Founded in 1870 through the merging of the Canterbury and Maidstone clubs, the Kent team have enjoyed success in the County Championship as well as various cup competitions. Kent's greatest era began in 1967 and lasted through until 1978, during which time the team were one of the most prominent forces in the domestic game. With a selection of over 220 images including memorabilia which illustrates the team's history since the nineteenth century, this book will appeal to all fans of Kent CCC.
0 7524 1871 8

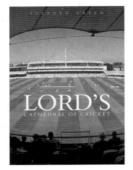

Lord's The Cathedral of Cricket
STEPHEN GREEN

Containing over 150 illustrations, this follows the history of the ground from its foundation right up to the present day. Including visits by royalty, the construction of the Media Stand and countless great occasions in domestic and international cricket – it is sure to appeal to anyone who has an interest in the game.

This is the story of the ground, the MCC – and of cricket itself.
0 7524 2167 0

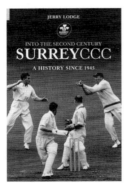

Into the Second Century Surrey CCC, A History Since 1945
JERRY LODGE

Celebrating their centenary just seven days after the Second World War, the county club has won more County Championships than anyone else since 1945. This delightful book contains comprehensive statistical information and over 100 superb illustrations.
0 7524 3177 3

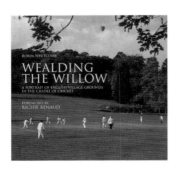

Wealding the Willow
A Portrait of English Cricket Grounds in the Cradle of Cricket
ROBIN WHITCOMB

In the Weald area of South-East England, cricket, along with the church and the local pub, is at the very centre of village life. Former *Cricketer* and *Daily Telegraph* writer Robin Whitcomb has travelled around the counties of Kent, Surrey, Hampshire and East and West Sussex collecting anecdotes and photographing the cricket. With a foreword by cricket commentator Richie Benaud, this is a worthy record of the great game and the places where it all began.
0 7524 3457 8

If you are interested in purchasing other books published by Tempus, or in case you have difficulty finding any Tempus books in your local bookshop, you can also place orders directly through our website

www.tempus-publishing.com